THE
PROGRESS
PRINCIPLE

THE PROGRESS PRINCIPLE

USING SMALL WINS TO IGNITE JOY, ENGAGEMENT, AND CREATIVITY AT WORK

TERESA AMABILE
STEVEN KRAMER

Harvard Business Review Press

Boston, Massachusetts

Library of Congress Cataloging-in-Publication Data

Amabile, Teresa.
    The progress principle : using small wins to ignite joy, engagement, and creativity
at work / Teresa Amabile, Steven Kramer.
        p. cm.
    Includes bibliographical references and index.
    ISBN 978-1-4221-9857-5 (alk. paper)
    1. Employee motivation.   2. Creative ability in business.   3. Corporate culture.
I. Kramer, Steven.   II. Title.
    HF5549.5.M63A58 2011
    658.3'14—dc22   2011004516

To our fathers,

Charles M. Amabile and *Louis S. Kramer,*

for whom making a living was important,

but making a life was the real goal.

And to our mothers,

Carmela C. Amabile and *Manja Kramer,*

who made that life with them and for us.

Together, they taught us to value progress and

never forget the people behind it.

Contents

Introduction

IN 2008, Google accomplished a rare feat among companies in any industry. Perched in *Fortune* magazine's lofty ranks of the top five most admired companies in America, Google also ranked among the top five of the magazine's best companies to work for. Millions of people around the world used Google's search engine daily, and ad revenues streamed in at an astonishing rate. The company's Mountain View, California, headquarters took on almost mythical status, tempting many business observers to assume that lavish perks led to employees' outstanding performance.

Media accounts made the ten-year-old Internet powerhouse seem like an employees' paradise, albeit one that relied on fabulous wealth. World-class chefs served up three free meals a day in several cafés spread across the two dozen buildings of the Google campus. Hourly shuttles with Wi-Fi access transported employees, free of charge, between Mountain View and San Francisco. Ping-pong games enlivened workdays, dogs tagged by their owners' sides, and the free state-of-the-art gym never closed. How could other companies possibly aspire to this double nirvana of business success and employee delight?

Our research shows how. And the secret is not free food or athletic facilities. The secret is creating the conditions for great *inner work life*—the conditions that foster positive emotions, strong internal motivation, and favorable perceptions of colleagues and the work itself. Great inner work life is about the *work*, not the accoutrements. It starts with giving people something meaningful to accomplish, like Google's mission "to organize the world's information and make it universally accessible and useful." It requires giving clear goals, autonomy, help, and resources—what people need to make real progress in their daily work. And it depends on showing respect for ideas and the people who create them.

As Google founders Larry Page and Sergey Brin said during the company's magical early years, "Talented people are attracted to Google because we empower them to change the world; Google has large computational resources and distribution that enables individuals to make a difference. Our main benefit is a workplace with important projects, where employees can contribute and grow."[1] In other words, the secret to amazing performance is empowering talented people to succeed at meaningful work.

This book reveals just what that means—for any enterprise. We have written the book for leaders and aspiring leaders curious about inner work life and what they can do, day by day, to support the kind of inner work life that leads to extraordinary performance—an inner work life marked by joy, deep engagement in the work, and a drive for creativity. We incorporate, and expand far beyond, our previous writings on these issues in *Harvard Business Review* ("Creativity Under the Gun," "Inner Work Life," and "Breakthrough Ideas for 2010: 1: What Really Motivates Workers").[2]

Drawing on over thirty years of research, this book focuses on a recent study that looked deeply inside seven companies, tracking the day-by-day events that moved the inner work lives of their people. Although we did not study Google, we did include one company that achieved Google-like success, reigning at the top of its industry for years and breeding highly motivated employees who are proud of their work and enthusiastic about the company. Another one of those companies set the low point of our study; consistently frustrated in their work and disgusted by their organization, its employees despaired as they watched their company's fortunes wane like the *Titanic* sinking beneath the Atlantic.

Throughout this book, you will see many examples of poor management that could ultimately cause companies to go under. This is not because we think managers are evil or incompetent, but because management is both very difficult and critically important. We value the work of good managers, and our aim is to help managers improve by highlighting hidden pitfalls. Management, when done well, can propel an organization toward success while enhancing the lives of people working within it. And when managers accomplish these two goals, their own inner work lives will be uplifted.

Too often, our culture and our organizations place managers and subordinates in opposition. Witness the wild popularity, in the first decade of this century, of the television show *The Office* and the comic strip *Dilbert*. But we have found that this is a dangerous stereotype. In this book, you will also see good managers who transcend the stereotype. Such leaders are crucial to effective organizations because they serve as a powerful positive force supporting employees' inner work lives.

As inner work life goes, so goes the company. We discovered that people are more creative and productive when they are deeply engaged in the work, when they feel happy, and when they think highly of their projects, coworkers, managers, and organizations. But there's more. When people enjoy consistently positive inner work lives, they are also more committed to their work and more likely to work well with colleagues. In other words, work-related psychological benefits for employees translate into performance benefits for the company.

Conventional management wisdom is way off track about employee psychology. When we surveyed hundreds of managers around the world, ranging from CEOs to project leaders, about what motivates employees, we found startling results: 95 percent of these leaders fundamentally misunderstood the most important source of motivation. Our research inside companies revealed that the best way to motivate people, day in and day out, is by facilitating *progress*—even small wins. But the managers in our survey ranked "supporting progress" dead last as a work motivator.[3]

In this book we will share our surprising research discoveries and illuminate the right track for every leader eager to bring maximum benefit to employees and to the company.

Revealing Inner Work Life:
Scenes from 12,000 Days

We never intended to study inner work life. One of us, Teresa, has spent thirty-five years researching creativity at Stanford, Brandeis, and Harvard, focusing initially on how the social environment—including the work environment—can influence creative output. At Harvard Business School, that interest evolved into a pair of burning questions: how do positive and negative work environments arise, and just how do they affect people's creative problem solving? Steven, a fellow psychologist who studied problem solving at the University of Virginia, Vanderbilt, and Brandeis, became captivated by this same question through hours of conversation with Teresa.

As we delved deeper, we realized that we could unravel the mystery of what really affects workplace creativity only by understanding the human stories behind inner work life: what happens to people's thoughts, feelings, and drives as they try to solve complex problems inside companies? This book, and the research program behind it, resulted from a confluence of these questions and our personal lives.

We have been married now for over twenty years. During those years, we have often discussed how our fathers built their own small businesses—businesses that not only succeeded but also brought much joy and pride to their employees. We have often pondered how they managed to pull it off, through good economic times and bad. We have been dismayed at how few modern organizations sustain both highly creative, effective performance and high employee satisfaction over the long run. We realized that, in probing inner work life, we might also discover what really makes the difference between organizations that pull off these feats and those that don't.

To get answers, we opened a window onto the thoughts, feelings, and motivations of people as they did their work every day. We spent years looking through that window, discovering the rich, complex world of inner work life, how it fluctuates as events at work change, and how it influences performance every day.[4] We invite you to look through that window with us and see the daily inner work lives of employees trying to do creative work. You will see how they perceive and react to the actions of managers, their colleagues, the organization, and even the work itself. Our focus on the inner work lives of *employees*, not managers, is designed to show you something you would typically never see. In the last chapter, we round out the picture by turning to the inner work lives of managers.

This book is the fruit of our psychological exploration. Searching for partners in that enterprise, we recruited 238 people in 26 project teams in 7 companies in 3 industries. Some of the companies were small startups; some were well established, with marquee names. But all of the teams had one thing in common: they were composed primarily of knowledge workers, professionals whose work required them to solve complex problems creatively. Most of the teams participated in our study throughout the course of a particular project—on average, about four months. Every workday, we e-mailed everyone on the team a diary form that included several questions about that day. Most of those questions asked for numerical ratings about their inner work lives—their perceptions, emotions, and motivations during that day.

The most important question allowed our respondents free rein: "Briefly describe one event from today that stands out in your mind." The event had to be relevant to the work in some way, but the diary narrative could describe any kind of positive, negative, or neutral event— ranging from the actions of managers and coworkers, to the person's own behaviors, to something that happened outside of work. To maximize candor, we promised complete confidentiality—which is why we disguise the identities of all companies, teams, and individuals in the book. (We collected much additional data besides the e-mailed diaries. You can find more details about every aspect of the research in the appendix.)

Amazingly, 75 percent of these e-mailed forms came back completed within twenty-four hours, yielding nearly 12,000 individual diary reports. These daily journals turned out to be a researcher's goldmine, giving us something that no researcher had enjoyed before—real-time access to the workday experiences of many people in many contexts over a long period of time. Several performance measures indicated that some of these people, and some of their teams, ended up doing very well; some did very poorly.

Inner Work Life Discoveries

The daily journals revealed what made the difference. They were a porthole showing what many managers, such as the captains of that *Titanic*-like company, are seldom able to see:

- Inner work life is a rich, multifaceted phenomenon.

- Inner work life influences people's performance on four dimensions: creativity, productivity, work commitment, and collegiality. We call this *the inner work life effect*.

- Inner work life matters for companies because, no matter how brilliant a company's strategy might be, the strategy's execution depends on great performance by people inside the organization.

- Inner work life is profoundly influenced by events occurring every day at work.

- Inner work life matters deeply to employees. A testament to this is the extraordinary participation of the volunteers in our research, who completed the diary form day after day, for no more compensation than the insight they would gain into themselves, their work, and their team's work.

In addition to revealing how much inner work life matters to employees—and thus to companies—our research turned up another, deeper layer of meaning, concerning *events that are part of every workday*:

- Three types of events—what we call the *key three*—stand out as particularly potent forces supporting inner work life, in this order: *progress* in meaningful work; *catalysts* (events that directly help project work); and *nourishers* (interpersonal events that uplift the people doing the work).

- The primacy of progress among the key three influences on inner work life is what we call *the progress principle*: of all the positive events that influence inner work life, the single most powerful is progress in meaningful work.

- The negative forms—or absence of—the key three events powerfully undermine inner work life: *setbacks* in the work; *inhibitors* (events that directly hinder project work); and *toxins* (interpersonal events that undermine the people doing the work).

- Negative events are more powerful than positive events, all else being equal.

- Even seemingly mundane events—such as small wins and minor setbacks—can exert potent influence on inner work life.

From the highest-level executive offices and meeting rooms to the lowest-level cubicles and research labs of every company, events play out every day that shape inner work life, steer performance, and set the course of the organization.[5]

Tales from the Front: Inner Work Life in the Trenches

Fascinating stories lie within the 12,000 daily surveys that provided the grist for our statistical analysis mill. No numerical results, no matter how significant, can tell those tales. In each chapter, we will introduce you to the people, teams, and companies behind the numbers.

Chapter 1 offers your first glimpses of inner work life, as you watch a lauded company heading for disaster. You'll see the men and women of one team in a world-renowned consumer-products company struggle to innovate as new management takes control of their product development agenda.

In chapter 2, you'll watch the devastating effects of this mismanagement on the team's perceptions, emotions, and motivations. These scenes will illustrate what inner work life is and how it operates. You'll begin to see the force that even small events at work can exert on daily inner work life.

Chapter 3 introduces a team of software engineers serving internal customers across a vast hotel empire. As you read of their delight in customer compliments, their discouragement in the face of a pending takeover, and their disdain for corporate management when terminations decimate their company, you will see the *inner work life effect*—how inner work life influences all aspects of individual performance.

Chapter 4 begins with a startling turn of events for these software engineers—a steep uptick in their inner work lives. Their story will show you the *progress principle*—the power of progress to steer people's thoughts, feelings, and drives. You'll see how the software engineers needed a massively positive project to lift their inner work lives out of the polluted stream of bad news that had engulfed them. Analyses across all teams' diaries will reveal that progress in meaningful work is the most important of the key three positive influences on inner work life.

Chapter 5 reveals how the progress principle works. You will see why even small progress events can be so powerful—but also why setbacks are even more powerful. In general, when it comes to events influencing inner work life, bad is stronger than good. Chapter 5 introduces the most important tools for leveraging the progress principle, and shows how progress and inner work life can fuel each other.

In chapter 6, you will see the second of the key three influences, the *catalyst factor*. This includes the myriad ways managers can support projects, such as setting clear goals, allowing autonomy, and providing sufficient resources. This chapter contrasts two teams that differed enormously in the support they received during their projects. One team, laboring in the consumer products "*Titanic*" to develop an innovative kitchen appliance, was hamstrung in its quest by indecisive top management, uncommunicative organizational support groups, and competing agendas. This team's inner work lives were among the worst we saw. The other team, working in a well-respected chemicals firm, found support at every turn as it worked to create a new weatherproof coating for fabric. Top managers responded promptly to requests for resources, gave honest feedback on ideas, and ensured that all organizational groups worked to support the team. Despite serious technical snags, that team triumphantly produced two breakthroughs, and its members enjoyed superb inner work lives throughout the project. This company continued to thrive. The consumer products company did not.

Chapter 7 immerses you in the roiling atmosphere of insults and mistrust endured by a team of mechanical engineers in a hardware company before taking you to the oasis of camaraderie created by the leaders of the hotel company's software team. These tales illustrate the third of the key three influences on inner work life—the *nourishment factor*, or the different ways of providing interpersonal support, such as encouragement, showing respect, and fostering collegiality.

Chapter 8 gives you a tool and a set of guidelines for ensuring that the people you manage get the catalysts and nourishers they need to make steady progress in their work. These catalysts and nourishers are the lifeblood of good inner work life, which sustains superior long-term performance. You will meet one team leader, in a different chemicals firm, who managed to keep his team going—creatively, productively, and happily—in the face of demanding customers and unsettling corporate rumors. Intuitively, he followed a set of practices that chapter 8 codifies into a daily discipline.

Chapter 9 shows you how to apply these guidelines not only to managing people, but also to supporting your own inner work life.

The New Rules

According to the conventional rules of management in the current information age, leaders manage people. They recruit the best talent, provide appropriate incentives, give stretch assignments to develop talent, use emotional intelligence to connect with each individual, review performance carefully, and retain those who clear the bar. As important as these activities are, relying exclusively on them means relying on the flawed assumption that individual performance depends solely on something inherent in the employee. Management guru Jim Collins advises that it's crucial to get "the right people on the bus."[6] Many managers leap to the temptingly simplistic conclusion that doing so is their most important job.

Unfortunately, the conventional rules miss the fundamental act of good management: *managing for progress.*

According to the new rules born of our research, real management leverage comes when you focus on progress—something more direct than focusing on an individual's characteristics. When you do what it takes to facilitate progress in work people care about, managing them— and managing the organization—becomes much more straightforward. You don't need to parse people's psyches or tinker with their incentives, because helping them succeed at making a difference virtually guarantees good inner work life *and* strong performance. It's more cost-effective than relying on massive incentives, too. When you don't manage for progress, no amount of emotional intelligence or incentive planning will save the day. The tales of our teams give testimony to this, in spades.

The first of those tales begins at an auction.

1

Scenes from the Organizational Trenches

THE AUCTIONEER approached the microphone under a harsh July sun. Before him, much of a vast parking lot had become a tented showroom, crammed with sleek modular desks, Aeron chairs, computers, CAD equipment, machine shop tools, and the smaller factory items that had not already been sold. All the pieces had been efficiently tagged, grouped, and cleaned to attract the highest bidder. Potential buyers stood ready, some having come from miles away to this rural Michigan town, their sights set on particular items and their intuitions sensing a good deal. Behind the auctioneer loomed the former headquarters of Karpenter Corporation, ten brick stories of offices towering over a three-level plant that stretched far into an expanse of former farmland. The offices were empty, the manufacturing plant silent. Weeds sprouted beside the front door.

Toward the back of the parking lot, behind the equipment and the buyers, stood a smaller group, mostly silent: about fifty former Karpenter employees, some of whom had been with the company for more than thirty years. Bruce, an engineer and amateur photographer, had stationed himself near the front, his trusty Canon camera around his neck. Lucas, a financial analyst who hid his bald spot with a Detroit Tigers cap, hovered nearby. Lisa, a young product designer who had worked with Bruce and Lucas, joined the pair and clutched her Snapple ice tea as she squinted at the scene before them. These "Karpenteers," as they had called themselves not so long ago, had once been proud to work at a company respected around the world for innovative products that touched the lives of so many: small power tools, kitchen appliances, manual and electrical cleaning devices, houseware gadgets that went beyond "cool" to nearly essential. Its brand had been recognized by 90 percent of American adults, and its wares were still found in almost 80 percent of American homes. In their days on the Domain team at Karpenter, Bruce, Lucas, and Lisa had designed cleaning gadgets that they continued to see in almost every home they visited, anywhere they traveled on the continent.

As the auctioneer began his task, some former Karpenteers shook their heads in disbelief, grimaced with disgust, or cursed in anger. A few wept. Designers, product managers, technicians, engineers, plant workers—many were still stunned by the company's demise. Karpenter had been their second home and a beloved employer for many years; it had once felt like an extended family, where they mattered and their work counted. It was also the lifeblood of their community and several others that were home to Karpenter facilities. Now it was gone. Although many of them had found jobs in nearby cities, they mourned the loss and saw the auction as a garish funeral.

Just four years earlier, the consumer products company that we call Karpenter had been named one of the ten most innovative, successful companies in America.[1] That parking lot had brimmed with cars, the landscaping was impeccable, and the front door swung with a steady stream of visitors—not only customers and suppliers, but also journalists, researchers, and others eager to learn the secrets of Karpenter's five-decade-long success. But something had gone wrong. Although the signs were not yet visible to most observers, people working in the trenches, including Bruce, Lucas, and Lisa, knew that Karpenter had become a terrible place to work. Their work lives had become nearly intolerable, and the work they were doing just didn't meet the same standards. And so now, while the rest of the industry and the economy continued to boom, Karpenter lay dead.

On a Course to Disaster

What had precipitated that spectacular demise?

Four years previously, Karpenter had brought in a new top executive team, which reorganized all divisions into cross-functional business teams, with each team managing a set of related product lines. When interviewers asked for the company's success formula, these executives told a compelling story about this model. Each team was to function as an entrepreneurial group, autonomously responsible for everything from inventing new products to managing inventory and profitability. Best of all, they would have the resources of a substantial corporation to back them up, with minimal interference.

But it didn't play out that way. Consider a quarterly product review meeting held at the end of June, when the company was still an industry darling. Jack Higgins, the general manager of the Indoor Living and Home Maintenance division, called these meetings with his vice presidents for each divisional team four times each year. Higgins, a trim forty-eight-year-old golfer fond of sports metaphors, claimed that these meetings would allow management to help the team "refine its playbook" by receiving information and giving constructive feedback on the team's new product development efforts. That day, it was review time for Domain, a team whose product lines focused on manual housecleaning devices.

Things did not go well.

The windowless ground-floor conference room was stifling, its ventilation system broken. The sound of ringing phones, eight receptionists, and more than twenty jocular visitors in the adjacent main lobby made for constant distraction. When Higgins signaled, team leader Christopher, product development manager Paul, and the other invited members of the Domain team began showing the materials that the team had worked diligently to prepare. After listening to the presentation for a while, politely viewing CAD renderings and handling prototypes, the executives took over. They had their own ideas about products the team should be developing. Jack Higgins began with a brief statement about the team needing "a new game plan." But it was the divisional management team—the vice presidents of R&D, manufacturing, finance, marketing, and HR—who laid out that game plan. The spokesman was Dean Fisher, vice president of R&D. (To help our readers keep track of who's who, we use full-name pseudonyms for managers outside the teams, and first-name-only pseudonyms for everyone else.)

Domain's product designer, Lisa, senior product engineer, Bruce, and several other team members had been working feverishly on a radical new design for floor mops, a program they had defended at the previous quarterly meeting, received funding for, and moved through key milestones. Three other new products had been in the works for months as well. But now, with little explanation, Fisher and the rest of the management team decreed that the Domain team should focus on four completely different ideas. One was revitalizing a line of window squeegees, which generated little excitement in the team. No matter—the dictates had been pronounced.

The Domain people attending the meeting made little fuss. They had learned that, with these executives, protests were futile. But private reactions were another matter. Extremely distressed, most of these people felt angry, frustrated, disappointed, and sad, or all of the above. Lisa, then twenty-six, had enthusiastically joined Karpenter right out of a college design program. But she found her motivation for the work that day suddenly sapped. As she described later in her digital daily journal (which we excerpt here, virtually verbatim), all the progress she thought she had been making on designing a new product was for naught: "After the [. . .] product review meeting this morning, Ralph [the operating design manager] came over and told me that the Spray

Jet Mops were killed. So, after several weeks of work on the project, it just dies, and all of my team priorities change."[2]

Lucas, Domain's finance manager, reflected the private views of many Karpenteers when he perceived the management team (MT) as overly controlling:

> During our new product review meeting, the MT basically told us
> what our top priorities were [for] new product development. [. . .]
> It was discouraging that our "freedom" to choose our direction/
> priorities was taken away from us as a team and we were given
> our direction, rather than being allowed to make more decisions
> on our own. [Lucas, 6/30]

Michael, the team's supply chain manager, had seen several abrupt, seemingly arbitrary goal shifts since new Karpenter management had come in three years earlier. He ended his description of the meeting with vivid irony:

> The needle still points north, but we've turned the compass again.
> [Michael, 6/30]

And Bruce, a long-time senior product engineer, was deeply saddened by this and other incidents that he saw shrinking Karpenter's core strength:

> After working on the Spray Jet Mop program for a period of time,
> I learn that we are not going to do it now. They say it has been
> put on hold, but I know we will never do it. It would be nice if we
> could go back to being the leader in product innovation and not
> the follower. [Bruce, 7/1]

This product review meeting proved to be a major event for the people of the Domain team. Like the slash of a sword, it cut down months of the team's product development work. Not only did it provoke unhappiness and frustration, it soured people's views of management and drained motivation for the work.

But even small events—more like nicks than slashes—could be just as damaging to workers' thoughts, feelings, and drives. A few weeks later, when upper management began to exert pressure on the teams to show results in Karpenter's cost-reduction program, the Domain team met to assess the program for its product lines. Although Michael had suggested a brainstorming approach to consider cost-cutting ideas beyond those under way, team leader Christopher insisted that the team focus on how best to present what it had already done—even if this meant inflating performance a bit. Although most team members said little in the meeting, their private reactions were explosive, including damaged regard for Christopher, frustration at having their ideas dismissed at the start of the meeting, and hopelessness about the team's ever meeting management's cost-reduction goals.

Product engineer Neil didn't rattle easily. Although he was only twenty-nine, his teammates saw him as an island of stability, an agreeable extravert who calmed fears in times of stress. But this is how he described the scene:

> Today, our whole team met to discuss cost reductions for our product line. There has been lots of pressure from upper management to take cost out of the business. [. . .] Christopher's relational style dictated the mode the entire time. (Tense!!) He seemed more concerned with cheating the system just to make our team's numbers look good. (Make him look good!) He was pushing his title around and telling us all what to do. I wasn't motivated to follow his leadership at all. Instead, I wanted to do just the opposite! I want to follow someone with courage, but today Christopher didn't have any! [Neil, 7/27]

These meetings were but two events in the organizational life of Karpenter Corporation—one major and one minor. They give a glimpse into the strategic decisions that top management struggled with at that time, decisions that undoubtedly contributed to the company's downfall. They show how the challenges of a changing marketplace rippled down from the top to team management. But is strategy in a challenging market the whole story behind that auction in the parking lot, the liquidation of this once-proud company just four years later?

No, and our research explains why. There is a deeper story to the success and failure of this organization, springing from its very heart—its people. These two noxious events—Jack Higgins's product review meeting and Christopher's cost-reduction meeting—were part of a drama that played out day after day in the final years of this organization, deeply affecting people and their work.

Well-meaning as we know they were, Karpenter's managers did not understand the power of what we call *inner work life*—the perceptions, emotions, and motivations that people experience as they react to and make sense of events in the workday. These managers did not understand how their own actions—even seemingly trivial ones—could have a potent effect on people working in the trenches of the organization. Because inner work life is mostly hidden and because human beings generally want to believe that all is well, Karpenter's managers had no idea how bad inner work life really was inside the company. They did not know how much workers' performance could suffer as a result. And they did not grasp how inner work life could affect the fate of the organization itself.

The Hidden Bulk of the Organizational Iceberg

When a corporate icon like Karpenter Corporation dies during good economic times, it seems like the sinking of the *Titanic*. Yet no single cataclysmic event was responsible for Karpenter's downfall. No accounting scandal, no market collapse, no design flaw caused the disaster that had seemed impossible just a short time earlier. Analysts in the consumer products industry scrambled to find explanations, and they pointed to the usual suspects. Some blamed flawed product-market strategy, a turn away from true innovation to incremental changes to the existing cash cow products. Others claimed that the new wave of Karpenter executives, who had started about three years before the company began to falter noticeably, lacked expertise in dealing with the big-box retail customers on whom the company depended. Poor strategy and lack of expertise no doubt contributed. But some also blamed an unusual source: bad morale, which they said contributed to exceptionally high turnover among valuable middle managers and professionals as well as poor performance among those who stayed.

We know that these latter analysts were right, although we eschew the vague "bad morale" terminology. Our decade-long research on Karpenter and other companies reveals the power of workers' unspoken perceptions, emotions, and motivations, the three components of inner work life. In the short term, bad inner work life compromises individual performance; in the long term, bad inner work life can sink even a titan like Karpenter.[3]

Observable actions in an organization merely form the tip of the iceberg; inner work life is the enormous bulk that's hidden beneath the water's surface. When you walk the halls of your workplace, you might see and hear people giving presentations to managers, conferring with colleagues, doing Internet research, talking to customers, participating in meetings, or running experiments. That's *observable work life*, the visible part of what each individual does, what you could see by looking at everyone's daily activities. What you probably won't observe are the judgments about managerial indifference during the presentation, the feelings of triumph during the customer conversation, or the passionate motivation to crack a bedeviling problem in the experiment. Inner work life is the mostly invisible part of each individual's experience—the thoughts, feelings, and drives triggered by the events of the workday.

Each person has a private inner work life, but when people go through the same events at the same time, they often have extremely similar private experiences. Over days, weeks, and months, if the same sorts of events keep happening in a group or an organization, those similar experiences can combine to become a formidable force—even if each event, by itself, seems trivial. "The Power of Small Wins (and Losses)" reveals the surprising strength of apparently trivial events.[4]

At Karpenter, the quarterly product review meeting during which Domain team members attentively took notes while divisional executives changed all of the team's priorities comprised the visible tip of the organizational iceberg. The team meeting on cost reduction a month later, when many of those same workers stopped contributing ideas near the beginning and instead quietly listened as the team leader laid out his plan for gaming the system, was still just part of that tip. But the perceptions these people formed of their managers as over-controlling, ignorant, weak, or unethical? Their emotions of anger, sadness, and disgust? Their dwindling motivation to come to the office each day and work like the dickens? These made up the hulking, hidden bulk of the iceberg. Eventually, that mass was big enough and bad enough to sink the organizational ship.

Unfortunately, like Karpenter's top execs, most managers do not understand inner work life well enough to ensure clear sailing and avoid onrushing disaster. Many mishandle employee inner work life not because they are mean-spirited, but because they do not appreciate how deeply people care about it. In 1993, flight attendants for American Airlines went on strike to protest the company's policies. The issue was not really pay or benefits—it was lack of respect. "They treat us like we're disposable, a number," said one flight attendant. Another said, "My self-respect is more important than my job."[5] Four years later, things had not changed much. This time, it was the pilots who were protesting: "As long as you treat your employees as merely 'unit costs,' like the Styrofoam cups we throw out after every flight, morale will remain at rock bottom."[6] Companies are still making the same mistake. In fact, in 2010, a global survey found that employee engagement and morale declined more in that year than at any other time in the fifteen years of the survey.[7]

This book reveals the reality of inner work life and the effect it can have on the performance of your organization. You will see that managers at every level affect the inner work lives and, consequently, the creativity and productivity of people throughout the organization. Most importantly, you will learn how to support inner work life in a way that maintains both high performance and human dignity.

The Power of Small Wins (and Losses)

Little things can mean a lot for inner work life. You can probably think of important events in the history of your own inner work life that might seem objectively trivial. Examples abound in the daily diaries we collected—reports of minor workday events that powerfully elevated or dampened feelings, thoughts, and motivation. There was the scientist who felt joyful after the top technical director took a few moments to discuss his latest experiment; the product manager who began to view her boss as incompetent when he waffled on a decision about pricing; the programmer whose engagement in the work leapt when he finally managed to defeat a pesky bug—a mighty *small win* in the grand scheme of things.[a]

In analyzing the diaries, we found that people's immediate emotional reactions to events often outstripped their *own assessments* of the event's objective importance. We found that, not surprisingly, most events (nearly two-thirds) were small, and most reactions (nearly two-thirds) were small. And, as you would expect, most reactions to big triggering events were big, and most reactions to small events were small. But here's the surprising part. *Over 28 percent of the small events triggered big reactions.*[b] In other words, even events that people thought were unimportant often had powerful effects on inner work life.

A growing body of research documents the power of small events.[c] A 2008 study found that small but regular events, including church attendance and physical exercise at a gym, can yield cumulative increases in happiness. In fact, the more frequently that study's participants went to

What Is Inner Work Life?

Inner work life is the confluence of perceptions, emotions, and motivations that individuals experience as they react to and make sense of the events of their workday. Recall your own most recent day at the office. Choose one salient event and consider how you interpreted it, how it church or exercised, the happier they were.[d] Even though any one small event by itself might have a minor effect, that effect doesn't disappear as long as similar events keep on happening: a person who works out regularly feels a little happier each time he leaves the gym, and he stays happier than he was in his pre-gym days. Similarly, a product manager who repeatedly witnesses her boss's indecisiveness will have a darker view of him than she did before she joined his team. Small positive and negative events are tiny booster shots of psychological uppers and downers.[e]

In managing people, you really do have to sweat the small stuff.

a. We borrow the phrase *small wins* from Karl Weick's classic paper "Small Wins: Redefining the Scale of Social Problems,"*American Psychologist* 39 (1981): 40–49.

b. You can find details on this study and all studies we report from our diary research program in the appendix.

c. In general, scholars argue, little things really do matter a lot. In Karl Weick's seminal 1981 paper he argued that social problems could be tackled in more innovative ways if they could be approached successfully on a small scale initially. Suggesting that the enormous scale of most social problems causes paralyzing emotionality and overwhelms cognitive resources, he proposed that there are great advantages in the small wins that can be gained from breaking down such problems into manageable pieces.

d. This paper reported studies of how "good" and "satisfied" people feel—their emotional state or sense of well-being (D. Mochon, M. I. Norton, and D. Ariely, "Getting Off the Hedonic Treadmill, One Step at a Time: The Impact of Regular Religious Practice and Exercise on Well-Being," *Journal of Economic Psychology* 29 [2008]: 632–642). Research has also shown effects of small events—astonishingly small events—on intrinsic motivation (internal motivation) and performance. (I. Senay, D. Albarracin, and K. Noguchi, "Motivating Goal-Directed Behavior Through Introspective Self-Talk: The Role of the Interrogative Form of Simple Future Tense," *Psychological Science* 21 [2010]: 499–504.)

e. This drug analogy comes from D. Mochon, M. I. Norton, and D. Ariely, "Getting Off the Hedonic Treadmill, One Step at a Time."

made you feel, and how it affected your motivation. That was your inner work life at that time. Each word in this phrase reveals a key aspect of the phenomenon.

Inner work life is *inner* because it goes on inside each person. Although it is central to the person's experience of the workday, it is usually imperceptible to others. Indeed, it can go unexamined even by the individual experiencing it. But part of the reason that inner work life hides from view is that people *try* to hide it. Most organizations have unwritten rules against showing strong emotions or expressing strong opinions—especially if they are negative or contrary to prevailing views. And even if people are comfortable confiding in a peer, they are usually loath to reveal themselves to superiors. For example, even if your blood boils when the chairman of the board dismisses the careful analysis you have just presented, you will probably smile pleasantly as you inquire about additional data that might be helpful. Being "professional" means concealing your outrage.[8]

Inner work life is *work* because that is both where it arises—at the office—and what it is about—the tasks that people do. At some level, we are all aware that we have inner work lives, even if we spend little time focusing on them. Inner work life can be affected by events in our personal lives, but only when those triggers influence our perceptions, emotions, or motivations about the work. For instance, an argument with your spouse in the morning can dampen your spirits and your engagement in work later that same day. Conversely, your inner work life can spill over to influence your feelings outside of work—a bad day at the office can spoil the evening's barbeque with friends. But, spillover aside, inner work life refers fundamentally to workday reactions to on-the-job events.

Inner work life is *life* because it is an ongoing, inevitable part of the human experience at work every day. We continually react to everything that happens at work. We determine whether the work we are doing is important and how much effort to exert. We also make judgments about the people we work with, including our superiors. Are they competent or incompetent? Should we respect their decisions? Inner work life is *life* for another reason, as well: because we spend so much of our lives at work, and because most of us are so invested in the work we do, our feelings of success as individuals are tied to our day-to-day sense of ourselves at work. If we believe that our work is valuable and we are successful, then we feel good about this key part of our lives. If our work lacks value or if we feel we have failed at it, then our lives are greatly diminished.

Perception, Emotion, and Motivation

Consider the inner work lives of Lucas, Lisa, Michael, and Bruce and their Domain teammates in Karpenter Corporation as they prepared for the quarterly product review meeting with Jack Higgins and the vice presidents of their division. Members of a cross-functional business team ostensibly managing their own product lines, they were proud of their headway on new products, especially the Spray Jet Mops. At the same time, although challenges loomed, they believed that they had effective plans for the ongoing business. Most of them had good inner work lives as the meeting approached. And the meeting seemed to start well, with the executives listening to the team's presentation about existing product lines and viewing prototypes (as well as progress charts) for the new products.

Before long, though, Lucas's inner work life took a blow, and so did that of his comrades. Jack Higgins made some general remarks about his conviction that the team needed to change direction, and then Dean Fisher unilaterally presented a list of new priorities. It became clear that these top managers had had no intention of allowing the Domain team the autonomy that it supposedly enjoyed. Although they may have betrayed little outwardly, Lucas and his teammates immediately tried to make sense of what was going on. Were they hearing correctly? The Spray Jet Mop program was to stop immediately? Were *all* of their new product development projects coming to a halt? Were they really supposed to revitalize a line of boring window squeegees that still had good sales?

This kind of sensemaking is a continuous part of people's inner work lives. When something unexpected or ambiguous happens, people will try to understand it and will draw conclusions about the work, their colleagues, and the organization based on that event. In this way, a single incident can continue to reverberate and impact people and their work long after the triggering event itself is over.

Some on the Domain team already saw Karpenter's top managers as ill-informed dictators; this meeting only strengthened that view. Newer employees promptly saw themselves as powerless subjects. They began to view the team's mission as incremental, not innovative. *Inner work life is about perceptions—favorable or unfavorable (and sometimes quite nuanced) impressions about managers, the organization, the team, the work, and even oneself.*

At the same moment, the team members—still controlling themselves outwardly—started reacting emotionally. Their reactions were immediate, reinforcing (and being reinforced by) their simultaneous negative perceptions. They were frustrated that their hard work had been negated by people who, in their view, knew so much less about the business than they did. They were discouraged that their autonomy was being stifled. They were sad to see a company known for innovation shrink away from creating new products. *Inner work life is about emotions— positive or negative—triggered by any event at work.*

Both their emotions and perceptions influenced the motivation of the people on the Domain team. They had been making real progress on the Spray Jet Mops, solving multiple design and cost problems, and their drive to complete the project had been high as they entered the review meeting. They believed that many of their other projects were feasible—and attractive, too. The sharply negative thoughts and emotions sparked by what management did in that meeting deflated the team's motivational balloon. In talking about this abrupt halt to the team's progress, Lisa employed terms of death; recall her lament that ". . . the Spray Jet Mops were killed. So, after several weeks of work on the project, it just dies . . ." *Inner work life is about motivation—the drive to do something, or not.*[9]

After that meeting, the Domain team dutifully halted all activity on the Spray Jet Mop program and the other terminated projects and focused on the new priorities. As it turned out, despite the team's efforts over a period of several weeks, the revitalization of the window squeegee program went poorly. From design to marketing, from pricing to packaging, performance was lackluster, missing any innovative spark. People on the team didn't need managers or customers to express disappointment; they were disappointed in themselves.

It was no coincidence that performance suffered on the Domain team after people's inner work lives took such a hit. Individual performance is closely tied to inner work life. If people do not perceive that they and their work are valued by a trustworthy organization, if they derive no pride or happiness from their work, they will have little drive to dig into a project. And without a strong drive to deeply engage the problems and opportunities of a project, people are unlikely to do their best work.

———————

As they watched Karpenter's remains being auctioned off, Lucas, Bruce, Lisa, and their fellow Karpenteers remembered how unbearably difficult simple progress had become in the company's final years. To their minds, that daily suffering had been as needless as Karpenter's ultimate demise. But the company's managers never understood the dynamics of poor inner work life.

Because inner work life, which matters so much for performance, is mostly unobservable, even managers who understand it have a dilemma. What can you do about it when you can't even gauge it? The findings in this book, and their implications, are based on human psychology. But rest assured—supporting inner work life does not require you to hold a psychology degree or invade the privacy of your employees. On the other hand, it is not something you can outsource to the human resources department. Regardless of your job title or level, you can boost inner work life every day. It is as simple, and as difficult, as creating the conditions for people to succeed at important work, because few things can nurture inner work life as much as being successful.

This book will serve as your guide in the quest to gain the understanding that Karpenter's managers lacked. It will help you avoid Karpenter's fate but, more importantly, it will help you build a successful organization—one that people love working in, because they have the chance to accomplish something that matters every day.

Your journey begins with a brief tour of inner work life.

2

The Dynamics of Inner Work Life

I NNER WORK life is difficult to see, but our research captured it "in the wild." A simple but salient example came from Neil, the product engineer on Karpenter Corporation's Domain team introduced in chapter 1, when he described his annual performance review by the product development manager. Although Neil was generally calm and unflappable, everyone was a bit anxious during the late-spring "review season." To his great relief, the meeting went well:

> Paul, "the Boss," gave me my performance appraisal today. He was encouraging and highly complimentary. Paul is a breath of fresh air here at Karpenter, when it comes to management. I feel truly motivated by him and I am even more willing to help him and our team succeed. [Neil, 6/15]

This example is one of only a handful of the 12,000 diary entries that explicitly mentioned all three inner work life components—emotions, perceptions, and motivation. Neil *felt* encouraged; he *thought* well of Paul, and he was *driven* to help Paul and the team succeed. Most likely,

Paul had only an inkling—at best—of what was going on with Neil's inner work life during the performance review. He might have seen a smile and gotten some words of thanks from Neil, and concluded correctly that Neil felt good. But he probably had no idea that Neil held him in such high esteem relative to other managers, nor that his words had been such a powerfully positive motivating force.

Because managers' actions generally had negative effects on inner work life at Karpenter, Paul was something of a rarity; he triggered *positive* inner work life, at least for Neil. Although Karpenter was, by nearly any measure, the worst company in our study, most participants from this organization did experience days of good inner work life. In the context of the other Karpenter stories we've presented, Neil's diary shows just a bit of the complexity of inner work life and the many forces that influence it.

Neil's diary entry reveals another important point: *inner work life is not the same as personality*. Recall that, in the Domain team meeting on cost reduction described in chapter 1, Neil had felt demotivated by what he saw as Christopher's cowardly team leadership—aborting idea generation and trying instead to make the team's numbers look good. This was the same Neil. Neil was not *always* motivated or unmotivated, not *always* happy or unhappy.

Conventional wisdom holds that, at work as in life, there are happy people and unhappy people; that's just the way they are, and there isn't much that will change them short of life-altering events. In fact, research has shown that pleasant or unpleasant temperament does remain relatively stable over time, and certain aspects of motivation are stable, too.[1] But the big news from our research is that most people's inner work lives shift a great deal over time as a function of the events they experience—*not* as a function of their personalities. Unwelcome events will trigger down days even for people who are basically upbeat. Nearly everyone in our study had days when inner work life soared and days when it plummeted. Such changes can happen quickly.

Conversely, different people can react differently to the same event, but only part of that difference can be explained by their personalities. In fact, we discovered that personality isn't the major determinant of inner work life responses to events.[2] Rather, the interpretation of the event is critical—how people make sense of it in the context of their individual positions, work, plans, history, and expectations. Because Neil and many of his teammates had similar expectations, plans, and positions going into Christopher's cost-reduction meeting, they had similarly negative inner work lives coming out of it.

The Three Components of Inner Work Life

To explore inner work life more fully, we'll take a closer look at each of its three components, which are depicted in figure 2-1. Notice that our conception of inner work life does *not* include all psychological processes that a person could experience during the workday. We focus on the three major processes that, according to psychological research, influence performance: *perceptions* (also called *thoughts* or *cognitions*), *emotions* (or

FIGURE 2-1

The components of inner work life

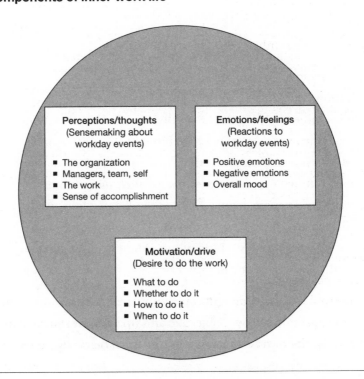

Perceptions/thoughts (Sensemaking about workday events)
▪ The organization
▪ Managers, team, self
▪ The work
▪ Sense of accomplishment

Emotions/feelings (Reactions to workday events)
▪ Positive emotions
▪ Negative emotions
▪ Overall mood

Motivation/drive (Desire to do the work)
▪ What to do
▪ Whether to do it
▪ How to do it
▪ When to do it

feelings), and *motivation* (or *drive*).[3] These are far and away the major internal processes that our participants described in their diary narratives, aside from the basic work they did that day and their specific "event of the day." Although inner work life includes a broad range of mental activities, we will not discuss all of them in this book. For example, although daydreaming undoubtedly contributes to creativity, we leave it out of the discussion because virtually none of the 12,000 diaries mentioned it.

Many diaries recorded emotions, however. That's where we'll start.

Emotions

Emotions are both sharply defined reactions and more general feelings, like good and bad moods.[4] Emotion is the joy you feel when you finally solve a difficult problem; the frustration when your solutions fail; the disappointment when the board rejects your strategic plan; the pride when a fellow manager recognizes your creativity at a company meeting; the gratitude when an assistant helps you find critical information; and the anger when you discover that your subordinates have missed a milestone because another team failed to do its work. Emotion is also the overall positive mood you feel when everything seems to be going well on a particular day, or the negative mood when a day starts with a setback and goes downhill from there.

Emotions vary along two key dimensions: degree of pleasantness and degree of intensity.[5] You can be mildly annoyed by a brief outage of the corporate intranet or enraged by a flippant response to a new idea you floated in a management meeting. Both are unpleasant emotions, but the latter is much more unpleasant *and* much more intense.

Lucas, the Domain team's finance manager, often expressed emotion, disproving the jokey stereotype that all people who work with numbers are emotionless automatons. When the Domain team saw unexpectedly good sales one month, Lucas expressed his feelings this way:

> I received our gross margin report for April, which showed sales
> for our team up 3% over objective and up 11% over prior year. It
> was a *pleasant surprise* to learn that our April results were an

improvement over objective and prior year. It showed that our hard work over the last few months, in trying to get additional sales or new accounts, has paid off. [Lucas, 5/18] *[emphasis added]*

As pleased as Lucas was by his teammates on this occasion, two months later, he was terribly frustrated by two of them as he strained to meet a tight deadline:

Our team had scheduled a morning session to review the Quarterly [Report] package. I had put together the financial piece, but Michael and Christopher had not completed anything for the text portion of the package. I was *frustrated*, since I had worked hard over the last 2 days to put together the financial piece. [Lucas, 7/20] *[emphasis added]*

Lucas was not an outlier. Nearly all of our 238 research participants expressed emotion in at least some of their diary narratives—*even though we never told them to do so*. The question on the diary form asked them only to "Briefly describe one event from today that stands out in your mind," not to say how they reacted to the event. Yet over 80 percent of the diary entries did express feeling in some way, either through words or punctuation. (We saw plenty of "!!!" and "???" as well as a few "*!$@*#!.") This is part of the reality of inner work life: you can't turn off the emotions. Even though many managers—and employees—would like to ignore emotions, pretending that such "messy" things do not belong in the workplace, such studied ignorance is a dangerous gamble.

Recently, much of the management literature has highlighted the long-neglected role of emotions at work. Most savvy managers have read about the need for emotional intelligence—an understanding of one's own and others' emotions and an ability to use that understanding to guide managerial thought and action.[6] Recent research has also revealed that emotions can have both positive and negative effects on a range of work behaviors, including creativity, decision making, and negotiations.[7] For instance, positive feelings can lead to greater flexibility in problem solving and negotiations. Clearly, emotions are crucial.

But beware. It's tempting to classify the entire inner work life phenomenon as "feelings," partly because emotion has become such a hot topic in management. Moreover, emotions are what you're most likely to see when inner work life does come to the surface. Recall the bereft expressions on the faces of Lehman Brothers employees as they left their building that day in September 2008 when the firm filed for bankruptcy. And when, in 2010, the 3-D film *Avatar* broke all box-office records, it was easy to imagine the elation rippling through everyone at 20th Century Fox.

However, inner work life is *not* simply about emotions. Emotions are only one piece of the puzzle, and managers who rely on emotional intelligence to build high-performance organizations are dealing with only a fraction of the inner work life picture. Our theory of inner work life builds on theories of emotional intelligence by placing emotion in the context of two additional components: perception and motivation. Both, like emotions, are essential.

Perceptions

Perceptions can range from immediate impressions to fully developed theories about what is happening and what it means. They can be simple observations about a workday event, or they can be judgments about the organization, its people, and the work itself. When something happens that grabs your attention at work, you start *sensemaking*—trying to figure out what it means. Your mind poses a series of questions, especially if what happened was ambiguous or unexpected; these questions and their answers make up your perceptions.[8] Interestingly, you are usually unaware of this process. These questions might bubble up unconsciously if upper management canceled your team's project without warning or explanation: Do these managers know what they are doing? Are my teammates incompetent? Am I? Does the work that I do have real value?

Bruce, the Domain team's senior product engineer, found himself in this situation in the aftermath of the June 30 product review meeting. When he wrote that putting the Spray Jet Mop program on hold was tantamount to canceling it, he noted, with some bitter irony, that "It would be nice if we could go back to being the leader in product innovation and not the follower." He perceived the project as a lost cause, his efforts as wasted, and the company as a fallen giant. Why was Bruce so sure that the program was dead? Why did he suspect the company could no longer lead the industry in innovation?

In films and plays, characters are given a *backstory* to help the actor understand how to play the part—for example, Scarlett O'Hara's pampered, restrictive childhood in the antebellum South of *Gone with the Wind* or Luke Skywalker's innocent upbringing on his uncle's farm in the *Star Wars* films. The backstory is the character's accumulated experience in a particular milieu over a particular period of time. We borrow the term because it helps illustrate how the perception component of inner work life operates. Real people have real backstories at work, and they form perceptions against those backstories.

There was a long backstory to Bruce's perceptions when he heard that the Spray Jet Mop program was off his team's priority list. After nearly twenty years at the company, he knew that something had changed dramatically after the new management regime took over. He had watched their pattern of decisions. He knew that Jack Higgins and his corporate boss, COO Barry Thomas, had seemed skittish about developing radically new products. Bruce compared their style, unfavorably, with the relentless innovative spirit of prior generations of top Karpenter management, who had driven the company to the pinnacle where the rest of the world still held it. Against this backstory, as he interpreted what happened to his favorite project in the product review meeting, Bruce drew his decidedly pessimistic conclusions.

Each of us interprets each workday event against our own backstories in our organizations.

Motivation

Motivation is a person's grasp of what needs to be done and his or her drive to do it at any given moment. More precisely, motivation is a combination of a person's choice to do some task, desire to expend effort at doing it, and drive to persist with that effort.[9] Many possible sources of motivation exist, but three stand out as most relevant to work life.[10] First, *extrinsic* motivation drives most of us in our work to some degree—the motivation to do something in order to get something else. This is your motivation to take a position because the pay and benefits can't be beat; to work fourteen-hour days all week just to meet a deadline that you consider arbitrary; to do whatever it takes to win an industry award; or to produce a position paper that you know will look good for your performance review. Lucas's two days of hard work on the financial piece had probably been extrinsically motivated by the tight deadline.

Intrinsic motivation is the love of the work itself—doing the work because it is interesting, enjoyable, satisfying, engaging, or personally challenging. Intrinsic motivation—deep *engagement* in the work—can drive people to surprising displays of seemingly unrewarded effort. Witness the phenomenon of open-source programming innovation, in which thousands of programmers collaborate online to create and improve computing platforms—with absolutely no tangible compensation.[11]

The stifling organizational atmosphere in which the Domain team was living at the time we studied them snuffed out intrinsic motivation at every turn. But, even in that atmosphere, some intrinsic motivation survived. Alvin was a forty-seven-year-old senior product engineer who had come to Karpenter right out of high school. Hardworking and determined, he had earned his college degree while learning product development hands-on at the company. He had idolized his mentors, and beamed with pride while naming the famous products he had helped invent. On a particularly frustrating day in May, a Domain product manager had asked him to resize a prototype for the third time in an effort to further reduce raw material costs. Alvin knew the exercise was useless because the product simply wouldn't work if it were any smaller. Yet even in the face of this, one more in a series of obstacles to creating the product, he retained his intrinsic motivation:

We have more roadblocks put in our way, and more redundant work, than you can imagine. Oh well—fortunately, I love *product development*. [Alvin, 5/26]

Finally, *relational* or *altruistic* motivation arises from the need to connect with and help other people.[12] The camaraderie that comes from collaborating with congenial colleagues can drive us in our work, and so can the belief that our work has real value to a person, a group, or society at large. Altruistic motivation can be fairly general ("My work helps people with Type 1 diabetes") or quite specific ("My research could lead to a treatment for my diabetic child"). Usually, the reason behind relational motivation isn't nearly as compelling as treating disease—but even less dramatic reasons can be forceful ("My collaboration helps this struggling junior designer"). Many people are driven to do well for a person or a group they like and respect. This was the case for Neil when, after Paul complimented his progress in the performance review, he wrote, "I feel truly motivated by [Paul] and I am even more willing to help him and our team succeed."

The different forms of motivation can coexist in the same person, at the same time, for the same work. In fact, nearly all intrinsically motivated tasks on the job have some extrinsic motivators attached. For example, you can be intrinsically motivated by the challenge of creating a marketing strategy for a new service, while still driven by next week's deadline for presenting the strategy to the board—an extrinsic motivator.

Unfortunately, there is a nasty underside to extrinsic motivation, one that many managers don't recognize: if extrinsic motivators are extremely strong and salient, they can undermine intrinsic motivation; when this happens, creativity can suffer.[13] Let's say that the CEO reminds you of that marketing strategy deadline twice a day. Now overwhelmed by the sense that you are working primarily to make the timeline, you can lose the excitement of creating something great. You may begin to focus narrowly on just getting the job done, rather than exploring for a truly novel "killer" strategy.

Most people have strong intrinsic motivation to do their work, at least early in their careers. That motivation exists, and continues, until something gets in the way. This has a startling implication: as long as the work is meaningful, managers do not have to spend time coming up with ways to motivate people to do that work. They are much better served by removing barriers to progress, helping people experience the intrinsic satisfaction that derives from accomplishment.[14]

Because intrinsic motivation is essential for people to do their most creative work, we focused our attention on intrinsic motivation in the diary research.

The Inner Work Life System

Inner work life is not a fixed state. It is the dynamic interplay among a person's perceptions, emotions, and motivation at any point during the workday. Because the three elements influence each other to create an overall subjective experience, this means that inner work life is a *system*, a set of interdependent components that interact over time.

The Dynamics of Inner Work Life

As an example of a much simpler system, consider a car's air conditioning. Fundamentally, the system consists of four main elements: the thermostat; the compressor that converts hot, humid air into cool, dry air; the fan that blows air from the compressor into the car; and the air in the car. A key aspect of any system is that you can't explain what is going on by looking at just one or two elements. The thermostat continuously reacts to changes in temperature caused by the fan and compressor; the compressor needs a signal from the thermostat; the fan can't deliver cool, dry air unless the compressor functions well; and proper car temperature requires all of these elements working harmoniously.

You can understand the air-conditioning system as a whole once you identify its elements and their dynamic interactions. Similarly, inner work life is a system that can be understood by looking at every element within the context of the whole. If the CEO pops his head inside your office door for the second time today to ask how you're coming along on the marketing strategy for next Monday's board meeting, you can't compartmentalize your frustration or your deflated intrinsic motivation any more easily than you can separate either from your perceptions of the CEO as overcontrolling and this task as make-or-break. It's impossible to understand your inner work life at that moment without considering the interplay of all three elements.

Figure 2-2 depicts the inner work life system. When something happens at work—some workday event—it immediately triggers the system: the cognitive, emotional, and motivational processes.[15] Recall what happened during the Domain team's cost-reduction meeting. Upper management had demanded that the team develop new ideas for greater cost savings in its product lines. But Christopher, the team leader, shut down a brainstorming session that the team tried to have for generating those ideas. He insisted that, to satisfy the demands of upper management, they instead figure out a way to better present the numbers on what they had already done. His aim was to convince the

FIGURE 2-2

The inner work life system

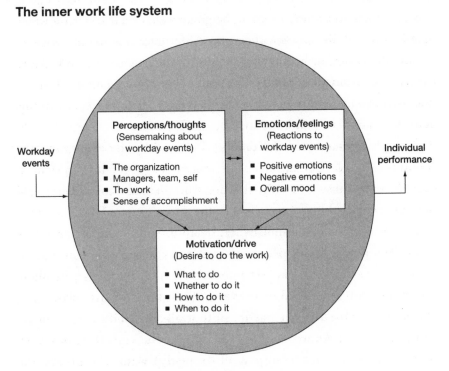

management team that the team wasn't really in trouble, that it didn't really need further cost reductions.

This event triggered plenty of sensemaking in Domain team members. Against the backstory of other recent incidents in which managers at one level had tried to wriggle out from under the demands of their own managers—putting subordinates in untenable positions—Christopher's behavior was particularly distasteful. Neil wrote that Christopher was "cheating the system," and viewed him as a self-interested coward who lacked courage in the face of management pressure. *Those* are perceptions that Christopher surely would never want to hear—and likely never did. He probably had no idea that his actions in that meeting led to such low opinions of him.

At the same time that people are forming perceptions (or thoughts), they are reacting emotionally to the event.[16] If the trigger is something specific and time-bound, they will probably experience a distinct emotion like happiness or frustration. If it is more drawn out, like a good day on which everything seems to be going well, or a bad day on which one failure follows another, they may experience a generally good or bad mood. Neil's diary entry on the day of the cost-reduction meeting was full of exclamation points—and not positive ones, either. "Tense!!" was the term he used to describe the meeting's atmosphere, attributing it to "Christopher's relational style."

The perceptions feed the emotions evoked by the event, and the emotions feed the perceptions. The more tense Neil felt in that meeting, the worse his view of Christopher. And the more cowardly or self-serving Christopher seemed to be, the more agitated Neil became. Negative impressions intensify frustration, for example, and vice versa. Happiness biases people toward more positive interpretations of an event, and vice versa. Depending on what happens with these cognitive and emotional processes, motivation for the work can skyrocket or nosedive (or hardly shift at all). In Neil's case, motivation shifted a lot. Of working for Christopher, he said, "I wasn't motivated to follow his leadership at all. Instead, I wanted to do just the opposite!"

The entire inner work life system influences performance, because the components are so closely interlinked. But the primary source of influence is motivation. Motivation not only determines what people will do and when and how they will do it, but *whether* they will do their work at all. Without some degree of motivation, the work simply will not happen. People on the Domain team had extrinsic motivation—the demands of management—to reduce costs; but they had little intrinsic motivation. Not surprisingly, Christopher's dressing up the numbers didn't work with management. So team members continued to half-heartedly grope their way toward dramatic cost reductions, to no avail. Management continued to find their performance unsatisfactory.

The Neuroscience of Inner Work Life

Any event that triggers a change in one component of the inner work life system is likely to influence the others as well, because perceptions, emotions, and motivation are so tightly interwoven. Brain science helps explain how the three components interact to shape performance. The inner work life system operates as it does because this is how the human brain operates. Areas of the brain that are responsible for emotions are connected in complicated ways to areas responsible for perception and cognition. For instance, brain imaging research reveals that when people are shown emotionally charged pictures, more of their visual cortex is activated than when they are shown emotionally neutral images.[17] This means that the way people *think* about what they see is affected by how *emotional* it makes them feel. Even the amount of attention the brain gives to an event is affected by the emotional content of that event.

Rational thought and decision making cannot function properly unless emotions are also working properly. Despite the *Star Trek* premise that Mr. Spock's purely rational, emotionless thought processes led to better decision making, in fact the opposite is true—at least for humans. Research on patients suffering damage to emotion centers in the brain reveals decision-making impairment even though they are quite normal cognitively. They can make complex calculations, understand language, and read and write, but they can have great difficulty deciding between even simple alternatives like taking a taxi or a bus.[18] They cannot decide which option is better, because all choices seem equally good. Without the emotion of fear, for example, they find it impossible to weigh the risks of one choice over another. Similarly, if they cannot feel joy in their accomplishments, they have little intrinsic drive to work. In either case, their motivation for taking action stalls.

Feelings inform values which, in turn, inform decisions. An emotionless pilot who, in an emergency, calmly weighs the cost of the aircraft against the lives of the passengers is not what we want. We want a pilot who cares passionately about life and never considers the cost of the plane.[19]

As a result of these neural interconnections, individuals' performance—the work they choose to do, how hard they work at it, how creative they are, how they behave toward coworkers—depends on a complex interaction of their thoughts, feelings, and drives. This is the reality of inner work life: because it is intimately bound up with the brain's architecture, it is an inescapable part of being human.

Inner Work Life and Human Dignity

As we read the diaries pouring into our computer system day after day, we came to realize the dynamism, urgency, and centrality of inner work life. As we noted above, we had only asked each of these people to describe one memorable work event from the day, yet most also told us how the event affected their feelings, their thoughts, or their drive—and sometimes two or three of these interconnected. Something compelled them to tell us about their inner work lives, as if the newscast would be incomplete without this crucial bulletin.

We know from our analyses that inner work life affects how people perform. But we also know that it affects the people themselves. The former Karpenter employees who showed up in the parking lot on the day of the final asset auction weren't there for a voyeuristic thrill. Their grimaces, their tears, and their curses revealed that a piece of themselves was on the auction block. For years, many Karpenteers had taken pride in doing good work at an impressive company where their inner work lives thrived. Then, in the dismal final years, it all went to pieces. Stymied in their work and treated as half-wit commodities by management, they came to think badly of the organization, their managers, their coworkers, their projects, and eventually themselves. Finally, they lost the inner spark of motivation for the work they had once loved. Their inner work lives had soured and their performance had flattened. A piece of their identity had been bound to their work at Karpenter, but that piece had been hollowed out. Their human dignity had taken a blow.

Inner work life is an important part of human *life*, affecting the quality of daily existence in significant ways. Beyond their value to contribute to organizational performance, people have value as human beings. Because they spend so much of their lives working, people deserve the dignity of having positive lives at work. In reading the diaries, we saw how personal work can be to the people putting their time and effort into it, daily risking failure to achieve their goals. Having meaningful work that is supported by management can enhance life immeasurably. Work that is devoid of meaning, interest, and joy can lead to lives that feel very empty indeed.

Managers who realize this have a valuable opportunity. By taking actions that support inner work life, they can simultaneously become heroes to their employees, build the long-term success of their organizations, and add meaning to their work as managers—which in turn will nurture their *own* inner work lives. So, in the interest of these triple goals, let's dig deeper into how inner work life influences people and their performance.

3

The Inner Work Life Effect

How Inner Work Life Drives Performance

H ELEN SMILED and raked her fingers through her short blonde hair as she finished her journal entry at the end of a busy workday. Her husband had just phoned to say he had picked up the kids at day care and, although exhausted, the forty-one-year-old software engineer was deeply satisfied as she reflected on the previous ten hours. A fifteen-year veteran of DreamSuite Hotels, now working for a subsidiary, Helen had started the day grateful that her team leader had told her she could take time in the afternoon to see her second-grade daughter star in the class play:

> I was so very appreciative that my project manager works with me so that I can have time off during the day to attend important personal, family functions like these. It gives me a boost thru the day. [Helen, 3/3]

Because of her manager's small deed, Helen's inner work life had had a jump-start before she even set foot in the office. The positive

effect of the boost was evident in her emotions (gratitude), her perceptions (having a reasonable, understanding project manager), and her
motivation (to stay until she finished the work she'd planned for the
day). In fact, Helen summarized her sense of the day by saying, "It was
a good day for me! I got a lot of work done."

One of her major tasks that day had involved educating an internal
customer who had questions about a complicated programming job
that had recently been delivered by her team, Infosuite. The job was
part of a new electronic billing system for clients of the DreamSuite corporate discount program. Helen performed so well in serving that customer's needs that she received a spontaneous lunch invitation:

> Our customer [. . .] told me how wonderful I was, and said she'd
> buy me lunch to show her appreciation! I was blown away by her
> kind thoughts. It made me want to work harder to get the job
> done [. . .] and I feel I did get more work done [. . .] than I
> usually do. [Helen, 3/3]

Helen's inner work life mattered for her personally; it gave her "a
good day." More importantly, from a managerial perspective, it seems
to have mattered for her performance. She got more work done than
usual *because* she started the day feeling upbeat, viewing her team
leader positively, and gearing up to tackle the work. Helen wrote in her
journal that the project manager's accommodating attitude gave her a
"boost thru the day." She wrote that she wanted to work harder for her
customer *because* the customer "blew her away" with kindness.

Helen's external work life wasn't rosy. Her team, a group of skilled
professionals who collaborated well under a pair of excellent coleaders,
supported internal customers within DreamSuite Hotels—a global
company that included several name-brand hotel chains. The nine-
person Infosuite team comprised the top-level programmers and statistical analysts for the company's financial units, handling all of these
units' information-gathering, storage, search, retrieval, and statistical
analysis. Nevertheless, despite the importance of the work they did, the

team worked in a remarkably ugly cubicle encampment in a corner of a converted warehouse in suburban Dallas. They were usually ignored by DreamSuite personnel, and even by the managers of their own subsidiary. So the DreamSuite customer appreciation that Helen received on March 3 was particularly noteworthy; Helen's work must have been truly outstanding.

Helen believed that her work was unusually good *because* she felt so great that day. But does good inner work life *actually* boost a person's performance? Does poor inner work life have a negative effect? Scientists have been debating the effect of emotions and (separately) the effect of motivations on performance for years, but our research is unambiguous.

As inner work life rises and falls, so does performance.

Stress or Joy: What Triggers Great Performance?

Every moment that they are performing their jobs, employees are "working under the influence" of their inner work lives. But what is the nature of that influence? Conventional wisdom seems to hold contradictory views on this, as does academic research. The nineteenth-century essayist-philosopher Thomas Carlyle famously wrote, "No pressure, no diamonds"—a somewhat more elegant form of the contemporary bromide, "When the going gets tough, the tough get going."[1] This powerful strain of Western cultural beliefs holds that high performance requires tribulation. A number of organizational psychologists support this view. They argue that dissatisfaction, discomfort, and distress galvanize performance—that people do their best work when they feel negative emotion, pressure, or extrinsic motivation based on rewards, expected evaluations, or competition with peers.[2] For instance, Jennifer George and Jing Zhou have demonstrated that brief periods of negative mood can enhance creativity. They argue that negative moods signal that a problem must be solved.[3]

But an equally strong strain of conventional wisdom maintains that success comes from enjoying the work. As British billionaire business-man Philip Green, owner of the Arcadia Group, put it, "You've got to love what you do to really make things happen."[4] Like Helen, many people have experienced especially productive or creative days when they started out in a positive frame of mind. And most people have ex-perienced times when stress or unhappiness has interfered with their ability to get their work done well, or at all. Adding weight to this per-spective, many studies show that people perform better when they are satisfied with their jobs, happier, and intrinsically motivated by love of the work, and do worse when they are not.[5] For example, in 2008, Michael Riketta analyzed dozens of studies on job satisfaction and per-formance. He found that, overall, higher job satisfaction predicts better subsequent performance.[6] Focusing specifically on emotions, Barry Staw and his colleagues found that employees who expressed more pos-itive emotions in their workplace at one point in time received more fa-vorable supervisor evaluations and larger pay increases at a later time.[7] The conclusion of researchers on this side of the debate? Happy, satis-fied workers make better workers.

Because scholars are clever at marshalling evidence, and because both arguments do have some validity, you can find studies to support each of these positions.[8] The problem is that none of the previous studies was as comprehensive as ours. Some were experiments in which students did brief, one-time tasks concocted by the researcher. Others focused on em-ployees doing real work in real organizations, but relied on a few one-time survey measures and studied just one aspect of inner work life (usually emotion). None collected data from as broad a sample as ours; none had a view into employees' daily experiences over a long period of time; none analyzed as many dimensions of performance across time. The impoverished measures of prior research have rendered it unhelp-ful in definitively answering the question of how inner work life influ-ences performance. The true nature of the link has remained elusive.

Our diary study clearly tips the weight of evidence to one side of the debate: it shows unambiguously that positive inner work life promotes good performance. This is *the inner work life effect*: people do better work when they are happy, have positive views of their organization and its people, and are motivated primarily by the work itself. For short periods, people can perform at very high levels under extreme stress, but this happens only under special conditions that we will discuss later. Over the long haul, and under most conditions, people perform better when their inner work lives are positive. Helen's experience on March 3 truly illustrates the inner work life effect.

This is not to say that positive inner work life renders work easy or eliminates frustration. Struggles are inevitable, because most contemporary work is nontrivial. That new billing program that Helen had to explain to her internal DreamSuite customer was extremely complex. The electronic ink developed for Amazon's Kindle took nearly a decade to perfect. And customized cancer treatments for most tumors still remain an elusive goal, years after the first promising studies. There will always be significant hurdles to leap. But the more positive a person's inner work life, the better able she is to clear those hurdles; in fact, trying to accomplish some really difficult goals can be exhilarating. On the other hand, when the events unfolding around a person spoil her inner work life, performance is likely to suffer.

Don't Chalk It Up to Personality

Just as personality can't fully explain inner work life, neither can it fully explain the *connection* between inner work life and performance. But here, too, the personality explanation is seductive. Isn't it possible, managers sometimes ask us, that certain people actually perform better when their inner work life gets worse—when they are unhappy, view their managers as adversaries, and feel motivated by fear or anger rather than the work itself?

Because it *is* possible, we took pains to measure personality and several demographic characteristics of each participant in our research, including education, sex, and organizational tenure, before the study began. Although they sometimes make a difference, these characteristics cannot explain our findings.[9] We saw a great deal of variation *within the same individuals doing the same jobs*, depending on what was happening in their work lives. Fluctuations in performance depend on fluctuations in inner work life that arise from events in a person's work situation, regardless of her personality traits or other characteristics.

Consider Helen's example. Was she just a consistently cheerful, hard worker, always upbeat, always performing at the top of her game? Was she incapable of negative reactions? Hardly. Let's fill you in on a bit more of the DreamSuite Hotels story.

At the start of their four-month participation in our study, the members of the Infosuite team worked in a DreamSuite subsidiary called HotelData, an eighteen-month-old joint venture between DreamSuite and Collander Data Systems. The aim of the joint venture was to use Collander's strength in managing information technology to better provide for DreamSuite's heavy information needs. HotelData was initially staffed by people who had been DreamSuite employees at the time— including most of the Infosuite team members—and a smaller number of former Collander employees (mostly in top management positions).

Just eighteen months after the joint venture was finalized, however, Collander divested its portion of the venture. On March 29, less than a month after Helen's "good day," HotelData became a wholly owned subsidiary of DreamSuite. The people of Infosuite learned officially about this divestiture just a few weeks before it took effect. With considerable bitterness, they described this change as a "takeover" by DreamSuite.

That bitterness stemmed, in large part, from the fact that, when HotelData was formed, Infosuite members were given no choice but to join HotelData and relinquish their status as DreamSuite employees—and the benefits they had accrued—if they wanted to have a job. Helen, like many of her teammates, considered this a termination by DreamSuite. Now, with the Collander divestiture, they were told—by letter, with no follow-up meetings—that they had to essentially start all over again as DreamSuite employees; no benefits would be reinstated. The team deplored the

DreamSuite "takeover," feeling devalued by this parent organization. This is how Helen reacted when she first heard the news:

> We heard a strong rumor today from outside the company that our HotelData [HD] president had resigned and taken his friends who are now in power with him, leaving us at the mercy of some boneheaded former DreamSuite types who are in high-up positions here at HD. Even though I know I don't have any kind of power over this situation, it bugs me that DreamSuite can still get to me. I was a DreamSuite person for over 12 years and I guess I loved the company. I must still have some bitter feelings about being "terminated." It bothered me to hear this news. It had an effect on my work after I heard the rumor. [Helen, 3/12]

Notice two important features of this journal entry. First, Helen's reaction to this unpleasant situation makes it clear that her mood switch was *not* permanently stuck in the "happy" position. Events changed, her inner work life changed, and her performance changed. Second, the last line provides additional evidence that inner work life affects performance. This time, the evidence reveals the downside, suggesting that negative inner work life dampens the ability to work effectively.

Measuring Performance

Project team work in most contemporary organizations is collaborative and complex, requiring ongoing problem solving and deep engagement. This was certainly true of the work that our study participants were doing. In settings where people must work together to solve challenging problems, high performance has four dimensions: creativity, productivity, commitment, and collegiality. These are the same dimensions that many modern organizations include in their performance reviews.

Creativity—coming up with novel and useful ideas—is probably the most crucial aspect of performance in today's business world. But creativity alone is insufficient. *Productivity* means getting work done on a steady basis, turning out consistently high quality work, and ultimately completing projects successfully. *Commitment* to the work, the project, the team, and/or the organization is something people demonstrate when they persevere through difficulties, help their coworkers succeed, and do what it takes to get the job done. *Collegiality* is any action that contributes to team cohesiveness; it is what team members demonstrate when they support each other interpersonally, act as if they are all part of the same team and work effort, and show that they care about how well the team functions.

Because inner work life is *inner*, it can be assessed only by self-reports. For our study, these came from various measures of thoughts, feelings, and drives on the daily diary form. We obtained assessments of all four dimensions of performance—creativity, productivity, commitment, and collegiality—from monthly ratings made by team supervisors and teammates. In addition, because creativity and productivity are generally viewed as key contributors to companies' bottom-line performance, we obtained additional daily measures of these two performance dimensions.

The Evidence

Analyzing thousands of data points from all of our participants enabled us to understand the details of the inner work life effect—the relationship between each component of inner work life and all four dimensions of on-the-job performance. You can find the details of our measures and analyses in the appendix. Here, we will highlight our main findings.

We found that each dimension of performance fluctuates with each component of inner work life—emotions, perceptions, and motivation. We will focus our attention on *creativity* here for two reasons. First, creativity is the most important performance dimension, given the need for pathbreaking work in twenty-first-century organizations. Second, there are no major differences between creativity and the other dimensions of performance in the pattern of results. Creativity, productivity, commitment, and collegiality are all higher when the three components of inner work life are positive. We present the creativity results for each inner work life component, starting with emotions. Even though we illustrate our findings with a few diary entries from our participants, the findings themselves are based on statistical analysis of data from all participants.

Emotions

Our diary study revealed a definitive connection between positive emotion and creativity.[10] We looked at specific emotions as well as overall mood (the aggregate of a person's positive and negative emotions during the day). Overall, the more positive a person's mood on a given day, the more creative thinking he did that day. Across all study participants, there was a 50 percent increase in the odds of having a creative idea on days when people reported positive moods, compared with days when they reported negative moods.

To pinpoint creativity, we searched each of the 12,000 "event of the day" journal narratives for evidence of whether a person actually did creative thinking on a given day. We defined *creative thinking* as coming up with an idea, solving a problem, engaging in problem solving, or searching for an idea. We did not count anything that was obviously routine. For instance, an R&D scientist in one of the chemical companies we studied reported creative thinking when he wrote:

> I tried everything I knew to do on the [equipment] in order to compound the resin and nothing worked. Then I tried something that had not been done before, to my knowledge, and it is working wonderfully at this moment.

Keep in mind that we did not ask our participants to report creative thinking, or even tell them that we were interested in creativity. Only when they happened to spontaneously report something like this as their "event of the day" were we able to say that they did creative thinking. These instances of creativity were significantly more likely on days of positive emotion (see "Happiness Boosts Creativity").

FOOD FOR THOUGHT

Happiness Boosts Creativity

You might wonder whether emotions really *cause* changes in creativity. Psychologist Alice Isen of Cornell University, a pioneer among researchers studying emotion and creativity, discovered that the answer is yes. In the 1980s, while at the University of Maryland, Isen and her colleagues designed a series of ingenious experiments to look at the effect of emotion on creative problem solving. In one experiment, when the participants arrived individually at the psychology laboratory, the researchers put each of them—randomly—into a particular emotional state.[a] To induce positive emotion, the researchers showed a five-minute clip of a comedy film. To induce negative emotion, they showed a five-minute clip of a documentary film about Nazi concentration camps. The students in the neutral emotion condition randomly received one of three treatments; they either watched a five-minute clip of a math film, exercised for two minutes (by stepping on and off a cement block), or received no particular treatment in this phase.[b]

Then, working individually, all thirty-three men and eighty-three women in the experiment were asked to solve the same problem: given a box filled with tacks, a candle, and a book of matches, they had ten minutes to affix the candle to a corkboard on the wall in such a way that the candle would burn without dripping wax onto the floor beneath it.[c] Students who had

We even found a surprising carryover effect showing that creativity *follows from* positive emotion. The more positive a person's mood on a given day, the more creative thinking he did the *next* day—and, to some extent, the day after that—even taking into account his moods on those later days. This may be due to what psychologists call an *incubation effect*.[11] Pleasant moods stimulate greater breadth in thinking—greater cognitive variation—which can linger and even build over a day or more.[12] Such cognitive variation can lead to new insights at work. In watched the comedy film were significantly more likely to solve the problem. Because of the random assignment and careful laboratory control of the situation, this experiment—like others by Isen—demonstrates cause and effect: positive emotion leads to better creative problem solving.[d]

a. A. M. Isen, K. A. Daubman, and G. P. Nowicki, "Positive Affect Facilitates Creative Problem Solving," *Journal of Personality and Social Psychology* 52 (1987): 1122–1131.

b. The researchers had determined separately that watching the comedy film induced more positive feelings, and the Nazi film more negative feelings, than the neutral conditions.

c. This is a classic creative problem-solving test, dubbed the Duncker candle problem after the psychologist Karl Duncker (who used it in a set of 1945 experiments). The problem can be solved by emptying the box and tacking it to the corkboard, then lighting the candle to melt some wax to the inside bottom of the box and sticking the candle bottom to the molten wax. Thus, the empty tack box serves as a candle-holder (and drip-catcher) for the candle.

d. In another of Isen's experiments, the subjects were physicians who participated individually (C. A. Estrada, A. M. Isen, and M. J. Young, "Positive Affect Improves Creative Problem Solving and Influences Reported Source of Practice Satisfaction in Physicians," *Motivation and Emotion* 18 [1994]: 285–299). The physicians randomly assigned to the positive mood condition scored significantly higher on a standard creativity test than those in the control condition. Moreover, on a questionnaire, those in the positive mood condition attributed relatively more importance to humanism (versus making money) as a reason for their practicing medicine. Most experiments on emotion and creativity enlisted undergraduate students as participants, however, not professionals like physicians. Many of these studies are reviewed by Alice Isen in the following works: A. Isen, "On the Relationship Between Affect and Creative Problem Solving," in *Affect, Creative Experience and Psychological Adjustment*, ed. S. W. Russ (Philadelphia: Brunner/Mazel, 1999), 3–18; A. Isen, "Positive Affect," in *Handbook of Cognition and Emotion*, eds. T. Dagleish and M. Power (New York: Wiley, 1999), 521–539.

other words, although new ideas might emerge soon after you experience a positive emotion, you might find them popping up much later.

We saw the carryover effect repeatedly in the journal of Marsha, a teammate of Helen's. Marsha, a petite, extraverted software engineer who had joined DreamSuite more than thirty years earlier, put in as much effort as anyone on this hardworking team. And she had plenty of fresh ideas. A little more than one-fourth of Marsha's diary entries showed creative thinking. The vast majority (80 percent) of these "creative performances" seem to have been sparked by positive emotional states on the previous days.[13]

For example, on March 9, Marsha was assigned to collaborate on a new project with Helen. In her journal, Marsha reported that she felt jazzed by the challenge; she would be learning a new system, and she would be writing new code. Also, she would be working with Helen: "I love to work with Helen because I always learn so much from her and we have a lot of fun!" On the day she received the assignment, she rated her own mood as well above average.[14] The next day she reported solving a problem creatively as well as contributing some new ideas:

> Today I attended a meeting with Harry (our team leader) and Helen, concerning our new project. I was able to report that I had found a way to clone some old code that is in our system, and this will cut many hours off our projected project time. I was also able to contribute some good suggestions concerning this planning phase of our project [. . .] I think I was pretty darn creative today! [Marsha, 3/10]

The pattern in Marsha's journal illustrates our findings across all the participants in our study. She felt good one day, and creativity followed the next day. She was excited about the challenge and about working with Helen; those feelings sparked creativity.

Perceptions

Creativity was higher when our study participants had more positive perceptions of their work environment—from the highest levels of management and the entire organization, to their own jobs. People were more creative when they saw their organization and its leaders in a positive light—as collaborative, cooperative, open to new ideas, able to develop and evaluate new ideas fairly, focused on an innovative vision, and willing to reward creative work. In other words, when people saw that a new idea was treated as a precious commodity—even if it eventually turned out to be infeasible—they were more likely to contribute suggestions. By contrast, they were less creative when they saw the organization and its leaders as driven by political infighting and internal competition, harshly critical of new ideas, and risk averse.[15]

Perceptions of the team and its leader mattered, too. People were more creative when they felt they had support from their team leader and teammates. For example, Infosuite software engineer Tom, though nearing retirement after more than twenty years with DreamSuite, had great respect and affection for much-younger project leaders Ruth and Harry—both in their thirties. They had earned this respect with their competence and the consideration they showed everyone on the team. Consequently, Tom performed particularly well on days when he expressed positive views of an interaction with either Ruth or Harry.

Perceptions of the work itself influenced creativity as well. On March 12, Marsha was given yet another new assignment. Some of the data from one of the DreamSuite hotel chains was missing. The data had to be found and flagged so it could be handled properly, without creating problems in the rest of the data set. As Marsha said, "Writing a quick program on the fly like this is called an ad hoc . . . it can be hairy because you need to do it quick but it has to be perfect or else you could really screw up the database. I like this kind of challenge." Marsha knocked off the task that same day. Like Marsha, most people were more creative when they perceived their assignments as challenging, and when they had autonomy in carrying out those assignments.[16]

Other key elements supporting creativity included sufficient resources for doing the work and sufficient time. We will have more to say about these work environment effects in chapter 6, including some rather surprising findings about the effects of perceived time pressure. (Hint: Sufficient time is necessary, but Marsha's experience of being creative "on the fly" wasn't entirely aberrant.)

Motivation

Motivation, the third component of inner work life, also influences creativity. Over the past thirty years, we and our colleagues have conducted several studies showing that people are more creative when they are driven primarily by intrinsic motivators: the interest, enjoyment, satisfaction, and challenge of the work itself—and not by extrinsic motivators: the promise of rewards, the threat of harsh evaluations, or the pressures of win-lose competitions or too-tight deadlines. Most of the evidence comes from experiments, allowing conclusions about cause and effect: if we lowered intrinsic motivation, or increased extrinsic motivation, lower creativity resulted.[17]

For one experiment, we recruited seventy-two creative writers.[18] When they arrived (individually) at the psychology laboratory, they all wrote a brief poem on the topic "Snow" (after all, it was Boston in the winter). We used these poems as a pre-measure of creativity, before we altered the writers' motivational state. Then we randomly assigned one-third of the writers to the extrinsic motivation condition. We gave them a short "Reasons for Writing" questionnaire that asked them to rank-order seven reasons for being a writer; *all* of those items, according to previous research, were extrinsic, such as, "You have heard of cases where one best-selling novel or collection of poems has made the author financially secure." The rank-ordering was irrelevant; the point was to have these writers spend a few minutes getting into an extrinsically motivated frame of mind. One-third of the writers filled out a "Reasons for Writing" questionnaire that had only intrinsic reasons, such as, "You enjoy the opportunity for self-expression." The final third of writers (the control group) spent a few minutes reading an irrelevant story.

Then, all of the writers wrote a second short poem on "Laughter." After all seventy-two writers had participated, a different group of twelve writers independently judged the creativity levels of all poems (without knowing which had been produced by whom). The results were simple and clear. Although the pre-measure poems showed no differences, the set of poems produced by writers who had contemplated extrinsic reasons for writing were significantly lower in creativity than the others. In other words, intrinsic motivation was more conducive to creativity than extrinsic motivation.

Think about it. Just spending five minutes focusing on extrinsic motivation temporarily lowered the poetic creativity of people who normally *loved* writing poems. This further highlights the power of small events. Imagine how much more strongly motivation and creativity can be depressed in workplaces that bombard employees with carrot-and-stick motivators every day.

Our diary study demonstrated that this finding is neither limited to the laboratory nor specific to creative writers; intrinsic motivation plays a role in creativity inside organizations. Participants in the diary study were more creative in their individual work on the days when they were more highly intrinsically motivated. What's more, the projects distinguished by the greatest levels of creativity overall were the ones in which team members had the highest average intrinsic motivation in their day-to-day work.

Here again, we can see the very real impact of inner work life through Marsha's eyes. On February 18, she was feeling rushed because she was leaving for a three-day weekend. She managed to find a creative way to get two tasks done in considerably less time than estimated—which not only pleased the customer, but also saved HotelData money. In her diary, she made it clear that her drive to get the work done in a timely fashion was intrinsic, not extrinsic. As she put it, "[. . .] it's not because of any external pressure. I put this mandate on myself to finish up these requests today before I leave."

From Individual Satisfaction to Organizational Success

Positive inner work life improves performance across industries—those that we studied, and those we did not. Consider the online shoe and clothing retailer, Zappos.com. A 2009 case study on Zappos emphasized the importance of employee happiness to the company's astonishing growth in revenues since 2000. CEO Tony Hsieh and COO Alfred Lin talked frequently about employee happiness. As Lin said, "Our philosophy is you can't have happy customers without having happy employees [. . .]."[19] Many at Zappos believed that the emphasis on happiness was responsible for the high quality work of employees across the company, from the customer service call center to the bustling warehouse. Like this Zappos example, our findings show that promoting positive inner work life doesn't only make people feel better; it also leads people to do better work.

In 2010, James Harter of Gallup Inc., along with several colleagues, published a study presenting hard evidence that positive inner work life for individual employees translates into better bottom-line performance for companies.[20] Working with over two thousand business units in ten different companies from industries as diverse as health care and transportation, the researchers used data on 141,900 employees' job satisfaction and perceptions of their work environment at multiple points in time. The researchers used these inner work life indicators to predict the business units' performance at later points in time. Results showed that employees' satisfaction and perceptions of their organization, their managers, their colleagues, and their work significantly predicted sales, profitability, customer loyalty, and employee retention. In other words, better inner work life for employees yields tangible benefits for companies, their customers, and their shareholders.

How Inner Work Life
Translates into Performance

In light of our results, managers who say—or secretly believe—that employees work better under pressure, uncertainty, unhappiness, or fear are just plain wrong. Negative inner work life has a negative effect on the four dimensions of performance: people are less creative, less productive, less deeply committed to their work, and less collegial to each other when their inner work lives darken. But why? How does inner work life translate into work behaviors?

Psychology and neuroscience yield some clues about one aspect of inner work life—emotion. Brain researchers have found that negative and positive emotions are produced by different brain systems; as a result, these emotions have very different effects on the way people think and act.[21] Psychologist Barbara Fredrickson theorized that positive emotions broaden people's thoughts and the repertoire of actions they pursue, but negative mood does just the opposite.[22] Working with colleagues, Fredrickson has tested her theory in a number of ways. In two experiments with 104 college students, she used film clips to induce either positive, negative, or neutral emotions, and then had them complete a task.[23] The task in the first experiment measured scope of attention by testing whether students took in the overall configuration of a geometric pattern or focused narrowly on its details. Compared with students in the neutral-emotion condition, those experiencing positive emotions were more likely to see the forest rather than focusing narrowly on the trees.

Fredrickson's second experiment used a fill-in-the-blank task to measure how many actions the students would like to engage in while feeling the particular emotion evoked by the film they had just watched. Compared with students who felt neutral, those feeling positive emotions listed many more actions they would like to undertake; those feeling negative emotions listed many fewer actions. Taken together, the two experiments showed that positive emotion can be liberating and negative emotion can be constraining. This research suggests how one component of inner work life might affect people at work.

By carefully analyzing our respondents' written journal entries, we were able to construct a more comprehensive picture of how all three aspects of inner work life influence creativity, productivity, commitment, and collegiality. We discovered that the inner work life effect operates in three primary ways: *attention* to tasks, *engagement* in the project, and *intention* to work hard. When inner work life is good, people are more likely to pay attention to the work itself, become deeply engaged in their team's project, and hold fast to the goal of doing a great job. When inner work life is bad, people are more likely to get distracted from their work (often by the inner work life killer), disengage from their team's projects, and give up on trying to achieve the goals set before them.

The worst days of the Infosuite team will help us paint the picture. We use negative inner work life in these illustrations because our study participants tended to write their most vivid journal entries about unpleasant events. But keep in mind that these are simply the converse image of positive inner work life. And keep in mind that these negative illustrations hold true not only for the Infosuite team, but also for teams across the various companies we researched.

Infosuite: Inner Work Life in Action

Overall, the day-to-day performance of the Infosuite team was average, with a great deal of variability. That performance variability echoes the extreme swings in Infosuite team members' inner work lives. They experienced many very good days, but they also had many very bad days.

Most of the negative events affecting the team were caused by upper management decisions at HotelData and the parent company, Dream-Suite. Earlier, we described team members' negative reactions to the "takeover" when DreamSuite reacquired HotelData as a wholly owned subsidiary. After that critical event, things got much worse, and quickly.

Soon after the DreamSuite reacquisition, rumors about terminations began to circulate, and then the terminations became a reality. They happened in waves, starting with higher-level managers, moving down to the project manager level, and hitting team members shortly after we ended our study. So, for approximately the last two months of our study, the members of the Infosuite team worried that their project manager (one of their two team leaders) might be terminated and that they might eventually lose their jobs, too. Worry was reinforced because management failed to explain adequately the basis for any new terminations; it even failed to invite the Infosuite team to the annual company picnic, increasing the team's sense of alienation and the fear that they were no longer to be part of the company. As it turned out, none of them got a pink slip. Still, the unfolding events wreaked havoc on team members' inner work lives and performance—particularly on days when the terminations took center stage.

Consider the excerpt below from Marsha's journal on the day that the terminations started. As you read it, keep in mind Marsha's back-story. She had a thirty-year history with DreamSuite, during which she had experienced—and survived—a number of lay-offs. They never became easier, as each time she feared for her own job and watched beloved coworkers get marched out the door with their boxes of personal belongings.

> It is very hard to work and get anything done around here today. 39 people lost their jobs [. . .] and it seems like this is just the beginning. They will get rid of people from the project managers' level next and then they will move on to us; they even came out with a letter saying as much! I feel like an abused spouse that will not leave the abuser. I keep giving them another chance and they keep socking us in the face. I'm ashamed at my own inability to just get up and walk away with a little dignity. Instead, I sit here and wait for them to decide my fate. [Marsha, 4/15]

Inner work life can hardly get worse than feeling like an abused spouse. The most obvious way in which this inner state affected Marsha's performance on April 15 was distraction from the complex cognitive processes that her Infosuite work required. Like many of her coworkers that day, Marsha's mind was hijacked. As the terminations continued, it became even more difficult for people to concentrate:

> 30 project managers got walked out today, throughout the morning until just after lunch. It was quite unnerving, and all anyone could talk about or think about for a good part of the day. Some of my teammates were even crying at their desks. [Helen, 5/20]

There is no need to invoke subtle neurological mechanisms to explain the effect of this day's negative emotions on Infosuite team members' performance. It's tough to pay attention to your work when everyone around you is talking about getting fired. It's impossible to focus on your programming job when the letters on the computer screen are swimming through tears.

The terminations also led Infosuite team members to disengage from their work. Marsha admitted apathy toward the task at hand when she said, on April 15, "I sit here and wait for them . . . " Marsha's abysmal perceptions of DreamSuite management—and of herself—led to this disengagement. She saw DreamSuite as a foe, and herself as a spineless fool. These perceptions drained Marsha's job of its positive meaning. Her identity as an employee of HotelData, and once again an employee of DreamSuite, had become a burden, her employee ID a badge of shame. No wonder she wanted to distance herself from the job.

When jobs have been robbed of personal meaning, the intention to work hard evaporates. This happens because the work is no longer intrinsically motivating—no longer interesting, enjoyable, or personally challenging. When people's motivation for a job has become purely extrinsic—when they are just putting in their time to make a buck or to get the benefits—they will do only what they must do, and no more. Goals have narrowed; going the extra mile for the job seems excessive. Here is what Marsha had to say when the layoffs had started, shortly after the DreamSuite reacquisition:

> We have heard some names, but of course no one is saying anything. The minute DreamSuite steps back into the picture, people are walking around scared and afraid for their jobs. [. . .] What kills me is, after this, they will turn around and wonder why everyone doesn't just throw themselves in front of a train for the company. What dopes. [Marsha, 4/14]

Marsha's bitterness sprang from the irony of the company treating HotelData employees as expendable while expecting highly motivated performance. To her mind, managers were duping themselves if they believed that these workers would have any desire to give their all for the company. Clearly—at least on this day—she had no such intention.

We saw reports similar to Marsha's almost daily during this period, from every member of the Infosuite team. This episode was not only extremely difficult for the team members; it was also hurting HotelData and DreamSuite. High performance cannot continue when inner work life suffers because, as we saw in the Infosuite journals and many others, people lose their attention to, engagement with, and

TIPS FOR MANAGERS

The Physical Symptoms of Emotional Health

In case you need more reasons to care about inner work life, beyond employee performance, here is another: employee health. Researchers have found a direct connection between health and emotion. Physical health is better when people experience more positive moods and fewer negative moods, possibly because mood influences the immune system. You might be surprised to learn that these findings cover illnesses as ordinary as colds and as life-threatening as strokes.[a]

Marsha's journal described health problems arising from the fear and uncertainty she felt during the Infosuite termination episode. "I'm feeling kind of tired and low-key [. . .] not like me at all. I woke up at 2 a.m. and couldn't get back to sleep last night, so that might be it," Marsha wrote in April. "My doctor asked me yesterday if I was under any stress and I just laughed. I am really trying to stay on track and get my work done, but everyone I meet in the hall wants to talk about the walk-outs. People are really, really scared."

Obviously, if people are sick, their ability to do productive, creative work—or even to work at all—is compromised. But you should pay attention to your employees' physical health not just because of its performance implications. It could be telling you something very important about the health of their inner work lives. Take it as a warning signal if, without any change in sick-day policy or any public health crisis, your employees are getting sick increasingly often.

a. A few recent papers provide good reviews of the literature linking aspects of everyday psychological experience, particularly positive and negative mood, to physical health (e.g., S. Cohen and S. D. Pressman, "Positive Affect and Health," *Current Directions in Psychological Science* 15 [2006]: 122–125; S. D. Pressman and S. Cohen, "Does Positive Affect Influence Health?," *Psychological Bulletin* 131 [2005]: 803–855; P. Salovey, A. J. Rothman, J. B. Detweiler, and W. T. Steward, "Emotional States and Physical Health," *American Psychologist* 55 [2000]: 110–121).

intention to work diligently on their projects (and more besides; see "The Physical Symptoms of Emotional Health"). But when inner work life thrives, people stay focused on the work, become deeply involved in it, and do what it takes to achieve their projects' goals. Performance hums.

Inner Work Life Lessons

The evidence is clear: inner work life governs how employees perform their work and behave toward their coworkers. Evidence on the inner work life effect favors the positive; if you want your people to perform at a high level over the long haul, you must avoid events that lead to poor inner work lives. For DreamSuite Hotels, dissolving the joint venture with Collander may have been a business necessity, but treating loyal workers badly at its inception and its dissolution was not.

Avoiding events that lead to negative inner work life applies to the entire range of events at work, from poorly handled reorganizations to neglected company-picnic invitations. On the upside, you can foster positive inner work life with a vast array of everyday events at work. Try to calculate the cost-benefit ratio of Helen's great workday that resulted from her project manager's granting time off to attend her daughter's school play. The calculation is impossible, because the cost was nil—and the benefit to Helen's inner work life and performance, enormous.

Lessons about the inner work life effect apply to any organization. Some years ago, we and our colleagues studied employees' perceptions of the work environment in a large, seemingly successful high-tech electronics firm.[24] Six months after we collected our first measures of this key aspect of inner work life, along with measures of creativity and productivity, the management announced a massive downsizing. Follow-up measures showed that creativity and productivity both suffered, and continued to suffer as much as four months after the downsizing was completed. Our follow-up surveys revealed that the event had a terrible effect on perceptions of the work environment. Our employee interviews revealed why: workers had become less engaged, less collaborative, and less mutually supportive.

Imagine what must have happened to the inner work lives of Sunbeam employees in 1996, when they learned that "Chainsaw" Al Dunlap was about to become their CEO. Dunlap had earned his proudly held nickname by slashing over eleven thousand jobs at Scott Paper Company, his prior CEO stint. It's unlikely that those Sunbeam employees were at their creative, productive best as they unhappily awaited the "Chainsaw's" arrival.

You may have long believed that happy workers are better workers. But not everyone thinks so, and many managers don't act as if it's so. When Carlyle said, "No pressure, no diamonds," he was suggesting that pressure is not just the best way, but the *only* way to produce excellent work. Similarly, when managers say they want their companies to be "lean and mean," they imply that excellence requires disregard for the human costs of maximal efficiency. And when Jack Welch, arguably the most respected manager of the twentieth century, wrote "Tough guys finish first," it became all too easy for managers to assume that this gave them license to ignore the impact of their actions on inner work life. In the extreme, managers conclude that it is necessary to treat at least some employees badly.[25]

Many modern organizations put enormous stress on their workers. But placing people under extreme stress, especially for long periods of time, is more likely to produce coal than diamonds. Undeniably, some pressure is unavoidable, but the best managers understand that, even in tough circumstances, it makes sense to take strategic measures to keep their workers creatively and productively engaged. At the very least, when they scale back, they communicate openly and respectfully with their employees. Repeated insults to inner work life, even small ones, can jeopardize the entire enterprise.

In the next chapter, we will begin to show how you can drive inner work life upward, advancing performance. Here we will leave you with a puzzle and a clue. Just five days after thirty HotelData project managers were terminated, sending some Infosuite members into tears, the team was handed an enormous, time-urgent project. Helen was called in from vacation to help get the job done. Although initially angry about being asked to give up her vacation, she willingly—even excitedly—put in fifty-eight hours on the project during her "week off." In fact, her inner work life reached peak levels. How was this possible?

4

Discovering the
Progress Principle

WHEN WE first saw Helen's May 25 diary entry, we were
stunned. Only five days had passed since thirty of her
firm's project managers had been laid off, and members
of HotelData's Infosuite team still feared their own heads might be on
the chopping block. Angry and bitter, Helen and her teammates had little reason to trust their firm's parent company, DreamSuite Hotels. And
yet something had changed:

> I was called in to work on the Big Deal project. So DreamSuite
> has to go to court. So Big Deal. What about my vacation? I'm
> angry about being called in. But I think I did some really good
> work under pressure. And I feel that I really supported the team.
> [Helen, 5/25]

The first part of the entry reflects the attitude you might expect:
Helen (the software engineer whom you met in chapter 3) was resentful
and a bit sarcastic. She had planned to spend five days relaxing and
spending late afternoons with her two school-aged kids. But what

should we make of her last two sentences? She seemed proud of her work and pleased that she helped her team. Moreover, she gave above-average ratings to all three elements of her inner work life that day—perceptions (specifically, her perceived progress in the work), emotions, and motivation. And this was someone who had just spent a "vacation" day at the office!

Infosuite was among the first teams we studied, so we had little basis for understanding such a dramatic shift. Was this just an isolated incident, something limited to Helen? Had events we weren't privy to somehow cheered her up? No. We would soon find out that other members of the Infosuite team were, like Helen, enjoying their workdays as they hadn't in some time. DreamSuite faced a $145 million lawsuit, and for several days, some of the team devoted all their attention, and much overtime, to compiling and analyzing the data needed to fight the suit. Some even worked over a holiday weekend—and loved it.

Initially, we looked for obvious motivators. Recognition, perhaps? No. Although the Infosuite team did receive some recognition from top management, it came at the end of this project. So that did not explain Helen's inner work life. Likewise, the team received no tangible reward for putting in extra time and giving up a long weekend.

Only when we analyzed the data from all twenty-six teams we studied did we fully understand the Infosuite team's experience during the Big Deal project; we had been witnessing the power of progress. This is one of the most important findings of our entire study: that making headway on meaningful work brightens inner work life and boosts long-term performance. Real progress triggers positive emotions like satisfaction, gladness, even joy. It leads to a sense of accomplishment and self-worth as well as positive views of the work and, sometimes, the organization. Such thoughts and perceptions (along with those positive emotions) feed the motivation, the deep engagement, that is crucial for ongoing blockbuster performance.

In chapter 3, we showed that positive inner work life leads to greater creativity and productivity.[1] In this chapter, we will show that making progress (being productive and creative) leads to positive inner work life. This creates *the progress loop*, the self-reinforcing process in which progress and inner work life fuel each other. We will explore the progress loop and its implications in chapter 5.

The Big Deal Project

The Infosuite team playfully dubbed the project that began on May 25 the "Big Deal," borrowing Helen's sarcastic label. Infosuite members with the requisite expertise for this project had just eight days, including the Memorial Day weekend, to come up with the data the company needed. The team was handicapped because Harry, one of the team leaders, was out sick, and Ruth, the other team leader (and project manager), was recovering from major surgery. Yet we know from the project records that four key members of the team (and four others in supporting roles) made steady progress from the very first day. And for the most part, their thoughts, feelings, and drives were remarkably upbeat. In the end, the project was a resounding success.

The details of the Big Deal project hold important clues about the impact of progress. As we reveal them, keep in mind this crucial fact: despite many setbacks along the way, the team made steady progress every day.

Because of its complex nature, the Big Deal project required the specific skills of Marsha, Ruth (a statistical analyst in her late thirties who had been with DreamSuite for ten years), and Chester (a programmer also in his late thirties who had been with DreamSuite for five years). Helen was called in as the fourth core worker because of her engineering expertise. Despite the angry tone of her May 25 diary entry, by the second day of the project, Helen didn't even mention her abandoned vacation:

> More work today on the big DreamSuite lawsuit problem. The Boss's Boss came by to offer encouragement. That was nice. He bought us bottled water! Not the cheap stuff I buy, either. We are getting tired! Nobody's snapped yet, though. I have to admit that I love working under pressure. [Helen, 5/26]

Stimulated by the high stakes, Helen rejoiced in this work. One factor seemed to be the high-energy atmosphere, where people were working hard—a prerequisite of fast progress. But the most important trigger, the one she mentioned first, seems almost trivial: a high-level manager came to the drab, cavernous Infosuite warehouse to offer encouragement and give the team "expensive" bottled water. Although some brand-name plastic bottles and a few supportive words seem like pitiful compensation for the demands being placed on Helen, the gesture made her happy and generated positive perceptions as well. Perhaps for the first time in a long while, a top manager was humanized; he had done something "nice." He had shown that he noticed her work and he cared.

But the manager's gesture altered *perceptions of the work itself*, which are even more central to the way that progress operates on inner work life. Because high-level managers almost never stopped by the Infosuite cubicles to encourage the team in any way, his action signified to the team how important this project was to the organization. The work now had more meaning, so every step forward gave Helen and her coworkers a greater *sense of accomplishment*—one of the key perceptual elements of positive inner work life. Even Clark, a recent college graduate in computer science with less than a year on the Infosuite team, was deeply affected by the attention management paid to his teammates working on the project. In his diary, he said it signaled to him that his office handled important work, that he had an expert team, and that management supported the team. Vicariously, he experienced the sense of accomplishment and found his perceptions of the team and its work growing ever more favorable. "Although I was not involved," he wrote, "it was a very positive experience."

The Big Deal project picked up steam on May 27, when several vice presidents visited to check on the project's progress; one brought both bottled water *and* pizza. Moreover, the top brass made it clear that people working on the Big Deal project could set aside other jobs without negative consequences, thus protecting the team from other demands.

Notice the motivational dynamics here. Top management did not have to create incentives to motivate the Infosuite team. The team was largely self-motivated by the important, challenging work. What management really had to do—and did effectively—was to remove the barriers that could have impeded that existing motivation—barriers like distraction from irrelevant tasks and even hunger pangs. In the process, management boosted inner work life by making people working on the Big Deal project feel like valued members of the organization. This was a far cry from the sense of alienation that Infosuite team members felt when they were not invited to the company picnic.

Like Clark, Tom—the quiet, loyal, oldest team member—played only a supporting role in the project. Nonetheless, his inner work life got a positive push from the team's forward movement, and from the support that he witnessed—particularly the involvement of what he called "corporate bigwigs," and Ruth's expert leadership. As he put it in his journal, "People are working crazy hours, vice presidents are a dime a dozen in our office, and wonderful Miss Ruth is doing a great job keeping us going."

The power of progress was operating in full force for Marsha, a core member of the Big Deal subteam; she seemed to revel in the "crazy hours." Remember, this is the person who, just six weeks earlier, reported feeling that DreamSuite treated her like an abused spouse.

> Today our entire office worked like a real team again. It was wonderful. We all forgot the current stressful situation and have all worked around the clock to get a big project done. I have been here about 15 hours, but it has been one of the best days I've had in months!! [Marsha, 5/27]

Working hard with the team, collaborating well, and progressing toward a clear and important goal pushed Marsha's dour thoughts and feelings into the background. The result, in her words, was a "best day"—outstanding inner work life.

Several Infosuite members demonstrated enormous commitment to the Big Deal project. On the last day of her "vacation week," Helen

stayed long enough to finish up loose ends on her part of the project
and assist other team members, noting how dedicated they all were:
"My vacation week: 58 hours on the job. And I put in less time than
everyone else."Amazingly, on the following Monday, a national holiday
(Memorial Day), Marsha, Chester, and Ruth spent their third consecutive fourteen-hour day at the office to finish up the project. And they
did finish, with high-quality work. Chester and Ruth shared the extraordinary inner work life reported by Marsha in her Memorial Day
journal: "The people I have been working with are wonderful and,
even though the hours have been stressful, the atmosphere has been
happy and light."

Chester's Memorial Day diary perfectly captured the impact of
progress. He described how the team's collaborative progress resulted
in powerfully positive perceptions, and he detailed the many elements
that facilitated their success:

> [. . .] The sense of accomplishment we felt after interacting so
> greatly throughout this entire ordeal is an event in itself.
>
> From 5/25 through 5/30, I put in over 70 hours of work, and
> some other team members did the same—including Ruth, which
> was a constant worry for us due to her health. However, as usual,
> she was great. We ran into all sorts of unexpected problems, and
> had to make all kinds of decisions. Several times, when we thought
> it was done, we would find a problem with the data, and some-
> times start all over again. [. . .] This involved at least 5 members of
> our team, who worked around the clock, giving up holidays and
> even vacation. It also involved people from other teams who were
> willing to help us (with a smile on their faces!), and what a fantastic
> help it was. [. . .] this not only brought our team even closer, but
> our efforts were noticed by [. . .] top management as well, having
> them here with us over the weekend for support to the point of
> going out of their way to bring us food. [Chester, 5/31]

Chester's first line went straight to the strong sense of accomplishment
arising from collaborative progress throughout the "entire ordeal."

Other positive perceptions, as well as emotions and motivations, are implicitly conveyed by punctuation and tone. He signals the importance of the project, detailing the above-and-beyond efforts of team members to forgo time off, put in extra hours, and overcome many setbacks. His narrative highlights several specific facilitators of the team's progress. First, Chester implies that team members had considerable *autonomy* to execute the project as they saw fit, making decisions along the way. Second, Ruth led the team in *dealing with problems* as they arose—even taking steps back, if necessary, to figure out the best way forward. Third, Chester notes that other teams *helped* the Infosuite team throughout its mission—even over the holiday weekend. Finally, he acknowledges that top managers *supported* the team, with a physical presence that mattered as much as the water and pizza.

The day after the project's completion, Ruth reported on the team's efforts to managers at both HotelData and DreamSuite Hotels—prompting hearty commendations for the team. She returned to the Infosuite cubicle camp, regaled them with the plaudits, and led them all in rousing applause for the entire team—with special thanks to the weekend "worker bees." The Big Deal project resulted in a major win for DreamSuite. Within days, the company successfully settled the lawsuit, due in large part to the work of the Infosuite team.

Consider how extraordinary the team's work on this project was. Only days before the Big Deal was handed to them, they were distraught over the organization's decision to terminate a number of highly respected project managers. Not long after the project ended, they once again faced the miseries of organizational change driven by uncommunicative upper management. And yet, during the project, the power of making progress in meaningful work, in a collaborative team, with supportive management, was sufficiently strong to overcome that trauma—at least temporarily—fuelling both peak inner work life and high performance.

Many factors besides the progress—the help they received, release from other demands, interpersonal and management support, recognition—boosted the team's inner work life. But, as we analyzed

the data from Infosuite and our other twenty-five teams, we came to realize that *making progress in meaningful work* is the most powerful stimulant to great inner work life.

Setbacks: The Dark Side

But just as progress is the biggest stimulant to inner work life, setbacks
are the biggest downer. Unfortunately, setbacks in any sort of meaningful work are a fact of life—hitting dead ends while trying to solve a vexing problem, being blocked in attempts to meet a goal, or failing to find
crucial information. Infosuite team members certainly had their share
of setbacks during the months we studied them. For example, well before the Big Deal project, Tom encountered a persistent bug while trying to make some changes to a billing program. His inner work life
ratings on the journal form made it clear that these frustrations cast a
pall on his day:

> No event today, just the continuing frustration of the week—
> trying to install a fairly simple change in code to an enormously
> complicated method of installation and production execution.
> Honest, you don't want to hear the details. [Tom, 4/9]

No one was to blame; Tom's setbacks were simply inherent in the
work. By contrast, on March 18 Marsha's work was stalled by her customers, the DreamSuite operations managers who had ordered a piece
of hotel booking software that Marsha and Helen were creating:

> Helen and I have been in meetings with our users all day!! [. . .]
> The purpose of the meeting was to nail down their requirements
> so we can charge ahead with the work. Their deadline is end of
> April; the only problem is that they don't know what they need or
> want. We have spent all day with them, and the end result is that
> they have gone off to confer among themselves, so they can come
> back to us once again and try to state their needs. I'm in Dilbert
> Hell!! [Marsha, 3/18]

Marsha's thoughts, feelings, and drive were all imperiled by her inability to move forward—or even get started—on this project. Moreover, Marsha had reason to question how meaningful the work was if the users themselves had no clear sense of what they needed. As for autonomy, she and Helen were handcuffed by their clients' hesitation. Marsha's experience here, like Tom's "continuing frustration of the week," stands in stark contrast to their inner work life experiences during the Big Deal project.

The Infosuite team was certainly not unique; we found setback events in every team we studied. Sometimes the cause seemed to be nothing more than bad luck or the inevitable difficulties of technology:

> My synthesis run went really wrong, and I made a pot of junk. I don't understand why this could happen, despite very careful planning and designing of the run. It irritates me when something like this happens. [Scientist, chemicals company]

At other times, the source was unresponsive upper managers or unhelpful coworkers:

> Tried to "sell" an idea to the MT [top divisional management], but they did not see my point of view. Were very rigid in their thinking, not open to a different opinion. At the same time, if I direct a question to one of them, they invariably do not have an answer. [Marketing specialist, team leader, consumer products company]

> In a meeting I was facilitating, Victor [a member of my team] showed a surprising lack of support for me (as a facilitator). In front of the client, Victor invalidated an exercise I was attempting to complete. This resulted in an inability to get a key result from the meeting. I believe this reflected poor judgment on his part. [Senior consultant, team leader, high-tech company]

In each of these examples, the setback itself evoked negative inner work life. In most cases, a deflated sense of accomplishment figured prominently in that response. If the setback resulted simply from the

difficult nature of the work itself, negative inner work life turned positive as people began to overcome the challenge, either on their own or
with help. Quite often, however, it was others' behavior—a manager or
a coworker undercut an idea, failed to offer help when it was needed, or
undermined the person's efforts—that led directly or indirectly to the
setback. In these circumstances, turning negative inner work life positive required the removal or reversal of the progress obstacle—meaning
that the person had to do something *else* before even starting to make
progress. An accumulation of such events could permanently taint the
person's backstory about the organization.

Although inner work life is hidden most of the time, it surfaced
clearly in many of the diary narratives reporting progress or setbacks.
We see the diarists' sense of accomplishment (or its absence), the perceptions of themselves as competent (or incompetent), the view of
others as supportive (or ill-intentioned). We see the emotions of happiness, joy, and pride after progress, versus anger, frustration, and shame
after setbacks. We witness the rise and fall of motivation. This is the
power of progress in its positive and its negative forms.

We see it potently in the journal of Tom, who was plagued by that
bug in Infosuite's complicated billing program. When the setback
turned to progress, his joy was nearly palpable:

> I smashed that bug that's been frustrating me for almost a calen-
> dar week. That may not be an event to you, but I live a very drab
> life, so I'm all hyped. No one really knows about it; three of the
> team [members who] would be involved are out today—so I have
> to sit here rejoicing in my solitary smugness. [Tom, 4/12]

Hard Evidence: Progress Feeds
Inner Work Life

The prominence of progress and setbacks resounded from the journals
of the Infosuite team. This pattern is what we call the *progress principle:
of all the positive events that influence inner work life, the single most powerful is*

progress in meaningful work; of all the negative events, the single most powerful is the opposite of progress—setbacks in the work. We consider this to be a fundamental management *principle*: facilitating progress is the most effective way for managers to influence inner work life. Even when progress happens in small steps, a person's sense of steady forward movement toward an important goal can make all the difference between a great day and a terrible one.

This pattern became increasingly obvious as the diaries came in from all the teams in our study. People's inner work lives seemed to lift or drag depending on whether or not their projects moved forward, even by small increments. *Small wins* often had a surprisingly strong positive effect, and *small losses* a surprisingly strong negative one. We tested our impressions more rigorously in two ways. Each confirmed the power of progress to dominate inner work life.

What the Numbers Reveal

Statistical analyses of our entire database supported the progress principle. Across the board, inner work life was much better on progress days than setback days. The daily diary forms yielded ratings of each of the three elements of inner work life: the person's *perceptions* that day of the work, the team, the work environment, and the supervisor; the person's *emotions* that day; and the person's *motivation* toward the work that day. Using these numbers from all 12,000 diaries, we compared inner work life on days when the diary reported a progress event, days when it reported a setback event, and days when it reported neither. (The appendix has additional information about our statistical analyses.)

Consider *motivation*. On days when they made progress, people were more intrinsically motivated—by the interest, enjoyment, challenges, and involvement in the work itself. On setback days, not only were these diarists less intrinsically motivated by interest, they were also less *extrinsically* motivated by recognition. Apparently, setbacks in the work can lead a person to feel generally apathetic toward doing the work at all. (See "Using the Progress Principle to Jump-Start Innovation.")

TIPS FOR MANAGERS

Using the Progress Principle to Jump-Start Innovation

You can use the connection between progress and intrinsic motivation to boost innovation. On days when people have made real progress in work that matters to them, they end the day feeling more intrinsically motivated—turned on by their interest in and enjoyment of the work. There's plenty of research showing that, when people are more intrinsically motivated, they are more likely to be creative.[a] This means that when your subordinates have pulled off a real accomplishment, they may be more open to new, challenging work that calls for creativity. In other words, they should be particularly eager to take on vexing problems and find creative solutions following days of notable progress.

Throughout the rest of this book, you will find ideas on how to facilitate such progress.

a. T. M. Amabile, *Creativity in Context* (Boulder, CO: Westview Press, 1996).

As we had suspected, our participants also experienced much more positive *emotions* when they made progress than when they had setbacks. Overall, they reported being in a more upbeat mood. And they expressed more joy as well as warmth and pride. When they suffered setbacks in the work, they expressed more frustration, fear, and sadness.

Perceptions differed in many ways, too. On progress days, people perceived significantly more positive challenge in their work. They saw the team as more mutually supportive, and they reported more positive interactions between the team and the supervisor.[2] On a number of dimensions, perceptions suffered when people encountered setbacks in their projects. They found less positive challenge in the work, felt that they had less freedom in carrying out the work, and reported that they had insufficient resources for doing the work. Moreover, on setback days, our participants perceived both their teams and their supervisors as less supportive.

Were all of these inner work life changes *caused by* daily progress and setbacks, or might some of them have *caused* progress or setbacks in the first place? There is no way of knowing from the numerical data alone. However, the diaries do tell us that more positive perceptions, a sense of accomplishment, satisfaction, happiness, and even elation, often followed progress. And we know that deteriorating perceptions, frustration, sadness, and even disgust often followed setbacks. Almost certainly, the causality goes both ways. As we showed in chapter 3, positive inner work life leads to better performance. These bidirectional forces provide managers with powerful tools—as we will describe in chapter 5.

Progress Versus Other Important Events

How important are progress and setbacks in the ongoing stream of *all* events that happen at work? When our participants wrote about the "event of the day" in their journals, they mentioned dozens of positive events across the diaries—not only progress in the work, but also getting help in the work, finding an important piece of information, gaining access to necessary resources, being recognized for an accomplishment, receiving encouragement, and many others. All of these positive triggers were associated with good inner work life; in general, they made for "good days" at work. Conversely, the journal narratives mentioned dozens of negative events—not only setbacks in the work, but also being micromanaged, having a resource request rejected, finding out that someone else's action had harmed the project, being ridiculed, being ignored, being overly pressured, and much else. All of these negative triggers were associated with poor inner work life; in general, they made for "bad days" at work.

Did progress and setbacks really stand out above all of these other events? Yes. To discover this answer, we categorized all of the different positive, negative, and neutral events reported in the diaries. For example, we flagged an event as *progress* when a diary reported that the person or the team moved forward or accomplished something.[3] When Chester, Marsha, and Ruth made their final push on the Big Deal project, their diaries reported a series of progress events. We flagged a *setback* when progress was blocked or the work moved backward in some way.[4] After refining and testing our event categorization scheme, we categorized all of the events in the journal entries from participants' very *best* inner work life days, and compared them to events on their very *worst* inner work life days.

Our findings could not have been clearer: progress and setbacks were the most prominent positive and negative events by a wide margin. When we systematically counted all types of positive events on the very best inner work life days, progress stood out as the most frequently reported event in those diary narratives. On the very worst inner work life days, setbacks were the single most frequently reported event.

More importantly, of all types of events, progress and setbacks showed the greatest *contrasts* on best and worst inner work life days. For example, we examined emotions by creating a measure of overall *mood* for the day; the measure was a combination of six different emotion questions included on the daily diary form. We looked at days when people reported their best moods and days when they reported their worst moods. We found that 76 percent of the best days involved progress, but only 13 percent involved setbacks; that's a difference of 63 percentage points. Worst days were the mirror image. Progress happened on only 25 percent of those days, but setbacks happened on 67 percent—a 42 percentage point difference. No other pairs of contrasting events showed as large a difference on the best- and worst-mood days.

Small wins—seemingly minor progress events—can yield significant inner work life benefits, sometimes as large as much greater leaps forward (and managers can facilitate such events; see "How Do You *Know* When You Have Made Progress?"). On the downside, even seemingly minor setbacks can—well, really set inner work life back. If people are in an excellent mood at the end of the day, it's a good bet that they have

How Do You *Know* When You Have Made Progress?

You can't get a sense of progress unless you're aware that you have actually *made* progress in your work. So how does this happen? According to researchers Richard Hackman and Gregory Oldham, there are two routes.[a] One—probably the route most managers would think of—is getting feedback. If a manager or knowledgeable peer tells the members of a project team that their work is creative or technically sound, they can be confident that they made real progress. Interestingly, though, the second route is preferable: getting feedback *from the work itself*. If a programmer labors to create some tricky new code and then runs the program through a series of tests, that debugging process gives her immediate and complete knowledge about how much progress she has made on that job. If she sees that there are just a few glitches, her motivation will surge, as will her joy and her positive perceptions. She doesn't have to wait for confirmation from anyone else; she doesn't even need *contact* with anyone else.

But if the testing is decoupled from the programming task, if it is done by someone else, that programmer cannot enjoy an immediate uptick to inner work life. The key, then, is to design each job so that, in the act of carrying out the work, people gain knowledge about the results of their effort. Ideally, this should be a feature of every job in every contemporary organization. Is it, in yours?

a. J. R. Hackman and G. R. Oldham, *Work Redesign* (Reading, MA: Addison-Wesley Publishing, 1980).

made some progress in their work. If they are in a terrible mood, it's a good bet that they have had a setback. To a great extent, inner work life rises and falls with progress and setbacks in the work. This is the progress principle and, although it may be most obvious on the best and worst days at work, it operates every day.

The Key Three Influences on Inner Work Life

Progress and setbacks are the most important triggers, but they aren't the only events that make a difference between sweet and sour inner work life. Other everyday events at work play important roles. Besides progress and setbacks, we discovered two additional categories of events that also turned out to be strong differentiators. We refer to them as *factors*, rather than *principles*, because they are not as prominent as progress and setbacks; nonetheless, all three exert important influences on inner work life.

The *progress principle* describes the first of these *key three* categories of events influencing inner work life. The second is what we call the *catalyst factor*. *Catalysts* are actions that directly support the work on the project, including any type of work-related help from a person or group—such as Chester's mention of other HotelData teams helping Infosuite during the Big Deal project. Other catalysts have to do with goals, resources, time, autonomy, idea flow, and dealing with problems in the work.

The third of the key three influences on inner work life is what we call the *nourishment factor*. Where catalysts are triggers directed at the project, *nourishers* are interpersonal triggers, directed at the person. They include respect, encouragement, comfort, and other forms of social or emotional support. The Big Deal project brought nourishers to the Infosuite team, as top managers stopped by to encourage the team with refreshments over the holiday weekend and commended them on their great work at the end of the project.

Just as setbacks are the opposites of progress, *inhibitors* are the opposites of catalysts, and *toxins* are the opposites of nourishers. These negative actions include failing to support the project or the person, as well as actively hindering the project or disrespecting the person in some way.

Figure 4-1 presents these key three influences on inner work life, in both their positive and negative forms. Each bar in the figure shows the percent of best-mood diaries that reported that particular type of event. You can see at a glance that progress is the most prominent event on best-mood days. Catalysts and nourishers also appeared frequently

FIGURE 4-1

What happens on best days (overall mood)?

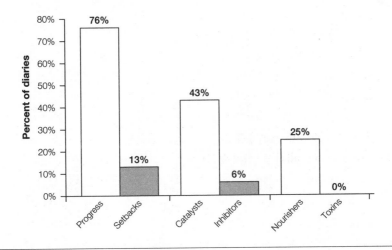

(sometimes in conjunction with each other or with progress). Clearly, the opposite types of events (setbacks, inhibitors, and toxins) are relatively rare. Aside from the key three event categories of progress, catalysts, and nourishers, no other types of events came close to being as important for positive mood. A whopping 85 percent of the best-mood days had one or more of these key three types of positive events.

The same best-days pattern holds for the specific positive emotions (joy and love), and for intrinsic motivation, too.[5] Great inner work life is much more likely on days when people make progress in their work, get help that catalyzes work progress, and find emotional and social nourishment.

Figure 4-2 shows that the pattern of prominent events on poor inner work life days is nearly the mirror image of that depicted in figure 4-1. Setbacks are the most prominent type of event on worst-mood days, with 67 percent of the diaries reporting them. Inhibitors and toxins also appear frequently. Not surprisingly, their opposites (progress, catalysts, and nourishers) are relatively rare on bad days. Again, aside from the key three event categories of setbacks, inhibitors, and toxins, no other

FIGURE 4-2

What happens on worst days (overall mood)?

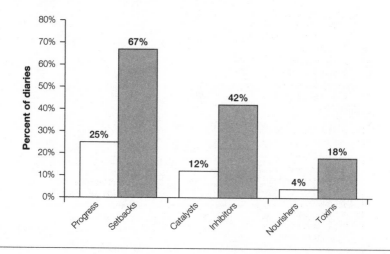

types of triggers came close to being as important for negative mood. Fully 81 percent of the worst-mood days had one of these key three types of negative events. The same pattern holds for the specific negative emotions (anger, fear, and sadness), and for low levels of intrinsic motivation, too. Terrible inner work life is much more likely on days when people have setbacks in their work, experience events that inhibit the work in some way, and suffer incidents that are toxic to their well-being as social animals.

Figure 4-3 summarizes the positive forms of the key three influences on inner work life.

People's inner work lives are influenced by a great many events, including triggers that don't happen at work—like changes in the company's stock price or hassles in their personal lives. But, mostly, inner work life revolves around the key three types of events that happen in organizations. In the next three chapters, we show how each of these key three works, and how you can use them to ignite joy, engagement, and creativity in your organization. Before turning to the catalyst factor and the nourishment factor, we reveal just why the progress principle is so fundamental.

FIGURE 4-3

The key three influences on inner work life

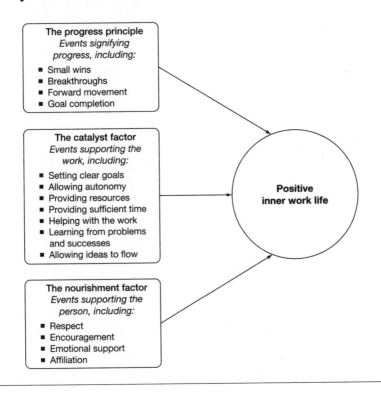

5

The Progress Principle
The Power of Meaningful Accomplishment

YOU MIGHT think it is obvious that managers should focus on supporting employees' work progress. It is not. Here's a startling fact: if managers were to draw the bar graphs you just saw at the end of chapter 4, *progress wouldn't even be in the picture.* We have asked dozens of managers, individually and in groups, to name their most important levers for motivating employees. They tend to favor the things that most management books tout: recognition, tangible incentives, and clear work goals. When we ask how they, as managers, might influence employee emotions, the list looks the same, although many add interpersonal support. Rarely—very rarely—does anyone mention progress in the work and how managers should support it. A 2009 McKinsey survey on motivating people at work yielded the same story—progress was completely absent from the results.[1] In other words, if we had group of managers draw a bar graph depicting what *they* think the key three influences on inner work life are, progress would be missing.

Secrets of the Videogame Designer

Managers may be unaware of how important progress is to human motivation, but it's the secret that every good videogame designer knows.[a] Of all entertainment forms, videogames are among the most addictive. People, especially young men between the ages of fifteen and thirty-five, spend enormous amounts of time and money to stay immersed in fantasy worlds like the massively multiplayer online game (MMOG) *World of Warcraft*. What keeps them hooked? To a large extent, it's two things: constant progress indicators and achievement markers. Both leverage the progress principle.

Virtually all videogames feature "progress bars" that are constantly visible onscreen as players engage in the game. These bars are tangible indicators of how close the player is to reaching the next major game level, the next step within the current level, and the next mini-goal within the current step. Achievement markers are a bit like the badges that Boy Scouts and Girl Scouts can earn for mastering particular tasks. In a videogame, achievements attained by each player—for any of a staggering array of ever-changing challenges throughout the game—are posted for all players to see.

Truly effective videogame designers know how to create a sense of progress for players within all stages of a game. Truly effective managers know how to do the same for their subordinates.

a. We are grateful to Andy Brown of Perfect World Entertainment for giving us these insights, and to Clive Thompson of *Wired* magazine for suggesting the link between videogames and our progress findings.

Puzzled, we wondered if our progress finding was just too obvious. Maybe managers didn't mention supporting progress because they saw it as so fundamental to leading people that it went without saying. Maybe more formal inquiries would reveal a recognition of the progress principle. To find out, we created a survey in which 669 managers ranked the importance of five factors that could influence motivations and emotions at work.[2] Four of the items were straight from conventional management wisdom: recognition, incentives, interpersonal support, and clear goals. The fifth was "support for making progress in the work." Surely, we thought, if we explicitly include progress in the list, managers will put it at the top.

But no. The results revealed unawareness of the power of progress, across all levels of management. Support for making progress was ranked dead last as a motivator, and third (out of five) as an influence on emotion. In fact, only 35 of the 669 managers ranked progress as the number-one motivator; that's a mere 5 percent. Instead, overall, these managers ranked "recognition for good work (either public or private)" as the most important factor in motivating workers and making them happy. Recognition certainly did boost inner work life, when it showed up in our diary study. But it wasn't nearly as prominent as progress. Besides, without work achievements, there is little to recognize.

Any manager's job description should start with facilitating subordinates' progress every day. Even if this imperative isn't big news for you, many managers are clearly unaware of it ("Secrets of the Videogame Designer" highlights one profession that does understand the importance of making progress).[3] In this chapter, we show why making progress is so central to good inner work life and high-level performance over time. And we describe the key to leveraging the progress principle: giving people meaningful work.

Why Progress and Setbacks Are So Powerful

People often say, "It's business, it's not personal." But work *is* personal. Many people, particularly professionals who have invested years of education preparing for careers, identify with the work they produce. Entrepreneurs often have great difficulty relinquishing top leadership positions when their companies have grown beyond their own managerial capacities, because they have invested so much of their personal identities in what they have built.[4] Twitter co-founder Jack Dorsey reported feeling like he was "punched in the stomach" after being replaced as CEO in the company based on his own idea.[5] In our own profession, scholars "are" their academic publications and awards. Through our research with the twenty-six teams we studied, we realized that the same applies to people up and down the organizational hierarchy. Work progress and setbacks matter so much because *work* matters so much. It's simply part of being human.

One of the most basic human drives is toward *self-efficacy*—a person's belief that he or she is individually capable of planning and executing the tasks required to achieve desired goals.[6] It begins to develop very early in life; in fact, the need for self-efficacy drives children to explore and learn about their world. This need continues and even grows throughout the lifespan as people compare their achievements with those of their peers as well as their own "personal bests." At work, people develop an increasingly strong sense of self-efficacy each time they make progress, succeed, or master a problem or task. Not surprisingly, mentally healthy people are predisposed to give themselves the credit when they make progress and attribute setbacks to external forces.[7] Nonetheless, setbacks on personally important projects can cause uncertainty, doubt, or confusion in people's sense of themselves and lower their motivation for the work.

The strong need for self-efficacy explains why everyday work progress stands out as the key event stimulating positive inner work life. It also explains why everyday work setbacks are particularly harmful. A 1995 study out of the University of British Columbia showed how research participants who encountered problems in their quest to achieve goals that were personally important to them (compared with goals that were less important) focused more attention on themselves and spent more time ruminating on those events.[8] Since self-focused attention has often been linked to depression, such findings suggest that people's emotional well-being can be damaged in the short run when they face discrepancies between goals that are important to their identity or sense of self-worth and what they have actually achieved.[9] The more negative the setback, and the more important the goal they were trying to achieve, the more likely they are to focus on that blocked goal; this rumination can cause even more negative emotion.[10]

Other research has confirmed the connection between setbacks on important projects and poor psychological states: negative emotion, dwindling motivation, and extended thinking about how poorly things went.[11] Interestingly, the journal entries in our research reveal a form of rumination: the more negative the "event of the day," the longer the entry.[12]

When people make progress toward, or actually meet, personally meaningful goals, the good match between their expectations and their reading of reality allows them to feel good, grow their positive self-efficacy, get even more revved up to tackle the next job, and mentally move on to something else.[13] Progress motivates people to accept difficult challenges more readily and to persist longer.[14] Recall how Helen of the Infosuite team attacked her work with extra zeal when a complex new assignment from a customer followed the successful completion of a previous project. If people feel capable, then they see difficult problems as positive challenges and opportunities to succeed. Put another way, they develop a "sense of empowerment."[15] If they suffer consistent setbacks, they see those same challenges as opportunities to fail, and avoid them ("The Power of Negative Events" shows why it is vitally important to reduce these discouraging setbacks).

Of all the teams we studied, the Sun-Protect team of Lapelle (a consumer products company) faced one of the most challenging assignments we saw: to develop a standard-setting face cream with excellent moisturizing properties and superior UV sun protection at half the cost of existing products. The team understood the strategic importance of this project. After weeks of refining the formula through a rigorous clinical testing regime, overcoming many setbacks along the way, team members anxiously awaited results of the ultimate test: consumer focus group data collected and analyzed by a neutral external research firm. Project manager Kathy described their reaction when they got the news:

We received [focus group] results on [our key] product. The results are extremely encouraging. Everyone feels very motivated because we delivered on what we claim the product can do, and this is clearly picked up by the consumer! Now we have [next steps] to move on.

The Power of Negative Events

If you want to foster great inner work life, focus first on eliminating the obstacles that cause setbacks. Why? Because one setback has more power to sway inner work life than one progress incident. Some surprising evidence:

- The effect of setbacks on emotions is stronger than the effect of progress.[a] Although progress increases happiness and decreases frustration, the effect of setbacks is not only opposite on both types of emotions—it is *greater*. The power of setbacks to diminish happiness is more than twice as strong as the power of progress to boost happiness. The power of setbacks to increase frustration is more than three times as strong as the power of progress to decrease frustration.

- Small losses can overwhelm small wins. The asymmetry between the power of setbacks and progress events appears to apply even to relatively minor triggers. Similarly, small everyday hassles at work hold more sway than small everyday supports.[b]

- Negative team leader behaviors affect inner work life more broadly than do positive team leader behaviors.

- The fact that people write longer diary narratives about negative events of all kinds—not just setbacks—compared with neutral or positive events hints that people may expend more cognitive and emotional energy on bad events than good ones.

- Other types of negative events—not just setbacks—are more powerful than their mirror-image positive events.[c]

Kathy and her teammates were ecstatic over the great progress they had made. They knew that they were far from done, but this event only whetted their appetite for tackling all the challenges that lay between that happy moment and the moment when they would see their product stocked on the shelves of major retailers worldwide.

- The connection between mood and negative work events is about five times stronger than the connection between mood and positive events.[d]

- Employees recall more negative leader actions than positive actions, and they recall the negative actions more intensely and in more detail than the positive ones.[e]

Precisely because they are less powerful in affecting inner work life, try to ensure that good events at work outnumber the bad. In particular, try to reduce daily hassles. This means that even your small actions to remove obstacles impeding the progress of individuals and teams can make a big difference for inner work life—and, thus, for overall performance. And be sure that *you* aren't the source of obstacles. Because negative triggers can have such a disproportionate effect on inner work life, you might do well to adopt the physician's creed: *First, do no harm.*

a. The first four pieces of evidence in this list come from our diary study. Details are in the appendix. Also see R. F. Baumeister, E. Bratslavsky, C. Finkenauer, and K. D. Vohs, "Bad Is Stronger Than Good," *Review of General Psychology* 5 (2001): 323–370; and P. Rozin and E. B. Royzman, "Negativity Bias, Negativity Dominance, and Contagion," *Personality and Social Psychology Review* 5 (2001): 296–320.

b. Researchers at the University of California discovered a similar effect: daily hassles were better predictors of unhappiness and psychological distress than either the daily uplifts or the major life stressors (A. D. Kanner, J. C. Coyne, C. Schaefer, and R. S. Lazarus, "Comparison of Two Modes of Stress Measurement: Daily Hassles and Uplifts Versus Major Life Events," *Journal of Behavioral Medicine* 4 [1981]: 1–39).

c. Baumeister, Bratslavsky, Finkenauer, and Vohs, "Bad Is Stronger Than Good."

d. A. G. Miner, T. M. Glomb, and C. Hulin, "Experience Sampling Mood and Its Correlates at Work," *Journal of Occupational and Organizational Psychology* 78 (2005): 171–193.

e. M. T. Dasborough, "Cognitive Asymmetry in Employee Emotional Reactions to Leadership Behaviors," *Leadership Quarterly* 17 (2006): 163–178.

Progress in Meaningful Work

Think of the most boring job you've ever had. Many people nominate the first job they had as a teenager—washing pots and pans in a restaurant kitchen, for example, or checking coats at a museum. In jobs like these, the power of progress seems elusive. No matter how hard you work in these jobs, there are always more dirty pots, always more coats coming in and going out. Only punching the time-clock at the end of the day, or getting the paycheck at the end of the week, yields any sense of accomplishment.

Now think about jobs with much more challenge and room for creativity, jobs like the ones our research participants had—inventing new kitchen gadgets, managing entire product lines of cleaning tools, or solving complex IT problems for a hotel empire. Simply "making progress"— getting tasks done—in these jobs doesn't guarantee good inner work life, either. You may have experienced this rude fact in your own job, on days (or projects) when you ended up feeling demotivated, devalued, and frustrated, even though you worked hard getting things done. That's because, in order for the progress principle to operate, the work must be meaningful to the person doing it.[16] In 1983, when Apple Computer was trying to hire John Sculley away from PepsiCo to be its new CEO, Steve Jobs asked him, "Do you want to spend the rest of your life selling sugared water or do you want a chance to change the world?"[17] In making his pitch, Jobs leveraged this potent psychological force and was able to entice Sculley to leave a wildly successful career at PepsiCo.

This desire for meaningful work creates the fundamental prerequisite for the progress principle. Recall how important the Big Deal project was to DreamSuite Hotels and to the Infosuite team members, even those not directly involved in the project work. Clark, the youngest team member, reported in his journal:

Our office has been asked to produce some ad hoc data [for the Big Deal project]. Our director, manager, and many users have been in the office all day to monitor our progress, while Ruth [the project manager] called Helen in from vacation to help address the problem. Although I was not involved, I've made this my event for the day because I was able to witness the extreme importance of the financial data that we handle in this office, the problem-solving capability of my team, and the supportive involvement of our immediate management. It was a very positive experience. [Clark, 5/26]

Because everyone, from top managers to middle managers to the project manager and Infosuite teammates, focused their attention and energy on this project, Clark knew how important it was—and, by extension, how important his team's work was in general. Not only did he see the Big Deal project as work that had real meaning, but he also saw all of these managers as supportive and his teammates as highly competent when they made progress in that meaningful work. Clark's vicarious experience is a perfect example of how, even when the gains are made by one's comrades, *progress in meaningful work* triggers the sense of accomplishment and the other positive perceptions, emotions, and motivations that comprise splendid inner work life.

Every year, *Fortune* magazine publishes its "100 Best Companies to Work For" list, based on extensive surveys of employees in U.S. public and private companies. Most of the companies on the lists do not offer lavish perks. As we review descriptions of them and think about the examples in our own study, we believe that the best companies to work for support inner work life by facilitating progress. For example, for several years, comparatively unknown Griffin Hospital in Connecticut made the list; in 2006, it ranked fourth. Interestingly, although Griffin offered salaries about 5 to 7 percent lower than other hospitals in the region, it received 5,100 applications for 160 open positions in 2005. Its voluntary turnover was a mere 8 percent. Apparently, health-care professionals were so eager to work at Griffin because of its stellar reputation for patient care; there, they would be supported in doing what mattered most to them. This attitude is also evident in a 2003 survey, which showed that important, meaningful work was valued by Americans more than any other job feature—including pay and promotions.[18]

What Is Meaningful Work?

To be meaningful, your work doesn't have to have profound importance to society—organizing all of the world's information, caring for the sick, alleviating poverty, or helping to cure cancer. What matters is whether you *perceive* your work as contributing value to something or someone who matters (even your team, yourself, or your family).[19] It can simply be making a useful and high-quality product for your customer or providing a genuine service for your community. It can be supporting a colleague. Or it can be saving your organization $145 million, as the Infosuite team did. Whether the goals are lofty or modest, as long as they are meaningful, then the conditions are set for progress to rule inner work life.[20]

Consider the case of Richard, a senior lab technician at a chemical company. Richard found meaning in his work when he believed that the project team depended on his intellect to help solve the complex technical problems it faced. However, in team meetings over the course of one three-week period, Richard perceived that his suggestions were being ignored by his team leader and teammates. As a result, he felt that his contributions were not meaningful, and his inner work life flagged. When, at last, he felt that he was again making a substantive contribution to the success of the project, his inner work life improved dramatically:

> I felt very much better at today's team meeting. I felt that my opinions and information were important to the project, and that we have made some progress. [Richard, senior lab technician, chemical company]

According to the mood and motivation numbers on his daily diary, this was one of Richard's best days during the project.

Four Ways to Negate Meaning

In principle, managers shouldn't have to go to extraordinary lengths to infuse jobs with meaning. Most jobs in modern organizations are potentially meaningful for the people doing them. However, managers should make sure that employees know just how their work is contributing. And, most importantly, managers should *avoid actions that negate the value of the work.* All the participants in our research were doing work that should have been meaningful. Shockingly often, however, we saw potentially important, challenging work drained of its meaning.

When we probed the journal entries to see just how this happened, we discerned four mechanisms. First is what Richard experienced: having one's work or ideas dismissed by leaders or coworkers. Second is losing a sense of ownership in one's work. This happened repeatedly to people on the Domain team in Karpenter Corporation, as described by team member Bruce:

> As I've been handing over some projects I do realize that I don't like to give them up. Especially when you have been with them from the start and are nearly to the end. You lose ownership. This happens to us way too often, time and time again. [Bruce, 8/20]

A third reliable way to kill meaning is to make employees doubt that the work they are doing will ever see the light of day. This can happen because management priorities shift or because managers simply change their ideas about how something should be done. We saw the latter in the Internet technology company VH Networks, after user interface developer Burt had spent weeks designing seamless transitions for non-English-speaking users. Not surprisingly, Burt's inner work life was seriously marred on the day he reported this incident:

> Other options for the international [interfaces] were [given] to the team during a team meeting, which could render the work I am doing useless. [Burt, 7/28]

Similar dynamics can occur when a customer's priorities change unexpectedly; often, this is the result of poor customer management or inadequate communication within the company. For example, Stuart, a data transformation expert at VH Networks, reported deep frustration and low motivation on the day he learned that weeks of the team's hard work may have been for naught:

> Found out that there is a strong possibility that the project may not be going forward, due to a shift in the client's agenda. Therefore, there is a strong possibility that all the time and effort put into the project was a waste of our time. [Stuart, 3/6]

Finally, otherwise valuable jobs can lose their meaning when people feel that they are overqualified for many of the specific tasks that they are being asked to do. Broderick, another VH Networks employee, had volunteered to work on a particular project because he felt his skills would allow him to make important contributions. But when his boss asked him to do "grunt work," his inner work life plummeted:

> I ran into my boss today, and he wants me to do a task that in-volves "grunt work"—his words, not mine. I didn't come onto this project to deal with this task [. . .]. To say the least, if I have to do this, my morale will be at an all-time low. Especially considering that I volunteered for this project. [Broderick, 7/10]

We all need to believe that our labor is actually contributing to some-thing that matters. When that belief stays firm, progress leads to real satisfaction, strong motivation to continue the work, and positive feel-ings. When our work is devoid of meaning, then even completing a long list of tasks cannot yield a genuine sense of accomplishment.

The Progress Loop

Progress and inner work life feed each other. Mathematician Norbert Wiener called this sort of interaction a positive feedback loop or "cumu-lative causation."[21] Progress enhances inner work life (the progress principle) and positive inner work life leads to further progress (the inner work life effect), creating a virtuous cycle. The loop can operate as a vicious cycle, as well. Just as inner work life and progress improve in tandem, when one goes downhill, so does the other. Figure 5-1 depicts both the positive and the negative form of the cycle that we call the *progress loop*.

Like any feedback loop, the progress loop is self-reinforcing. Just as a physical object in motion, such as a pendulum in a vacuum, maintains its momentum unless acted on by an outside force, the progress loop continues unless other events interfere. Just as air resistance or any

FIGURE 5-1

The progress loop

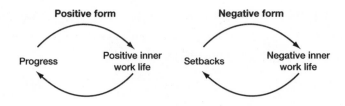

Note: For purposes of brevity, the model depicted here has been simplified. The way in which inner work life and performance interact is both complicated and fascinating. The interested reader can observe some of its true complexity in the interaction of emotion and creativity presented in T. M. Amabile, S. G. Barsade, J. S. Mueller, and B. M. Staw, "Affect and Creativity at Work," *Administrative Science Quarterly* 50 (2005): 367–403. That paper presents evidence, based on our diary study, that not only does emotion influence creativity, but creativity leads to emotional reactions.

other physical interference slows the momentum of the pendulum, many forces in the workplace can break the virtuous cycle of the positive progress loop. Happily, a vicious cycle can be broken by intervening events, as well. It isn't easy, but it can be done by removing obstacles to progress and providing the supports necessary for success.

The progress loop is a secret weapon of high-performance companies; it produces a powerful win-win for both managers and employees. Consistent daily progress by individual employees fuels both the success of the organization and the quality of those employees' inner work lives.[22] To harness this powerful force, you must ensure that consistent forward movement in meaningful work is a regular occurrence in your employees' daily work lives, despite the inevitable setbacks that all nontrivial work entails. In the real world, the pendulum of a clock keeps moving only if someone keeps the clock wound. Similarly, as a manager, you must keep the progress loop in motion by continually facilitating progress and removing obstacles. If you focus on supporting the daily progress of people working in your organization, you will not only foster the success of the organization but also enrich the everyday lives of your employees.

Managers can enhance inner work life in other ways—for example, by injecting playfulness into the workplace to spark happiness—but those methods pale in comparison to focusing on the power of progress. Not only is progress most germane to the organization's purpose but, of all the events that engender positive thoughts, feelings, and motivations, managers have the greatest control over events that can facilitate or undermine progress. That's good news because, as we have seen, nothing boosts inner work life like progress.

———————

The progress principle describes the most important influence on inner work life, but progress and setbacks are not the only work events that matter. In the next chapter, we explore the second of the key three influences on inner work life: the catalyst factor.

6

The Catalyst Factor

The Power of Project Support

A PRODUCT MARKETER named Sophie and an engineer named Tim never met during our study of their companies, and we doubt they ever will. But should they ever meet, they would surely have much to discuss. Sophie worked at Karpenter Corporation, the once-great consumer products company whose Domain team you have already met. Tall, bespectacled, and energetic, Sophie labored valiantly against ever-present obstacles to advance the new kitchenware products she was overseeing. Here is only one of the many tales that Sophie could have told Tim about inner work life at its worst:

> I don't understand why R&D kills so many of my projects, yet I
> am supposed to be measured on new product development! Dean
> Fisher [VP of R&D] killed my new handheld mixer three times
> before it was approved a couple of weeks ago. Very conflicting
> goals, causing us to start, stop, restart, etc. [Sophie, 5/10]

Tim, a senior research engineer at O'Reilly Coated Materials, would probably have listened attentively to Sophie's description of events at

Karpenter, stroking his beard as his deep blue eyes expressed sympathy. But Tim would have had difficulty truly empathizing with Sophie, truly identifying with her deep frustration, tattered motivation, and abysmal opinion of her organization. Consider, for example, Tim's account of an event from the first day of his current project:

> We had our first team meeting, and [. . .] decided that we will meet every Friday at 11 a.m. The group leader demonstrated his excellence in logical analysis, and [. . .] described what, in his mind, will happen in the next two to three months on the new project. [Tim, 10/9]

Tim's experience could not be more different from Sophie's—because from that very first day, Tim's team had something that Sophie's lacked: clear goals about where they were heading. When you don't know what you should be doing, it's tough to feel good about doing it. Having clear goals orients people as they approach any job, from the most self-contained task to the broadest-scope project. Disoriented and disheartened as another of her new projects was shot down in flight, Sophie felt little sense of direction and even less autonomy in her work. She began to lose her motivation to continue. By contrast, Tim was jazzed after his team's first meeting, ready to take off in the direction the group leader had begun to map with the team.

Clear goals are one crucial element of the *catalyst factor*, a broad category of events that is second only to the progress principle in the key three influences on inner work life. In chemistry, a catalyst is a substance that initiates or accelerates a chemical reaction. In our research, we use *catalyst* to describe anything that directly facilitates the timely, creative, high-quality completion of the work. We use *inhibitor* to describe the absence or negative form of a catalyst.

Catalysts support progress in the work. Inhibitors hinder progress or cause setbacks.[1] As we have shown, progress and setbacks are the major influences on inner work life. Surprisingly, though, *catalysts and inhibitors can have an immediate impact on inner work life, even before they could possibly affect the work itself.* As soon as people realize that they have, for example, clear and meaningful goals, sufficient resources, or helpful colleagues, they get an instant boost to their perceptions of the work and the organization, their emotions, and their motivation to do a great job. But as soon as goals are jumbled, resources denied, or the ball dropped by a colleague, their thoughts, feelings, and drives begin to crumble. Progress or setbacks will ensue later, but people feel the effects on their inner work lives instantaneously.

Figure 6-1 shows the direct and indirect effects of catalysts on inner work life. The direct effect (depicted by the bold arrow) happens as soon as the person becomes aware of a catalyst. The indirect effect on inner work life happens through the progress loop: as soon as the catalyst leads to actual progress, the sense of progress lifts inner work life. For example, if a programmer is told she will be receiving the new computer she had requested, there will be an immediate impact on her inner work life. Even before the computer arrives, she is likely to feel happy about the news, and she might perceive her employer as competent or herself as valued. But when she actually receives the computer and it helps her to make more progress, her inner work life will be lifted further by that progress and the accompanying sense of accomplishment.

Because the progress loop continues unless interrupted by some negative event, catalysts can have continuing positive effects on inner work life. Unfortunately, by the same mechanism, strong inhibitors can have continuing negative effects on inner work life.

FIGURE 6-1

The effects of catalysts on inner work life

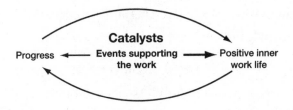

The Seven Major Catalysts

Catalysts can take many forms. Our analyses of the 12,000 "event of the day" narratives we received, along with participants' self-rated inner work lives on those days, revealed seven major catalysts that galvanize work on projects and inner work life—along with their mirror opposites, seven major inhibitors. Although these aren't the only kinds of triggers that catalyzed or inhibited the work our participants were doing, these seven stood out for their impact on inner work life and the work itself.

1. *Setting clear goals*.[2] People have better inner work lives when they know where their work is heading and why it matters. Un-ambiguous short- and long-term goals give teams tangible mile-posts that render their progress salient. When people have conflicting priorities or unclear, meaningless, or arbitrarily shift-ing goals, they become frustrated, cynical, and demotivated. Time is wasted as people spin their wheels, and the work suffers.

2. *Allowing autonomy*.[3] Setting clear goals can backfire if it amounts to nothing more than telling people what to do and how to do it. To be truly intrinsically motivated and to gain a sense of self-efficacy when they do make progress, people need to have some say in their own work. What's more, when employees have free-dom in how to do the work, they are more creative. A key aspect of autonomy is feeling that one's decisions will hold. If manage-ment generally overrides people's decisions, they quickly lose motivation to make any decision, which severely inhibits progress. Work gets delayed because people feel that they have to wait and check in before they begin or change anything.

3. *Providing resources*.[4] Lavish resources aren't required, but access to *necessary* equipment, funding, data, materials, and personnel is. When employees lack those catalysts, they realize that progress will be difficult or impossible and their inner work lives

dip. The fact is that "lean and mean" rarely succeeds over the long haul, especially when it comes to cutting personnel.[5] Providing resources has a twofold positive effect on inner work life. Not only does it allow employees to envision success on a project, but it also signifies that the organization values what they are doing. Withholding necessary resources or rendering them difficult to access engenders a sense of futility, anger at having to waste time scrounging or doing "grunt work," and a perception that the project must not be very important.

4. *Giving enough time—but not too much.*[6] Time pressure is one of the most interesting forces we studied. Although occasional time pressure for short periods can be exhilarating, using extreme time-pressure to stimulate positive inner work life, for weeks on end or even in the short run, is playing with fire (see "Time Pressure and Creativity"). If managers regularly set impossibly short time-frames or impossibly high workloads, employees become stressed, unhappy, and unmotivated—burned out. Yet, people hate being bored. Although it was rare for any participant in our study to report a day with very low time pressure, such days—when they did occur—were also not conducive to positive inner work life. In general, then, low-to-moderate time pressure seems optimal for sustaining positive thoughts, feelings, and drives.

5. *Help with the work.* In modern organizations, people need each other; almost everyone works interdependently. Employees left entirely to their own devices, without any assistance or support from someone else, accomplish very little—they need help.[7] Help can take many forms, from providing needed information, to brainstorming with a colleague, to collaborating with someone who is struggling. Employees become dejected when help is inaccessible, frustrated when it is withheld by someone important to the project—managers at any level, colleagues anywhere in the organization, teammates, and even suppliers

Time Pressure and Creativity

Like many of the people in our study, you may *feel* more creative on days of very high time pressure. But we found that people generally *do* more creative work under low time pressure. We discovered this by comparing journals written on days of very high time pressure with those written on days of very low time pressure.[a] Very high time pressure was much more common than very low time pressure, and few journals reported any creative thinking on high-time-pressure days. We describe these high-pressure, no-creative-thinking days as being *on a treadmill*, because people tend to work on many unrelated (and often unexpected) tasks on those days, constantly running from one thing to another without really getting anywhere—or at least anywhere that matters.

We describe the low-time-pressure days when people do creative thinking as being *on an expedition*. At those times, people tended to be exploratory in their work, often collaborating with one or two other people to approach a problem from different angles. Low time pressure can be perilous, though, if people find little support for innovative thinking from their managers. Then,

---

or customers—and infuriated when they perceive that someone is actively hindering their work. Conversely, getting the right sort of help, from the right people, at the right time, can give a significant boost to inner work life—even when that help has not yet resulted in progress.

6. *Learning from problems and successes.*[8] No matter how skilled people are, or how well designed and well executed their projects, problems and failures are inevitable in complex, creative work. We found that inner work life was much more positive when problems were faced squarely, analyzed, and met with plans to overcome or learn from them. Inner work life faltered when problems were ignored, punished, or handled haphazardly.

they can go into a condition of being *on autopilot*—a state producing little creativity and high boredom.

The rarest of all conditions is being *on a mission*, when people produce creative work under high time pressure. The circumstances have to be just right, though: an urgent, important project where other distractions are held at bay so that the people doing the work can concentrate on solving the crucial problem.[b] Unfortunately, even working on a mission for long periods of time can lead to burnout and degraded performance.

For optimal creative performance, go for low or moderate time pressure as a general rule—punctuated by occasional periods of focused urgency.

a. T. M. Amabile, C. N. Hadley, and S. J. Kramer, "Creativity Under the Gun," *Harvard Business Review*, August 2002, 52–61. Other research has shown that, when competitive rivalry coincides with heightened time pressure, people make poorer economic decisions (D. Malhotra, "The Desire to Win: The Effects of Competitive Arousal on Motivation and Behavior," *Organizational Behavior and Human Decision Processes* 111 [2010]: 139–146).

b. Other research has found that people may be able to do creative work under stress, if the work environment is supportive. In one study, employees were able to do creative work while in negative moods—but only if they also experienced positive moods in the same time period, and only if the organization encouraged creativity (J. M. George and J. Zhou, "Dual Tuning in Supportive Context: Joint Contributions of Positive Mood, Negative Mood, and Supervisory Behaviors to Employee Creativity," *Academy of Management Journal* 50 [2007]: 605–622).

Learning from success mattered, too. Our participants' thoughts, feelings, and drives fared better when successes, even small ones, were celebrated and then analyzed for knowledge gained. They fared worse when success was ignored, or when its true value was questioned. The ability to learn and move forward after failure is much more likely in organizational climates marked by *psychological safety*—a shared expectation, conveyed by the words and actions of leaders, that people will be commended for admitting or pointing out mistakes, rather than shunned.[9] Only in a psychologically safe climate can people take the risks necessary to produce truly innovative work.

7. *Allowing ideas to flow.*[10] Our research participants had some of their best days when ideas about their projects flowed freely within the team and across the organization. We found that ideas flowed best when managers truly listened to their workers, encouraged vigorous debate of diverse perspectives, and respected constructive critiques—even of themselves. When this crucial catalyst was missing or inhibited—when managers shut down debate or harshly criticized new ideas—people seemed to shrink into themselves. In self-protective mode, inner work life is dominated by fearful emotions, negative perceptions of the work environment, and stunted motivation.

Organizational Climate Spawns Everyday Events

Catalysts and inhibitors don't just pop up randomly. These everyday triggers that influence inner work life arise out of the organization's climate, the prevailing set of norms that shape the behavior and expectations of the people who work there. Climate (or culture) is an organization's "signature" to people inside and outside the organization.[11] It is created largely by the words and actions of leaders, beginning with the organization's founders.[12] Climate spawns the specific events that unfold within the organization; over time, similar specific events reinforce the climate.

For example, throughout Google's early years, its climate was characterized as both hardworking and fun loving. Many daily work events were marked by free-spirited exploration of new ideas and energetic collaboration toward the lofty mission of making the world's information universally accessible. By contrast, for years, the IBM climate was viewed as ultraconservative; employees dressed in dark blue suits, focused on serving large corporate customers, and carefully followed specified procedures. As long as leaders' and employees' behavior adhered to those norms and new recruits were socialized to follow them, the conformist climate prevailed. Whatever the specific climate of an organization, the norms are established by the actions of founders and early top managers; without significant changes in the style of managers or the status of the organization, the climate can endure for decades.

Three main climate forces shape the specific catalyst and inhibitor events that occur inside an organization:

- *Consideration for people and their ideas.* In word and deed, do top managers honor the dignity of employees and the value of their ideas? Do other managers, too, serve as examples of civil discourse and welcome every individual's contributions?

- *Coordination.* Are systems and procedures designed to facilitate smooth collaboration between individuals and groups? Is the organizational structure congruent with the organization's strategic goals and employees' skills to meet those goals?

- *Communication.* This is perhaps the most powerful force. Clear, honest, respectful, and free-flowing communication is essential for sustaining progress, coordinating work, establishing trust, and conveying that people and their ideas have value to the organization.[13]

Corporate climates can vary on many other dimensions, but when all three of these particular climate forces are strong and positive, specific events within the organization are much more likely to support inner work life. On the downside, negative climates engender negative daily events, and inner work life suffers. Repeated events of a similar type, positive or negative, reinforce and perpetuate the climate.

For example, consider the climate of Karpenter Corporation, the once-admired, now-defunct consumer products giant. Stemming from actions taken by the new top management team, an unfavorable climate prevailed during our study of the organization. A confusing, misaligned matrix and incentive structure at Karpenter meant that different people on the same team reported to different bosses, and that those bosses often had conflicting priorities. This made it extremely difficult for teammates to *coordinate* their efforts or align their actions toward the same goal. If a team leader tried to help one team member, he would inevitably get in the way of another. A fiercely competitive atmosphere inside Karpenter stifled *communication* within and between groups, as people jealously guarded information for their own uses. And certain top managers' frequent *lack of consideration* for individuals and their ideas set a norm of dismissing and harshly criticizing divergent viewpoints.

A Tale of Two Teams: How Catalysts and Inhibitors Affect Inner Work Life

To reveal specifics about how work catalysts—and inhibitors—affect inner work life and progress, we'll contrast one of the worst teams in our study—Karpenter Corporation's Equip team—with one of the best—the Vision team at O'Reilly Coated Materials. Sophie and Tim, whom you met at the beginning of this chapter, were members of Equip and Vision, respectively.

O'Reilly is a chemical company whose laminated and polyurethane-coated fabrics can be found in products ranging from soft-sided luggage and weatherproof clothing to circus tents and store awnings. It has thrived for decades and continues to lead its industry. Headquartered in a small city in west Texas, O'Reilly has corporate, research, and manufacturing buildings sprawling across a campus of nearly sixty acres.

At the start of our study, O'Reilly and Michigan-based Karpenter appeared to be similar corporations from the outside. Like Karpenter, O'Reilly was among the most successful and respected companies in its industry, considered an innovative leader. Its products were ubiquitous. Both were public companies, staffed by well-educated professionals and headed by experienced managers. During the time we studied them, both companies faced many of the same challenges, including rapidly increasing production costs and competition from foreign manufacturers. Recall that Karpenter had had years of great financial and innovative success and had been named one of America's ten most successful companies just two years before our study. But its fortunes began to turn the year after we began the study, three years after new management had taken over, culminating in the disaster we have already described. In contrast, during the fiscal year before our study began, O'Reilly had its twentieth consecutive year of increased dividends, and its profits had increased by over 20 percent. The year the study ended, the increase was over 15 percent. O'Reilly remains one of the best-known brands in its field.

What made the difference? As we analyzed the diaries from Karpenter and O'Reilly, it became clear that the companies were *extremely* different on the inside, with climates like night and day. We were struck repeatedly by marked contrasts in the presence of everyday catalysts and in the daily inner work lives of employees—contrasts that prefigured the two companies' sharply divergent futures.

The Teams

The cross-functional Equip team comprised the four women and nine men responsible for Karpenter's small-kitchen-appliance product lines. The team's official mandate included every phase of this business, from developing innovative new products through managing inventory and deciding which products to retire. Like all Karpenter business teams, Equip was accountable for the profitability of its product lines. During our study, it was focused on a radically redesigned handheld mixer, an electric knife, and a compact knife sharpener.

The Vision team, composed of four male scientists and technicians, was one of four that we studied at O'Reilly. All teams were based at headquarters, in the corporation's primary R&D unit, which was responsible for developing the chemistry and the prototype products to fuel the company's future innovation and meet changing customer needs.

The Vision team's mandate involved early-stage work on a crucial project for the company: modifying a polyurethane-based coating used for all of the company's outdoor clothing and shelter products. The team's goal was to explore new formulas that would reduce costs in the face of rising raw material prices. This work was extremely complex, fraught with technical challenges. But if the people of the Vision team could succeed in creating a lower-cost coating of comparable quality—including durability, water-resistance, and flexibility—they would revolutionize the company's product lines.

Stark Inner Work Life Contrasts

Our "tale of two teams" displays the best of times and the worst of times for inner work life. On each aspect of inner work life—perceptions, emotions, and motivations—the Equip team was at or near the bottom on most of the measures in our study, and the Vision team was at or near the top of our sample. As you can see from table 6-1, Vision outranked Equip across the board.

The Vision and Equip teams differed to a staggering degree on work progress—the number-one influence on inner work life. Vision was working on a complex chemical engineering problem with many unknowns. It struggled with numerous technical obstacles. Yet, throughout the study, the ratio of progress events to setback events reported in

TABLE 6-1

Inner work life comparison of Equip team and Vision team

Elements of inner work life from daily diary scales	Rank out of all teams 1 = best, 26 = worst	
	Equip	Vision
Perceptions of:		
Autonomy in the work	21	2
Team support	23	7
Supervisor support	24	2
Organizational support	24	1
Emotion (overall mood)	21	1
Motivation (intrinsic)	20	10

its diaries was 5.33—one of the highest of all the teams we studied. For each setback the Vision team encountered, it took more than five steps forward.

The Equip team, too, was doing difficult work. It was supposed to introduce a stream of innovative kitchen appliances that were both ergonomic and attractive. But in terms of progress, it was the worst team in our study. The Equip diaries reported an alarming 0.47 ratio of progress to setback events—or about twice as many setbacks as progress events. On this measure, Equip was the worst of all 26 teams in our study.

The two teams even differed widely in the way their members wrote the daily journal entries. The Equip diaries were much longer, on average, describing inhibitors to the work almost as often as they described the work itself. This higher word count fits with our finding that study participants wrote longer entries when they were reporting more negative events. The Equip narratives also tended to be much more expressive of the thoughts, feelings, and drives the writers had experienced during the day.

The Vision team's entries were brief, straightforward, and focused on the work itself. Team members seldom complained about inhibitors, leading us to deduce that these were not an issue.[14] When they did describe something besides an event in the day's work, it was likely to be a catalyst. Although the Vision members seldom wrote about their feelings in the narrative portion of the diary—making for rather cryptic, dry, "just the facts" entries—they tended to give positive ratings to their thoughts, feelings, and drives on the daily diary form.

The Equip and Vision team members had similar personality profiles and education levels, according to the tests we gave at the start of our study. In other words, both teams had "the right people on the bus."[15] Both teams were doing difficult, complex work under the same economic conditions. Then what made the difference between the great inner work lives (and significant progress) in the Vision team, and the horrendous inner work lives (and frequent setbacks) in the Equip team? The answer lies in the catalyst factor.

The Best of Times: O'Reilly's Vision Team

Vision was a newly formed team whose four members worked out of a common office crammed with their desks, computers, technical manuals, and supplier catalogues. Music emanating from an iPod docking station was either classical, jazz, or bluegrass, depending on which team member had arrived first that day. Vision's laboratory, shared with another team, was located across the corridor, on the ground floor of a four-story O'Reilly research facility. A line of laboratory-scale manufacturing equipment, for pilot-testing new formulations, was housed in the basement.

Tim, who had earned both an MS in chemical engineering and an MBA in marketing, was the senior research engineer. The team leader was Dave, an agreeable, soft-spoken thirty-four-year-old PhD chemist who enjoyed growing bonsai trees as a hobby. Senior technician Richard held an MS in chemistry and, at age thirty—with seven years of O'Reilly experience—was working on a part-time MBA. Rounding out the team was Will, a lean and gregarious marathon runner who served as the Vision team's experimentalist. Although Will lacked a college degree, he was the most experienced member of the team; during his eleven years at O'Reilly, he had assisted in running experiments for seven projects.

Catalysts abounded in this team. On the first day of Vision's existence, Dave, Tim, Richard, and Will met to begin planning how to achieve the project's aim: creating a high-quality, lower-cost coating for the major O'Reilly products. They discussed both what they were aiming for and possible pathways to get there:

> The entire team drew a decision tree that clarifies what work will
> be done on our first product. [Dave, 10/9]

Dave rated his mood as good that first day.[16] As Vision's leader, he was glad that the team had both the capability and the freedom to create a map for its own project. The team's creation of the decision tree was just the first of many instances demonstrating the *autonomy* that the vice president of R&D, Mark Hamilton, had given the Vision team. (Note: We will *italicize* the name of the specific catalyst or inhibitor in our discussion of each illustrative diary excerpt.) From the beginning, this team was highly motivated to make the project a success because they felt ownership in it.

However, this doesn't mean that management left the team entirely to its own devices. On the contrary, upper management had specified the team's original mandate and worked with the team to *clarify overall goals* at several points in the project's life. For example, the O'Reilly technical directors discussed goals with the team immediately after reviewing the team's proof-of-concept work. This is how Tim described it, on a day that brought him considerable happiness:

> The project passed start gate today. We discussed the direction of the project with our directors, and we got very good feedback from them. [Tim, 11/6]

Like other great companies, O'Reilly had struck the perfect balance by giving the team clear strategic *goals* along with *autonomy* concerning how to conduct the project. Every member of the team was enthusiastic as the official project work began. We saw this energizing balance of clear strategic goals and operational autonomy across O'Reilly.

Interestingly, the balance of these two catalysts also appears inside the legendary W. L. Gore & Associates, the creators of Gore-Tex fabric and other engineering marvels. In fact, many sources credit Gore's companywide practice of supporting autonomy for its scientists and engineers for that firm's dual forms of success: Repeatedly named one of America's best companies to work for by *Fortune* magazine, Gore also has a long history of bottom-line success.[17]

The Vision team's technical work got off to a rough start; Will had serious problems running the first few Vision experiments. Even so, the team soon began to make good progress. Will's diary describes one catalyst that contributed: members of the team frequently gave each other *help* as needed—even without being asked:

> Today when I was running the experiment, I was having some trouble feeding the machine. I was about to call for help, when Richard showed up and started helping without being asked. I think this project will be successful with this kind of team effort. [Will, 10/22]

Another catalyst of the Vision project was access to necessary, if not lavish, *resources*; management quickly approved appropriations when the team made well-justified requests.

By halfway through their timeline, team members knew they were likely to achieve the project's goals. At that point, they had created a coating formulation that was stronger and more waterproof, using less expensive raw materials. The next step was to determine whether fabrics could be coated with this formulation on a production line, using the industry-standard process of coating first one side of the fabric and then the other. But the production experiments were not going well. After the first pass through the equipment, the coating seeped through, leaving the fabric sticky and blemished in certain spots on the non-coated side and making it impossible to finish that side properly.

At first, the team was stymied. Then, at Dave's suggestion, they began sharing the odd results with their managers and colleagues. People across the company eagerly joined the conversation. A steady *flow of ideas* poured forth, and that triggered positive inner work life for the team members, who reported their appreciation:

> Discussion with project leader and another senior scientist helped to stimulate my thinking about the project. [I have come to] at least one conclusion [. . .]. It may help to make the project more feasible. [Tim, 12/16]

Over the ensuing weeks, this process generated dozens of ideas, and the team tested several of them. Finally, in a meeting to assess what they had learned, the group had a breakthrough—the new coating formulation could be tweaked to allow the production machines to evenly coat *both* sides of the fabric in one pass. This could revolutionize most of O'Reilly's coating processes, cutting production costs dramatically. Excitedly, the team tried out the radical idea, produced promising prototypes, and e-mailed a report to the technical directors.

The response was less than overwhelming. Although Mark Hamilton expressed interest, two high-level managers and two technical directors advised him that the team's conclusions had to be flawed. There was no evidence in the existing scientific literature to back up the team's claim. In fact, they argued, Hamilton should stop funding Vision's experiments with the coating process so the team members would turn their attention back to the original goal, the coating itself. Why chase an illusion?

Dave may have been soft-spoken by nature, but he was unafraid to *face problems and learn from them*. That's how the team leader reacted to this potential inhibitor. His response to the crisis was immediate, decisive, and straightforward. The very next day, he approached these managers and asked them about their concerns; they told him in detail. He then proceeded to address each problem the skeptics raised, showing the prototypes the team had produced using the new process:

> Demonstrated to two persons (who have expressed doubt about [the] success of our project) the quality of the prototypes. Demonstrated that the prototypes have sufficient properties for [our] planned applications. [Dave, 2/6]

By tackling the problem head-on, Dave was able to keep the project on track and obtain crucial new resources for the team. Moreover, his inner work life got a boost when he saw how effective his approach had been. And, by his example, Dave taught his team members the value of *dealing with problems* in a straightforward way. (For more on the role of team leaders in creating catalysts, see "The Special Role of Team Leaders in the Catalyst Factor.") That lesson was not lost on Tim who, a few weeks later, owned up to Dave about a mistake he and Will had made:

> I showed [Dave] the results I got and told him that there was a [. . .] mistake in one of the trials [. . .]. He said that is all right, as long as we know what we did [. . .]. [Tim, 3/27]

Even though the prospect of revealing the mistake to his team leader could not have been a comfortable situation for Tim, he actually experienced very good inner work life that day. Not only was he relieved by Dave's reaction, but he was motivated by the prospect of learning from the error.

The Special Role of Team Leaders in the Catalyst Factor

Our study revealed that—holding other factors equal—"local" sources of the catalyst factor, such as team leaders and immediate coworkers, had a statistically stronger influence on inner work life than "broad" forces such as top-level managers and organizational systems. This certainly doesn't mean that people were impervious to the effects of these broad forces, but it does mean that, if you are a team leader, you have special leverage on the inner work life of your team. In fact, you can be a more important day-by-day source of the catalyst factor than top managers.[a] By analyzing the team leader actions that led our research participants to see their team leaders as supportive (or not), we identified a set of catalyst factor leverage points.[b]

As a team leader, *do* . . .	As a team leader, *don't* . . .
• Gather information constantly that could, in any way, be relevant to the team's work	• Fail to disseminate project-relevant information to the team
• Involve the team in making important decisions about the project	• Micromanage; don't stifle team members' autonomy in carrying out their work
• Develop contacts with people outside the team who could be important sources of information and support for the project	• Fail to motivate and inspire the team by what you say and, especially, the example you set with your own work habits
• Sell the project; fight for a good project if it is threatened	• Avoid solving problems or cause problems through your own timidity or arrogance
	• Fail to provide clear, appropriate, meaningful assignments and goals

Source: T. M. Amabile, E. A. Schatzel, G. B. Moneta, and S. J. Kramer, "Leader Behaviors and the Work Environment for Creativity: Perceived Leader Support," *Leadership Quarterly* 15 (2004): 5–32.

a. Our results about the power of local context are supported by a study of nurses in seven large Australian hospitals, which showed that nurses' job satisfaction related more strongly to the subculture of the ward than the culture of the hospital overall (P. Lok and J. Crawford, "The Relationship between Commitment and Organizational Culture, Subculture, Leadership Style and Job Satisfaction in Organizational Change and Development," *Leadership and Organizational Development Journal* 20 [1999]: 365–373).

b. Here, we list the catalyst factor actions; nourishment factor actions appear in the next chapter. The research was reported in: T. M. Amabile, E. A. Schatzel, G. B. Moneta, and S. J. Kramer, "Leader Behaviors and the Work Environment for Creativity: Perceived Leader Support," *The Leadership Quarterly* 15 (2004): 5–32.

As the Vision team's research on both the formulation and the manufacturing process went into high gear, time pressure rose beyond tolerable limits. The project deadline was fast approaching, but the team still had much to do. Their serendipitous discovery had, ironically, increased their workload dramatically. Relief came when the team requested a temporary technician, and one was hired within a day. Diary ratings from both Tim and Dave showed that even this slight *release of time pressure* bolstered their motivation. Now the goal seemed attainable.

Almost miraculously, the team made its deadline, and the Vision invention turned out to be *the* major innovation in the coated fabrics industry over the entire decade. Of all twenty-six teams in our study, Vision was the only one to achieve a significant breakthrough during the months we studied it. The company won big, and so did each member of the team. Through cost cutting, the company improved its bottom line significantly; the team received meaningful recognition and enjoyed superb inner work lives throughout the project. On the last day of the project, after having taken his teammates out for a lunchtime *celebration of their success*, Dave finally gave us a glimpse of the elated emotions he was feeling:

> Held our project review. Basked in the glory of a job well done by our team! [Dave, 5/7]

The Worst of Times: Karpenter's Equip Team

Unfortunately, not all managers get it right. In fact, no group of managers in the companies we studied did as well at promoting work catalysts as Dave, other team leaders, and upper-level managers at O'Reilly. You already know enough about Karpenter Corporation to guess that its managers didn't even come close. Without meaning to, they consistently propagated inhibitors.

Like the other three Karpenter teams we studied, Equip was located at the company's Michigan headquarters—uncomfortably close to the autocratic new corporate executives who had taken charge three years earlier. The team and its administrative assistant and two interns

occupied an entire wing of the third floor in the primary Karpenter office building. Escorted through the bright hallways of that wing, visitors
gaped at display cases of colorful kitchen gadget prototypes, bulletin
boards festooned with sketches of the team's most famous products, and
state-of-the-art CAD equipment.

Sophie, the bespectacled and energetic product marketer, had an
MBA from UCLA and nine years of Karpenter experience under her
belt. She was responsible for two of Equip's major products, including
the new handheld mixer. Four other team members figure prominently
in our story. Steve, the thirty-two-year-old team leader, had enjoyed
considerable success in a variety of marketing positions during his two
years at Karpenter. Like Dave of the Vision team, Steve was in his first
stint as a team leader. Diminutive product development coordinator
Beth, a twenty-year Karpenter veteran, was known for her innovative
designs and her no-nonsense personality. Samantha, a thirty-five-year-
old Wharton MBA and mother of four, oversaw two other key products
in the Equip line. And burly packaging engineer Ben, with over three
decades of Karpenter experience, had invaluable connections both
within and outside of the company.

While the O'Reilly Vision team, a thousand miles away in Texas,
knew just what it was trying to accomplish, the Karpenter Equip team
was having a terrible time trying to clarify its goals. *Lack of clear goals* was
just one inhibitor plaguing Sophie's project to develop a radically
redesigned handheld mixer. The mixer saga could be a script for how to
dampen catalysts—and fire up inhibitors—during new product development (see "A Fly on the Wall: Observing Inhibitors at Work").

The Equip project encountered obstacles at every turn, and from
every corner of the organization. Boltman Corporation, the team's chief
competitor, was about to come out with a new model rumored to be
almost as good as the one Sophie and her subgroup had designed. But
after a year, her project still languished because of *lack of clear goals*:

> Had meetings [. . .] to discuss how to reposition our proposal for a
> new hand-held mixer. This project has taken over 1 year to develop,

mainly because the division's management team continually asked for more analysis, and R&D was slow in developing a reasonable technology to create a soft-grip handle. Finally, the team rallied to present a viable project, which the management team approved, only to have the COO say he wants a hard-grip handle [instead,] at a $5 lower retail. Steve waffles back and forth. [. . .] Beth is contrary on most points—really doesn't seem to care one way or the other. Very frustrating project, getting little support from Corporate, management team, or key team members [. . .]. Yet, all agree that the competitive situation is becoming desperate [. . .]. Allen [Equip's finance person] & I have prepared yet another proposal to show the management team tomorrow, but I need to get Steve to buy in; not sure which way he will go. [Sophie, 4/26]

Obstruction glares through nearly every sentence of Sophie's journal entry, and so does her frustration.[18] The new mixer project *had yet to receive significant resources* for development or production because the divisional vice presidents—the management team—*could not agree on goals* for the project.

As a result, Sophie began to view the project as a doomed folly, and herself as a pawn. She tired of *trying to get help* from the uncooperative R&D department. And, in contrast to the Vision team members at O'Reilly, who regularly helped each other, Sophie got *little help* from her own teammates, including product development coordinator Beth, who should have championed this effort.

After her day of fruitless meetings on April 26, Sophie was unable to experience any sense of accomplishment with this project. Increasingly frustrated by her confusion, *constrained autonomy*, and helplessness, she struggled to maintain her motivation in this "desperate situation." The April 27 meeting with vice presidents did nothing to improve the situation:

[. . .] Frustrating. Lack of decisiveness is driven by political pressure from corporate, making them [the VPs] very risk averse. Steve

A Fly on the Wall: Observing Inhibitors at Work

From our vantage point as recipients of daily work diaries, we watched life inside organizations much as the proverbial fly on the wall. We often saw things that no one else was aware of, except for the people directly involved. In fact, we suspect that many of the people involved weren't really aware of what they were doing. When managers trampled autonomy, blocked idea flow, or reacted badly to honest mistakes, did they know how their actions were coming across? Trying, as most of them were, to do a good job as leaders, did they ever question their approaches? Did they recognize the effects these inhibitors were having on their subordinates? Would you recognize inhibitors like these in your own behavior? Like us, you might feel an uncomfortable sense of familiarity in some of what we saw— either because you have done these things yourself, or you have been on the receiving end in the past. These examples come from different teams, in different companies:

> Today [the VP of R&D] tried to wipe out quite a bit of work we've done [. . .] he wants it another way because "he said so."
> [He] is like a steamroller—he wants his way and doesn't want to listen to anybody else. It is so frustrating!! Why pretend to give us

is not strongly leading the project, and appears to be afraid to come down on one side or the other in the argument. [Sophie, 4/27]

A chronic indecisiveness, fueled by fear of displeasing the seemingly capricious, dictatorial corporate executives—well-founded, given the COO's unexpected directive to nix the soft-grip handle—severely affected managers at all levels in Karpenter. Steve, the Equip team leader, was particularly vulnerable. Not timid by nature, Steve repeatedly had his *flow of ideas blocked* by the withering critiques of those executives, for example:

> [Barry Thomas] the COO told me I had my head up my ass during the [quarterly] review last Saturday morning. [Steve, 5/31]

autonomy if you're just going to make everything be done your way anyway???

We had a team meeting; the purpose was to formulate recommendations that we would give management later this week. We were TOLD by our team "leader" that, due to political sensitivities, we should present fact and some individual conclusions, but [. . .] we should not present a conclusion and recommendation. [. . .] This is ridiculous [. . .]. After all, we get paid for our fact-finding, processing, concluding, and recommending. He's just afraid of saying the "wrong" thing! No leader here!!

Jonah [a fellow chemical engineer] showed me samples of his first trial [. . .]. I thought his success was outstanding, since he was able to demonstrate that at least it can be done, even though there were problems with the process. Jonah, however, told me that he was discouraged because [the team leader] thought the trials were a bomb because the samples weren't all perfect. I think it is reprehensible that [the team leader] would say something like that to Jonah, who worked his butt off to get these trials done [. . .]. It just goes to show the type of poor "leadership" we have here and how they are so effective in stifling creativity.

This crude rebuke by a top executive, in a meeting attended by many managers and team leaders, was only the most egregious of many instances in which analyses, opinions, or new ideas met with a chilly reception, open insult, or blatant mockery. More often than not, the perpetrators were high-level managers. Rather than creating the psychological safety essential for making good decisions, exploring new ideas, and taking reasonable risks, Karpenter managers repeatedly *stanched ideas at their source.* This negativity had a particularly devastating effect on the inner work lives of inexperienced team leaders like Steve, who began to shrink from confrontation and taking a stand on any issue. The Equip team working under Steve was like a ship sailing rudderless.

At O'Reilly, Dave and his Vision team had no significant problems gaining the resources they needed. At Karpenter, every *resource* request involved a struggle. Sophie finally got the capital appropriation to buy machine templates for manufacturing the mixer, but the approval came weeks after that late-April meeting. And even when the Equip team did get a particular template, there was often a significant delay getting it engineered to fit in the manufacturing line. One such incident, concerning a different product line, added to Sophie's frustration:

> I can't get [the template for the new knife engineered into] a machine, to run parts for a large customer order, because R&D says they are lacking resources (people). [Sophie, 4/27]

Things only got worse for the Equip team's inner work life; roadblocks stood at every bend in the road. Even after the mixer made it to production, and customer orders began to flow, the team's woes with the product continued. Because the VP of R&D was feuding with the VP of Manufacturing, the manufacturing department dragged its feet on production. Beth—never reticent about her thoughts or feelings—became increasingly agitated in her daily reports. One day toward the end of our study, Beth's journal fairly exploded:

> We have been working very hard to get production running, so we can fill a huge order that has a very tight deadline. Yesterday, production was up and running, and everyone breathed a sigh of relief. But, when we came in this morning, we found out [. . .] that Manufacturing had shut down production and was refusing to start back up until all the packaging arrived. The packaging was due today, and they had an empty warehouse to stage the parts until it got there. But, without asking/threatening/informing anyone on the team, they just did what they damn well pleased. [. . .] They definitely knew this was a hot order, but they just shrugged their shoulders and said it wouldn't be their fault if the order didn't ship. [Beth, 6/18]

This incident highlights two inhibitors plaguing the Equip team. The team received *little help* from the manufacturing division; in fact, what it got was active *hindrance*. In the war between R&D and Manufacturing, the Equip team had become a hostage. Beth had lost faith in Karpenter's leadership—which, ideally, would have made the Manufacturing department jointly responsible for production of the team's products—and also lost her motivation to do much for the company or the team.

Extreme *time pressure* was another frequent inhibitor. It was usually time pressure of the worst sort, where people ran "on a treadmill" from one task to another, interrupted constantly by unforeseen demands, but getting nowhere. For example, Samantha and her Equip team colleagues, in consultation with Dean Fisher, had created an aggressive timeline to finish developing a new line of electric knives. But, with no warning or explanation, Fisher told Samantha to drop her other projects and finish developing the knives immediately—a month ahead of schedule.

> We are getting pressure from the VP of R&D to get going on launching the [knife] line, but we are unsure our approach is correct. [. . .] We are feeling pressured to move too fast [because Dean Fisher] wants a meeting in two days. [Samantha, 4/26]

As we compared the Equip team's daily journals with the Vision team's journals arriving during those same months, we couldn't suppress the notion that Dean Fisher was the misguided twin of Mark Hamilton, O'Reilly's VP of R&D. Similar in age, education, experience, and organizational tenure, the two men could scarcely have been more different in management approach. Hamilton consistently created catalysts for the Vision team's work. He worked collaboratively to set goals for the Vision project, and did not change those goals without fully consulting team leader Dave. He encouraged, and participated in, a lively flow of ideas.

Fisher, by contrast, consistently created inhibitors for the Equip team's work. His behavior vacillated between exasperating indecision on the team's plans and autocratic, seemingly arbitrary, dictates about what products to make and how to make them. The most obvious result was a string of setbacks, including projects abandoned close to the finish line and others rushed through design or development. The tangible result for consumers was a disappointing array of new products, which became less innovative and shoddier over time. The hidden casualty was the inner work life of each Equip team member.

When problems with a product arose at Karpenter, they were usually ignored or patched over; teams seldom had the time or autonomy to *learn from problems*, let alone fix them properly. Ben, Equip's packaging engineer, described a typical incident—one that substantially decreased his intrinsic motivation.[19] He found during routine testing that a new product broke frequently when it was handled. (A teammate had noted the possible weakness a month earlier, but had been afraid to mention it.):

> We [. . .] discussed what could be done to improve the product I have been breaking when testing. The consensus is that the product is poorly designed, but we will have to find a solution to the breakage through packaging, as it is too late to redesign the product. [Ben, 6/15]

Ben's diary excerpt is a fitting metaphor for the entire new product development process at Karpenter. Like the inner work lives of Karpenter's product development teams, it was broken. The company's stellar reputation would only conceal the break for so long, before the rest of the world would begin to see the damage.

It truly had become the worst of times. As people on the Equip team labored under every sort of inhibitor, their inner work lives withered. When people see that leaders can't or won't support their work, they view themselves like tightrope walkers working without a net. When leadership or other groups actively hinder their work, they feel like someone is shaking that tightrope. Motivation decays because such tenuous support provokes anxiety and signals that the work is either unimportant or doomed to failure—or both. Equip's people went to the office each day knowing that much of their hard work would be undermined and that, as a result, they were more likely to fail than succeed. Many of them had worked at Karpenter for years, thrilled that it was celebrated as one of the world's most admired companies. Their journals tell their tale of bitter disappointment as they watched the early death throes of the company for which they had once been so proud to work.

Deliberate Catalysts, Accidental Inhibitors

Imagine that Sophie, the product marketer from Karpenter's Equip team, found herself on a long airplane trip seated next to Tim, the research engineer from O'Reilly's Vision team. After introducing themselves and making small talk for a while, they might have begun to compare notes on their work lives. We imagine that they would have felt like they inhabited different planets. In a way, they did: Sophie and her teammates lived in a catalyst wasteland. If she came across as angry, unmotivated, and jaundiced, it would be an honest expression of her inner work life most days. Tim and his team, in contrast, worked in a veritable Promised Land. His contentment, his upbeat views of O'Reilly, and his deep drive to do the work stemmed directly from his knowledge, reinforced day after day, that he would get the support he needed to succeed—from his team leader, teammates, other groups, or top management.

In our meetings with these companies' top managers after we finished collecting data, we were able to gain some insight into how they thought about catalysts. At O'Reilly, we learned that the highest-level leader of the division we studied—Mark Hamilton, the VP of R&D—intentionally established catalyst mechanisms throughout the organization. Other high-level managers varied in how conscious they were of providing these catalysts; some said, "This is just how we do things here." It was a well-established part of the O'Reilly climate.

At Karpenter, the CEO and COO saw their jobs almost exclusively in terms of setting corporate strategy and managing the external environment; when they did speak about the business teams, it was only in vaguely ideal terms of "entrepreneurship" and "teamwork." No one at the top in Karpenter realized—or cared—how little help the business teams were getting from the rest of the organization. They seemed to believe that their teams were being paid to produce innovative, profitable products—so that's what should happen. They also showed no awareness that their own occasional interventions, such as revoking autonomy, or their failure to maintain clear goals for new products, could destroy inner work life and wreak havoc on team projects. In other words, the dearth of catalysts and abundance of inhibitors at Karpenter seemed accidental, rather than deliberate.

Dean Fisher, the VP of R&D in the division we studied, viewed the teams as unruly groups of children who had to earn decision rights over their projects. He was oblivious to his own failure to ensure that the teams had the resources and time they needed and to his role in causing the teams to avoid facing—and learning from—mistakes. Nor did he encourage the teams to celebrate and learn from any successes they did have. Where the Vision team reported frequent events to appreciate and debrief project successes, not one of the six hundred–plus Equip diary entries reported any such event at Karpenter.

To be fair, we must acknowledge that Fisher himself was being squeezed by his own bosses. The CEO and COO constantly second-guessed him, too, and frequently reversed *his* decisions without explanation. His behavior reflected the climate that had recently overtaken Karpenter.

For many of the teams we studied, work catalysts—or inhibitors—far outweighed interpersonal factors in elevating or depressing inner work life. For others, social, interpersonal interactions mattered more—the sympathy and smile, or the snarl and sneer that wait just outside the office door. Sometimes *that* is what sticks in the head and the heart long after the day's work is done. And that is the subject of chapter 7.

7

The Nourishment Factor

The Power of Interpersonal Support

O N   A N   O R D I N A R Y   workday in late March, Infosuite team member Helen put in a fairly routine request: she asked for a day off. Helen described in her diary entry just how much her manager's response affected her inner work life:

> In response to my request for a day off [. . .], I got a note from the project manager thanking me for what I had done and reminding me that I had a "free day" coming as a reward for hard work already completed. It made me feel good and made me want to work harder to make the project manager and team a success. It sounds corny, I know, but that's how I felt . . . it's nice to feel appreciated. [Helen, 3/22]

Helen's inner work life soared, motivating her to redouble her efforts for the Infosuite team and for Ruth, the project manager who had made the day so great.

But Ruth probably didn't give this incident a second thought; she didn't even mention it in her own diary. We might say that this was simply a manager doing her job. In reminding Helen that she had *earned* a "free day," Ruth was merely recognizing good work and following through on a commitment she had made to a valued team member. But—mundane as it may have been—this was an act of extraordinarily good management. By her simple action, Ruth was taking advantage of the *nourishment factor*, which ranks with the progress principle and the catalyst factor as one of the key three contributors to the quality of inner work life.[1]

The nourishment factor refers to something that everyone craves at work: human connection. You nourish the inner work lives of your subordinates when you reward or recognize their good work, encourage them, or offer emotional support. You might also help resolve interpersonal conflicts, provide opportunities for people to really know each other, or simply let them have some fun. Our guess is that, when you think about the best days of your own work life, many of them are days when you enjoyed that human connection. Indeed, sometimes what gets people most fired up about going to work and giving it their all is the interpersonal events—even small ones like Helen's interaction with Ruth. Great meaning can grow from the simple pleasure of enjoying colleagues.[2] As always, though, there is a negative side: interpersonal interaction can also lead to toxins, which poison inner work life. When nourishers are lacking—or worse, when people feel disrespected, underappreciated, or abused—inner work life sours.

Although nourishers may matter more to some people than others, none of us can truly thrive without them. As humans, we want others to respect, recognize, care for, and enjoy us. When they do, we revel in the positive emotions of joy, pride, and even love. And we are motivated to contribute to something wonderful. Over time, these inner work life reactions fuel superior performance. In other words, nourishers indirectly influence work progress, by influencing all three components of inner work life; in the instance from Helen's journal, Ruth's actions boosted Helen's perceptions of Ruth, her feelings, and her motivation to work even harder.[3]

The Four Major Nourishers—and How They Lead to Progress

Across all the teams we studied, when people found someone reaching out to offer them nourishers, their inner work lives blossomed—which increased the odds that they would make progress in the work.[4] The primary way in which nourishers fuel inner work life and progress is by infusing the work with greater meaning. When we care about the people we work with, we want to succeed for them. When our colleagues become a kind of family to us, work can take on new meaning in our lives. Human connections really can inspire people to "go the extra mile for the team." Creativity and productivity result.

We found that the nourishment factor can be divided into four broad categories of events, each directly impacting inner work life:

1. *Respect.*[5] Managerial actions can determine whether people feel respected or disrespected. Recognition may be the most important of these actions. However large or small the tangible value of rewards for good work may be, and however formal or informal the recognition for such work, people feel respected when their efforts are acknowledged. Respect is also conveyed when managers give employees' ideas serious attention, signaling that they and their insights are valued. In addition, although it can be very difficult, dealing with people honestly shows respect. When people realize that a manager is misleading them—even when attempting to spare their feelings—they can conclude that the manager does not trust their professionalism. Finally, basic civility signifies respect and—because negative events are so much more powerful than positive events—incivility signifies strong disrespect.

2. *Encouragement.*[6] Encouraging people can nourish their inner work lives in a couple of ways. First, a manager's own enthusiasm can help to increase employees' motivation for the work. This is

especially true when that encouragement includes statements about the importance of the work. Second, when a manager expresses confidence that people are capable of doing the work well, this message increases their sense of self-efficacy—their own belief that they are effective human beings.

3. *Emotional support.*[7] Because emotions constitute one of the three essential components of inner work life, people feel more connected to others at work when their emotions are validated. This goes for emotions arising from events at work, like frustration at stubborn technical problems, as well as events in personal life, like grief following a loved one's death. Managers who simply acknowledge people's sorrows and frustrations—as well as their joys—can do much to alleviate the negative and amplify the positive emotions. Empathy is even better than simple acknowledgment. Although managers may not see evidence of an employee's emotional state frequently, they can certainly—without prying—remain vigilant to expressions of emotionality as well as events that are likely to evoke strong emotional reactions. When someone directly tells a manager about an emotional experience, an empathetic word can go a long way toward easing his mind and allowing him to get back to the task at hand.

4. *Affiliation.*[8] Affiliation—actions that develop bonds of mutual trust, appreciation, and even affection with coworkers—is the most obvious way in which people feel the human connection at work. Affiliation is especially important in contemporary organizations where people telecommute, work virtually, or become project team members as contract workers rather than organizational employees. The need to bond with coworkers collaborating to achieve a shared mission does not evaporate when people do most of their work from their home offices or airport lounges. In fact, that need intensifies. Managers can

facilitate affiliation—and even warm camaraderie—by providing opportunities for people to become acquainted with their colleagues face to face and finding ways for them to have fun together. When people enjoy each other, there are fewer and milder interpersonal conflicts that can negatively impact the work. Building bonds between team members can also improve the flow of ideas and increase collaboration.

Many managers seem to know that interpersonal support is important for motivating employees and uplifting their emotions.[9] But the tricky thing about the nourishment factor is that it's more than the obvious pats on the back for a job well done and the pep talks at the end of a long week. It's not just how managers interact directly with subordinates. It's also establishing the foundation for subordinates to *give each other* nourishment. That means establishing a positive organizational climate and considering personalities and work styles as well as skills when assigning people to teams. It also requires ensuring that people understand their roles so that they can coordinate their efforts and communicate openly with each other. Otherwise, destructive conflict is almost inevitable. Although animated debate about ideas and civil discussions about the work itself can be extremely productive, personal clashes based on misunderstandings, resentments, mismatched personalities, or clashing work styles can destroy trust and bring down an entire team.[10] Good management means avoiding these problems altogether, or alleviating them when they crop up.

We discovered that many managers have great difficulty doing either, and in the worst-case scenarios, they create a toxic work environment (see "A Fly on the Wall: Observing Toxins at Work"). *Toxins* are the opposite of nourishers, and have the opposite effect. The four toxins are *disrespect*, *discouragement*, *emotional neglect*, and *antagonism*. The toxins can be negative behaviors—such as the Karpenter COO's remark that a team leader "had his head up his ass" at a review meeting. But the simple absence of nourishers—such as failure to recognize the contributions of a subordinate or colleague—can also be toxic to inner work life.

A Fly on the Wall: Observing Toxins at Work

If you become stressed in your management job, you can find yourself saying or doing the very things you most despised in your own previous managers. Even when calm, many managers find it difficult to empathize with subordinates' human needs or to handle dicey interpersonal situations.

With respect to nourishers and toxins, management training has a long way to go. Too seldom does it help managers internalize the perspective that interpersonal relationships matter a great deal for effective performance, and therefore require consistent attention.

Here are a few choice examples of toxic managerial behavior from the daily diaries. Ask yourself how many times you have been exposed to similar toxins. Then ask yourself how many times you might have been guilty of the same mistakes—even when you thought you were being friendly, helpful, or humorous. Think about the effects on others' inner work lives, and think twice in the future:

> In the "free and open" Q&A with the COO at the end of the divisional meeting [. . .], someone asked what was being done about the morale problem. He said, "There *is* no morale problem in this company. And, for anybody who thinks there is, we have a nice big bus waiting outside to take you wherever you want to look for work."

Such was the case in the Focus team at Edgell Imaging, Inc. Its managers failed to understand the power of Nourishers, and that failure cost the company dearly.

A Breakdown of Trust: Edgell's Focus Team

Barbara was a rising star at Edgell Imaging, a Maryland-based company that developed flatbed and sheet-fed image scanners. With a graduate degree from Caltech, five years of experience at a successful

I asked [a member of the top management team] about an offer I am expecting [to move to one of our R&D units across the country]. I have been waiting for the offer for two weeks now [. . .]. He put me off by saying, "Be cool, it's coming." This bugs me! My life is going to be thrown into upheaval soon [. . .] I don't think it's unreasonable to expect information about it!

Trying to talk to [a teammate] in meetings [is] extremely difficult. He interrupts, etc.—nobody seems to know how to interact with him. We had a *HUGE* diversion in this meeting because of this. People were looking to [the two team leaders] for help/guidance/action. They provided none, and nobody knew how to bring the mess to closure.

I had just started working on the [360° team assessment] when I received a call. As I was hanging up, Lance [the team leader] walked into my office, and started talking to me. As is his annoying habit, he made it a point (as he always does) to read what was on my screen, and he saw the ratings that I had given him. I was irritated with myself for forgetting that the questionnaire was on the screen. What a mess!

medical-device start-up, and two patents already under her belt, Barbara was considered one of Edgell's top mechanical engineers after just three years in the company. Outspoken, self-confident, and physically striking, with large brown eyes and jet-black hair, she radiated excitement about her work. She was particularly pleased when upper management assigned her to the company's top-priority project—developing a general-purpose scanner-copier. The project, dubbed Focus, was the first step in Edgell's new strategy to move from its current line of expensive custom-built machines for business customers (like magazines, libraries, large corporations, and the military) to the consumer and small-business markets. Edgell management told the Focus team at the outset that the future of the organization hinged on this project.

Unfortunately, because the people managing Focus failed to apply the nourishment factor, the project foundered. And Edgell lost Barbara. The Focus story illustrates how problems with nourishers led to these disastrous outcomes for the project and the company. We'll start just before Barbara's departure, and then rewind the story to show how things were bungled from the start.

Well before the Focus project had been conceived, Barbara had arranged for a six-month unpaid leave to join her husband on a European sabbatical from his faculty position at Johns Hopkins. Eager to retain Barbara, the Edgell HR department had guaranteed her position, plus a raise, upon her return.

But the support and confidence she received from HR was totally lacking in her immediate team. As the time approached for Barbara to leave, she tried to explain her project notes and unfinished prototypes to Roy and Matthew, the other two mechanical engineers on the team. Her efforts met with *disrespectful* apathy from her colleagues:

> There is a lot of work that I have made a good start on, that needs to be completed. As I uncover more and more of the intricacies of the design and work out details between the many mating parts, I wonder how someone else will be able to figure it all out [. . .] A few times in the past week I have asked teammates how/when they want to get information from me—and the essential answer is "leave us the files." [Barbara, 5/12]

As time passed, *the absence of any real affiliation* among members of the Focus team became painfully obvious to Barbara. Another full week went by, and still no teammate responded to her overtures:

> I have not had any contact with the team except for a few friendly inquiries about [my leave] and my last day. I am expecting to pass a lot of information on to the team, and am currently preparing

it. However, I am waiting for a request for the information. I do not want to force anyone to take work they do not see as valuable. [Barbara, 5/19]

Barbara never received any indication that her teammates saw her work as valuable. On May 21, the day before her leave started, she again suffered from their *disrespect* for her contributions, as she tried one more time—fruitlessly—to effect a meaningful transfer of information:

This is my last day on the project and I am very disappointed to say that not a single team member has requested to meet with me and have information passed on. I sent an e-mail to the team asking people to set up time to meet. The only response was from Roy, who said that he would be out all morning today and to leave notebooks. [. . .] I am really glad to be leaving this company. [Barbara, 5/21]

That May 21 was Barbara's last day at Edgell Imaging—ever. Angry and sad, she simply left her notes and walked out the door. In that instant, Edgell lost all of the tacit knowledge Barbara had amassed about the company and its products, as well as the future value of her expertise. She did not return after her leave.

Clearly, something had gone terribly wrong within the Focus team. Although poor communication and disrespect were not rare in the teams we studied, the stonewalling by Barbara's colleagues was the starkest failure of teamwork that we saw. How had this happened? How could a team get to the point where a highly competent member repeatedly tried, and failed, to pass on critical information to her colleagues? In many ways, the Focus team was top-notch. Aside from the mechanical engineering subteam—Barbara, Roy, and Matthew—there was Donald, the team leader, who had both mechanical and electrical engineering expertise, and four other engineers with electrical, hardware, and software expertise. Barbara, Roy, and five of their colleagues had master's degrees or were working toward them, and four members (including Barbara, Roy, and Donald) held patents. Donald's early diary entries praised Barbara and Roy's technical prowess. Our measures of the team's personalities at the start of our study revealed no reason for them not to get along and work well together. We expected to see an effective group focused on its new product innovation, its members working hard together toward a challenging goal—something like the low-drama success stories of the O'Reilly Coated Materials teams.

Yet reading the Focus diaries sometimes seemed like watching a bad soap opera with characters reading from different scripts; there was plenty of melodrama even though the characters were almost never on the same page. Severe interpersonal strife, inadvertently set up and fueled by management, bedeviled Barbara's subteam. As a result, the team's day-by-day progress suffered and long-term performance stalled.[11] In fact, in their own ratings of the project's success at the end of our study, the Focus team members' scores ranked eighteenth out of our twenty-six teams.

Disrespect and Antagonism

The script for the Focus soap opera took shape when the team was formed. Perry Redding, the VP of R&D, put the experienced but newly hired engineer Donald in charge of the project. All of the people that Redding selected for the team had good engineering credentials, but he paid no attention to their level of experience at Edgell or their widely divergent problem-solving styles. He also made the terrible error of allowing both of the top mechanical engineers, Barbara and Roy, to believe that they were going to play the lead role in the mechanical design effort. On their background questionnaires for our study, both of them indicated that they were the lead mechanical engineer for the project.

Neither was ideal for the role, because Roy had much less experience at Edgell, and Barbara's leave was going to start before the project deadline. Neither Perry Redding nor Donald—nor anyone in management—clarified Barbara or Roy's roles until two months into the project—a script for disaster. After Redding finally declared that Roy was the sole lead mechanical engineer, Barbara felt *disrespected* by both Redding and Roy. Although Barbara's own actions likely contributed to the dearth of nourishers in the Focus team, we will zero in on how this disrespect—and other toxins—affected her inner work life:

> I explained to Donald that I was feeling insulted by having the [lead mechanical engineer] "role" taken away from me, and by having Roy show very little respect for my ideas over the past 2 months. Donald told me that Perry (VP of R&D, my boss and someone whom I trusted) had arranged for roles to be switched that way. In the same way that Perry gave my responsibility for the concept design to [an outside consultant] in February without even telling me, he did this [role switch] without telling me. I think I would feel much less insulted if Perry [would] let me know in advance about these things rather than letting me find out in meetings and from people's behavior. [. . .] I am much less inclined to come back to this job after my six-month leave. [Barbara, 4/14]

Because she perceived her manager as someone she could no longer trust, Barbara began to see Edgell as unworthy of her loyalty. She felt devalued by both Perry Redding and Roy. Being relieved of a leadership role in the team served as powerful *discouragement* to her. Barbara's emotions were quite negative: angry, resentful, frustrated, disappointed, and sad.[12] Her motivation to work for Edgell began to ebb. All of these inner work life reactions followed from the *disrespect* she was shown: She was not treated honestly, as a trusted employee should be, and her intellectual contributions to the project went unrecognized.

The plot of the Vision story was further complicated by the fact that Barbara and Roy had very different problem-solving styles—a fact that became obvious to us as soon as we looked at the questionnaires they had completed before the study began.[13] People's problem-solving styles, deeply ingrained through inheritance and experience, are part of their uniqueness as individuals. Barbara preferred to generate multiple innovative ideas, think outside the box, try many solutions rapidly to eliminate the infeasible ones, and move problem solving along by challenging assumptions. Roy preferred to solve problems more methodically, working within established paradigms to analyze new ideas, and ensuring that they would work before presenting them to others.

Both Roy and Barbara had high levels of expertise and the potential to be creative. But their problem-solving style differences needed to be managed.[14] They were not. Several weeks after the project started, Matthew, the third mechanical engineer, was thrown into this mix. Matthew, whose style was closer to Roy's, took an immediate dislike to Barbara. Because no one helped the three understand their style differences or facilitated an appreciation of each other's strengths, antagonism grew, marked by conflict and a breakdown of trust.

Roy and Barbara's style differences played out in many ways, but they were most acute in a conflict over the mechanical design schedule. Donald tried to placate Roy and Barbara by asking them both to prepare schedules, hoping that the schedules could be reconciled easily. However, instead of cooling the *antagonism* between Roy and Barbara, Donald's action unwittingly fanned the flames by creating a zero-sum competition. As a result, the conflict over the basic schedule, which had ignited in February, still burned almost two months later. Donald and all three mechanical engineers noted it in their journals. Near the beginning, Barbara wrote:

> Roy proposed one schedule and we discussed it. I disagreed with the plan and suggested another. It looks like one plan must be chosen and there will be a win/lose situation between the two of us who must work very closely together. I feel we are wasting time and also feel that if his type of plan is followed, then this is not the type of company I should be working at. [Barbara, 2/24]

Matthew, who joined the team two months into the project, was incredulous that the schedule had yet to be decided:

> The schedule is [still] being debated and argued about, and I do not understand why it is happening this late in the project timetable. [Matthew, 4/13]

Barbara, Roy, Matthew, and Donald all suffered blows to their inner work lives each time one of these ugly incidents erupted. Yet, although the destructive effects on work progress were obvious, Donald seemed powerless to reduce the *antagonism*.

Spillover

Negative effects on inner work life were not limited to the principals in this central interpersonal conflict. Inevitably, there was spillover, infecting the entire team and slowing everyone's progress. The Focus diaries contained dozens of examples in which someone noted the *antagonism* between Roy and Barbara (and sometimes Matthew). Hardware engineer Dustin was a particularly keen observer:

> Getting technical information out of the ME [mechanical engineering] folks seems to be a problem lately. (I asked for some pretty basic dimensions.) Might be because they are not communicating between themselves. [Dustin, 3/17]

> With the open offices, I'm still hearing the mechanical people complaining about each other. I'm wondering when it's going to end, but I'm getting used to it. [Dustin, 4/10]

> It was hard for me to listen to Roy moan and groan about Barbara's [. . .] work. [Dustin, 6/8]

Dustin's own inner work life deflated on many of the days that he noted the struggles within the mechanical engineering subteam.[15] And it continued to hit troughs because of the *emotional neglect* that he and the other innocent bystanders on the team suffered. Donald didn't know that Dustin was so bothered by the conflict, because Donald treated it as an undiscussable topic. And the effects bled from inner work life to performance. Because team meetings were likely to ignite conflicts between the mechanical engineers, all teammates began to avoid each other, and communication across the team in general began to suffer. Indeed, communication problems created a significant drag on the progress of the Focus team, driven by the *antagonism*, *disrespect*, and resultant *mistrust* among the mechanical engineers. Donald didn't address these problems effectively, and neither did upper management. Consider this report from Nick, a Focus software engineer:

> The meeting at which the reorganization of engineering was announced by Perry Redding seemed pretty irrelevant to our group [. . .] The big problems—unreal schedules, team members that don't like or trust each other, the disconnects between authority and responsibility—were never mentioned. [Nick, 6/3]

For the most part, people worked alone and in the dark, isolated in their misery.

Leadership Failures

When we first read the Focus diaries, we were tempted to chalk up the prevalence of toxins to unusually disagreeable personalities. However, when we checked the personality test that participants took at the beginning of the study, we found that none of the three mechanical engineers scored terribly low on the "Agreeableness" dimension.[16] The problems lay more with team *management* than with team *members*.

Leaders at multiple levels failed the people of the Focus team by laying a foundation in which nourishing inner work life was almost impossible. Perry Redding made ill-considered decisions like assigning the inexperienced Donald as the team leader, ignoring Roy and Barbara's enormously different problem-solving styles, and—most destructively— leading *both* Roy and Barbara to believe that they would be the lead mechanical engineer. Moreover, Redding's dealings with the team were problematic throughout the project. For example, hoping to both assuage Barbara's concerns and exert control over a project he considered too important to fail, he would tell Barbara one thing to her face (such as praising her work) and then take actions that betrayed her trust (such as telling Donald to reprimand her).

More importantly, Redding encouraged team members to speak directly with him if they had problems, rather than with Donald. This

undermined Donald's authority as team leader, making it more difficult for him to resolve the growing conflict. Redding and Director of
Operations Joseph Callaghan repeatedly made secret personnel
plans—such as moving Barbara off the Focus project—that Donald
had to plead with them to change. In all of these ways, upper management displayed a lack of respect for the team members in general and
Donald in particular.

Donald, an excellent engineer with several patents to his credit, was
kind, well-intentioned, and motivated to lead the Focus project well.
However, he proved unable to provide nourishers to the Focus team.
New to Edgell, he lacked the political savvy and internal credibility to
lead such an important project. Eager to tackle the technical work, he
was blind to the long-term implications of the growing tensions in the
mechanical engineering subteam. He was slow to catch on to the magni-
tude of their interpersonal problems, even though they were quite obvious to nearly everyone else on the team. For weeks after the project
(and the conflict) started, Donald failed to talk with Roy and Barbara,
either separately or together, about their increasingly public attacks on
each other. He allowed their disagreements to overtake the agendas of
team meetings. When he did finally remark on the *conflict* in his journal,
his observations tended to be rather mild, clinical, and detached. He
did not view it as a problem to be solved:

> Another battle erupted between Roy and Barbara at the summary
> meeting after [a key customer] had left. Barbara and Roy have
> greatly different attitudes toward life and neither seems to accept
> the other's methods. [Donald, 4/7]

After several weeks and two threats from management to remove
Barbara, Donald decided to become proactive. He pleaded with Callaghan
and Redding for more time before making any personnel changes, and
he gently discussed the conflict with Barbara, Roy, and Matthew individually and together. Privately, each of the three mechanical engineers
dismissed Donald's remarks as hopelessly naive, and dug in their heels.
He tried to build team spirit by having everyone read short bios of

themselves in a team meeting, which only gave the warring engineers a public forum for mockery disguised as humor. Clearly, by the time Donald stepped in, the game had already been lost:

> Despite my admonitions, Roy and Barbara were still sniping at each other during our schedule meeting. [Donald, 5/7]

Donald had made one of the most common mistakes managers can make when it comes to nourishers and toxins. Trying to do something positive—attempting to build affiliation within the team—he did it so timidly, and so long after matters had gotten out of hand, that the impact was negative.

In the end, the new scanner-copier was delayed by more than a year, and had to be developed by a reconstituted team with a different leader and almost all new members. Why did Focus fail? The evidence points to the overwhelming predominance of toxins over nourishers. The team's journal entries were dominated by reports of personal insults, nasty arguments, and rampant mistrust. Team members' inner work lives were characterized by anger, dwindling motivation, and dim views of the team, the work, and the organization. Progress sputtered as team members proved unable to even create a project schedule against which progress could be gauged.

The Focus story is an extreme case, but dismissing it as irrelevant would be a mistake. The predictable fallout from lack of nourishers applies in more typical situations. In fact, in our study, managers got it wrong more often than they got it right. In constituting teams, they frequently failed to consider the likelihood of unproductive conflict. In managing teams, they frequently underestimated the significance of interpersonal problems. Many people see in the Focus story an all-too-clear reflection of their own organizations. Managing human connections is extremely difficult to do well, and it's tempting to ignore them. But beware: to the extent that nourishers are deficient in your own organization, inner work life will be degraded and, consequently, so will performance. Once trust has been lost, it can be quite difficult to repair.[17] In the extreme, there is a point of no return.

A Human Connection: DreamSuite's Infosuite Team

As Helen's diary entry at the beginning of this chapter illustrates, the Infosuite team at DreamSuite Hotels had mastered the nourishment factor. Despite being relegated to cramped cubicles within a windowless warehouse, and despite being generally mistreated by DreamSuite management, the people of Infosuite managed to maintain good inner work lives most of the time by nourishing each other. The contrast to Focus, where people seemed intent on hurting each other, is particularly striking.

In many ways, the Infosuite and Focus teams were opposites. As badly as the Focus members rated their own project's success, that's how well the Infosuite members rated theirs—second of all twenty-six teams in our study. Our analysis of nourishers in the two teams yielded an equally stark contrast. Many of the negative forces in Focus were completely absent in Infosuite, and many of the positive forces in Infosuite were completely absent in Focus. In both cases, managers' behavior laid the foundation for support—or lack thereof—within the team. Unlike the Focus team, where managers at all levels played a toxic role, high-level managers were a negligible source of nourishment for the Infosuite team. Here, the managers who made a positive difference—in the face of negative top management behavior—were the team coleaders (this is often the case; see "The Special Role of Team Leaders in the Nourishment Factor").

Models of excellent support, both for each other and the rest of the team, Ruth and Harry inspired a team climate of respect, encouragement, warmth, and understanding unique among all the teams we studied. Helen's journal entry is only one of dozens from Infosuite describing Ruth's or Harry's use of nourishers. In nearly all such instances, inner work life rose, as Helen's did when Ruth reminded her of the "free" day

The Special Role of Team Leaders in the Nourishment Factor

Because of their close working relationship with subordinates, team leaders can have an especially powerful impact on inner work life through the nourishers they provide or fail to provide. In fact, if you are a team leader, you may have even more power than top managers to create a supportive or debilitating work environment for members of your team. You can even attenuate the negative impact of an unsupportive upper management. Our research identified direct actions you can take—or avoid—if you want to support your team's inner work life through nourishers.[a] Even if you are not a team leader, you can apply the same tools—whatever your level in your organization.

Each guideline below has an example (*in italics*) from one of the diaries. Although these guidelines may seem obvious, it is well worth bearing them in mind. A disturbingly high percent of team leaders in our study failed to follow them consistently—even as they *thought* they were managing people well.

As a team leader *do* . . .	As a team leader *don't* . . .
Show that you respect people and the work they do: *Seth [the team leader] asked for my opinion on a problem he is facing. This, to me, is an encouraging sign of his enhanced trust in my technical ability.*	Act dismissive, discourteous, or patronizing: *Matt [the team leader] came by my office this morning and told me that he would be freeing up Jared from the project early so that he could work on another project. I don't mind Jared being freed up before me. What hurt was that Jared's share of the mindless, boring, wind-up activities were now transferred to me [. . .] Matt tried to patronize me by saying that I do this kind of job better than Jared anyway. I hated that, [. . .] because I don't want to be in competition for the noncreative, mindless, wind-up activities of the job. I felt like the cleaning lady!*

As a team leader *do* . . .	As a team leader *don't* . . .
Recognize and reward the accomplishments of your people: *In a team meeting, Gene [the team leader] recognized me for work I did. This felt good and is a motivating factor for me.*	Display apathy toward your team members or their projects: *I am feeling slightly frustrated . . . I tried to speak with Spencer [the team leader] about an idea for an experiment yesterday. He put me off and said he'd get back to me today . . . Still waiting.*
When needed, provide emotional support to those who work under you: *The positive side to this [upsetting conversation with a strategic alliance partner] is that Rob [the team leader] voiced support and offered comfort; [it] made me feel good that my manager would stick by me.*	Obfuscate roles, responsibilities, and formal relationships, or change them haphazardly: *During my meeting with [my team leader], he mentioned that [I will be doing something entirely different] within the next two weeks. Not much more was said except that there is [. . .] "more change coming."* *This is a normal occurrence around here. Rumors fly for about 6 months or longer, then one day—Pow! You have a new boss on a different team. [. . .] This type of change creates havoc with team continuity.*
Create opportunities for the development of friendship and camaraderie in the team: *Today, we posed for our team's June calendar photo. Since January, we've been posing for photos and picking the best one each month to use as our "calendar shot" for the next month. It's fun and it creates such good feeling! I enjoyed working with the team today.*	

Source: T. M. Amabile, E. A. Schatzel, G. B. Moneta, and S. J. Kramer, "Leader Behaviors and the Work Environment for Creativity: Perceived Leader Support," *Leadership Quarterly* 15 (2004): 5–32.

a. In chapter 6, we noted that local managers, such as team leaders, can actually exert a stronger influence than high-level managers on people's inner work lives through the catalyst factor. The same is true of the nourishment factor. Here, we list the nourisher actions that support people; catalyst actions that support the work appeared in chapter 6.

she had earned. But as far as we could discover through our DreamSuite interviews, upper management cannot be credited with laying a foundation for the sublime chemistry of the Infosuite team. The nine-person group had been cobbled together with little forethought. In this case, the company got lucky.

Recall that, in the Focus team, Barbara and Roy had very different problem-solving styles. Interestingly, Ruth and Harry had a similar, if not as extreme, style difference. But differing problem-solving styles do not have to clash as they did with Barbara and Roy. Barbara and Ruth's style involves producing lots of ideas, some of which might be hare-brained. Roy and Harry's more methodical style can help sort through those ideas and systematically develop and refine the best ones. However, to work together effectively, people with differing styles have to accept the validity and usefulness of the other's way of solving problems. This is what Ruth and Harry were able to do. As a result, they got along beautifully and, in our judgment, were the most effective team coleaders we encountered in our study.[18]

So why did Infosuite have the human connection that Focus lacked? One clear difference with the Focus team was that Harry and Ruth had, early on, deliberately worked to achieve a mutual understanding about their roles relative to each other. Ruth, who held the title of project manager, was formally Harry's superior. Nevertheless, Ruth treated Harry as an equal. After a second team was added to her responsibilities, Ruth trusted Harry completely with day-to-day Infosuite team leadership. Moreover, the two of them communicated frequently and openly about the Infosuite team, its projects, and any potential problems that appeared. In one example, Harry reported:

> Strategized with Ruth, our project manager, on how to divide
> tasks/responsibilities/resources, with the addition of a second
> office under her. I feel that we came up with a reasonable plan of
> attack. [Harry, 2/18]

Although they often had different perspectives at the outset, they respected each other's opinions and worked hard to find good solutions.

As a result, team members had great confidence in both Ruth and Harry. Moreover, they followed the example set by these two coleaders, who created three basic nourishers within Infosuite: *respect* for teammates, *affiliation*, and *emotional support*. The fourth nourisher, *encouragement*, was often part of the mix. In each of these ways, inner work life nourishers came to and flowed from each member of the team.

Mutual Respect

Respect refers to either explicit or implicit expressions of another person's value. For example, Harry was quite ill in late May, and then took a few vacation days with his family. Although many team members expressed *respect* for Harry through their concern for him and elation at his return, none was more effusive than software engineer Tom:

> Our Harry is home!!!! Our Harry is home!!!! Everything's going
> to be okay now. Okay, so I exaggerate a little, but Harry's return
> after almost two weeks (illness, then vacation) is such a relief of
> pressure on each of us. He's the big brother who guides, protects,
> and encourages us. [Tom, 6/7]

Tom and his teammates *respected* Harry as a highly effective leader who provided both catalysts (helping with the work itself, which we addressed in chapter 6) and nourishers (*encouraging* people and looking out for their interests). As a result, Tom's emotions and self-perceptions were nourished by Harry's mere presence. Clearly, Tom felt considerable affection for Harry and was motivated by his leadership. Everyone else on the team felt the same.

Ruth, too, was honored by the team. Her *respectful* accommodation of team members' needs was one of the many actions that triggered a reciprocal respect. Consider the following diary excerpt from Helen, who occasionally needed to work from home because of the schedules of her young children:

> I just love working from home. I feel like I'm not distracted by
> the regular work issues at all. I can focus on what I need to focus

on without being distracted by ringing phones or the questions of others. Plus, I think I do better work programming in my slippers with my comfy coffee mug at my side and my radio playing full-blast!! I am so very pleased that my project manager allows this for us. I feel like she trusts me to work away from the battle station, and that she needs me to do the work or she wouldn't work out deals with me like this. What a great boss! She is the best. [Helen, 3/29]

Notice Helen's explicit expression of appreciation for and trust in Ruth, at the same time she described Ruth's appreciation for and trust in *her*. Helen's inner work life was clearly uplifted by the *respect* for her individuality that she received from Ruth. Emotionally, Helen felt happy and grateful and perceived herself as a valued, productive, and fortunate employee. Ruth's support of Helen's needs had a direct impact on Helen's inner work life which, in turn, had a positive impact on Helen's work progress on the days she worked at home.

In the long run, Helen's performance—her creativity, productivity, commitment to the work, and collegiality—was high. The importance of that fourth dimension—collegiality—is difficult to overestimate. Ruth showed collegial respect for Helen when she accommodated her special workday needs. In turn, Helen showed *respect* for her teammates by generously sharing both her knowledge and her high spirits. Witness this diary entry from Marsha, when she heard she would be working on a new project with Helen:

I'm very excited about [the project] because I will be learning a system I know nothing about and I will be creating some new processing. I am working with Helen [. . .] I love to work with Helen because I always learn so much from her and we have a lot of fun! [Marsha, 3/9]

On March 9, Marsha's inner work life skyrocketed. And the project she worked on with Helen was a resounding success.

Affiliation

The second nourisher that distinguished Infosuite was strong *affiliation*. Generally, the more closely bonded team members are to one another, the better inner work life will be across a team, and the greater their progress. In discussing team *affiliation*, we include a number of behaviors: doing anything explicitly for the sake of the team (rather than simply the work or the project); doing something to increase emotional bonding within the team; having fun with teammates at work or outside of work; and demonstrated pride, affection, or warmth for a teammate or the team as a whole.

Not all of these factors need be present for a team to function well in terms of affiliation. For example, the members of all four of the teams at O'Reilly Coated Materials seemed to get along quite well without much friendship outside of work or much affection mentioned between team members. But there was clearly a sense of pride in being part of these teams, and team members did have fun together from time to time.

Infosuite showed extraordinary *affiliation*, with examples appearing throughout the team's diaries, including this one by Tom:

[. . .] the truth is, everyone is working crazy hours, doing impossible tasks, and still keeping on the cheery side of the street. God help me, I do love them so! [Tom, 5/28]

It was Ruth and Harry who inspired unflagging loyalty and roused the team to exhibit an unusual combination of warmth, humor, and fun, interwoven with a powerful work ethic. The team saw Ruth take on the extra load of managing a second team, and Harry take on unexpected team leadership duties, without complaint. The team laughed with glee at Ruth's self-deprecating humor—such as when, embarrassed by a slip of the tongue she'd made in a team meeting, she crawled inside a large shipping box that happened to be in the room. And the team witnessed Ruth working alongside two teammates throughout the Memorial Day weekend to finish the Big Deal project—all the while maintaining her good spirits.

Marsha was infected with Ruth's positive attitude perhaps more than any other Infosuite team member. Keenly aware that Ruth cared for, respected, and protected the team while maintaining the highest work standards, Marsha did her best to emulate those qualities and displayed her own commitment to the team and to Ruth, as well as fierce pride in her work:

> The [customers for our current project] have never given us written requirements for the project, and yet they just sent us a note asking if we will make the May 6th deadline. I am just forging ahead and coding like crazy. Here's hoping they like what they never have asked for. Ruth is trying very hard to get them to commit themselves. What is very important to me is that I make Ruth look good; we all protect each other on this team. [Marsha, 4/6]

These are the fruits of *affiliation* at its strongest.

In her April 6 diary entry and others, Marsha revealed something very interesting about her inner work life: it depended to some extent on how she perceived the inner work life of her teammates, especially Ruth. Marsha's inner work life was positive when she perceived the team as happy and well-functioning. These perceptions evoked positive emotions, and drove Marsha's internal motivation for excellent work. In other words, the direct effects of nourishers on Marsha's inner work life indirectly enhanced her progress.[19]

All members of the Infosuite team expressed trust and pride in their teammates, in multiple diary entries. This mutual high regard was also evident in their daily numerical ratings on the diary form. On average, they rated the Infosuite team's progress higher than their own individual progress. By contrast, the Focus team at Edgell Imaging showed exactly the opposite pattern.

Our final meeting with the Infosuite team, soon after the study ended, confirmed that Ruth and Harry were the primary source of the team's strong *affiliation*. When we talked about Infosuite's successes, many team members remarked that they owed these successes primarily to their team leaders, and noted that other teams were jealous of them because they had such great leadership. However, both Ruth and Harry argued that the Infosuite team as a whole deserved the credit. Harry remarked, "No, this is just a great team. Anybody who isn't a total bonehead could manage this team." But we know better. As we saw at Karpenter Corporation, even highly intelligent managers who fail to provide nourishers can turn good teams, whose people have worked well together for years, into teams beset by sniping and mistrust.

The good inner work lives Infosuite shared were right on the surface. Their joyful camaraderie allowed them to see the team environment as a place where they could be their authentic selves, where they didn't have to hide part of who they were. When people can bring different aspects of their identities to bear on their work, they are more creative.[20] With the Infosuite team, this link to performance was clear.

Emotional Support

The third major nourisher that we saw in the Infosuite team was *emotional support*—any situation in which a person's emotions or views are validated in some way, or the person receives some sort of comfort or empathy about the work or a personal matter. *Emotional support* enhances inner work life by soothing negative emotions—calming fears, reducing frustrations, or dispelling despair:

> Ended up calming Ruth in the morning, after another needless reminder note from her boss put her in tears. [Harry, 5/7]

> Our teammate whose father is in the hospital returned for the day. It was good to see her, and it gave all of us the chance to fuss over her a little bit. We are such a good team!! [Helen, 3/22]

Helen's entry shows that *emotional support* not only nourishes the inner work life of the person on the receiving end; it can also have positive effects on the inner work lives of the people giving it. In this particular instance, Helen's perceptions of the quality of her team were boosted by being part of the group's effort to uplift the teammate whose father was very ill—an excellent example of the sensemaking process of inner work life. These positive perceptions were intertwined with very positive emotions.[21]

This strong socio-emotional support created an almost absolute sense of trust and an open flow of communication. Team members remarked repeatedly that they could discuss any aspect of their professional work and most aspects of their personal lives with each other, including their two team leaders, and expect honest responses. With clear communication leading to reduced fear of the daunting challenges they faced, the Infosuite team was better able to focus on the job at hand.

Leading by Nourishing

The most successful leaders know how to nourish the inner work lives of those they lead. Sir Ernest Shackleton, who captained the *HMS Endurance* on an Antarctic expedition in 1915, was one such leader.[22] His ability to foster human connections allowed him to lead his twenty-seven men through one of the most incredible feats of survival in human history.[23]

The *Endurance* became trapped in the ice on January 18, 1915; eight months later, when the ice began to crack the ship, Shackleton and his men abandoned it for a nearby ice floe. Although the explorers were stranded in the harshest possible conditions until their rescue on August 30, 1916, not a single man was lost.

Their survival is largely credited to Shackleton's leadership. Intuitively, Shackleton employed nourishers in that role. Early in the voyage, he required each crew member to do every job on board ship. This reduced the differences in status between the men, leading to greater affiliation. Shackleton also went out of his way to help the crew feel as happy as possible. After they became stranded, he encouraged playing games, making music, and performing skits. Two months after the group had abandoned the *Endurance*, he determined that the party would trek from the ice to land, where provisions from previous expeditions might be found. Because it was just before Christmas, he decided that they should celebrate prior to leaving; they did their best to make a feast from the available provisions. Shackleton's efforts to bond the crew reaped benefits repeatedly, when their lives depended on absolute unity of purpose.[24]

Like Shackleton, the most effective business managers lead people by serving their needs as human beings.[25] Donald, the nominal leader of Edgell's Focus team, did not engage deeply enough with his team members on a human level to truly nourish their inner work life. By contrast, Infosuite team coleaders Ruth and Harry truly engaged with their people, consistently exemplifying all four of the nourishers. Their example of serving each other's needs, as well as those of the team, was infectious.

The great management scholar Peter Drucker once wrote, "The goal [of management] is to make productive the specific strengths and knowledge of each individual."[26] In Drucker's view, a manager's job is to serve employees by ensuring that their needs for challenging work and satisfying work lives are fulfilled. Leading by serving does not mean abdicating responsibility. But it does require a wholly different mind-set toward management—focusing not on traditional control of subordinates, but on contribution to real work progress by the organization's members.

You have seen that managers can foster positive inner work life and drive progress by meeting their subordinates' needs for both catalysts and nourishers. You have also seen that managers can create misery, apathy, and a sure path to failure by neglecting those needs. In chapter 8, we'll show how you can care for inner work life and foster great performance by following a simple protocol every day.

8

At the End of the Day

NOT LONG AGO, we addressed a convention of business executives—from Nokia, Microsoft, Intuit, Coca-Cola, and dozens of other top companies—gathered in a posh Atlanta hotel ballroom. During the session, we asked their views on the thoughts, feelings, and drives that people experience in reaction to events at work. We asked if they believed that inner work life affects performance. Most did. So we pressed—what can managers do to keep employees happy, enthusiastic about the company, and motivated to dig into their work each day? The first several people who raised their hands mentioned various incentives and benefits, including competitive salaries, bonuses, recognition programs, and perquisites like employee assistance programs for folks dealing with personal crises. All of these, our audience members agreed, show that the company cares.

After acknowledging that incentives and benefits do make a difference, we asked these executives whether they thought it was also important to facilitate employees' daily progress in their work. Many of the conventioneers looked puzzled. A man in the third row voiced the question that seemed to be on many minds: "What do you mean? *Of course* daily progress in the work is motivating. But if you've hired the best people, and structured your organization well, it's up to them to make progress in their work. You shouldn't have to worry about 'facilitating' it every day."

Oh, but you do. If people in your organization cannot make consistent progress in meaningful work, they cannot have good inner work lives. They cannot make that progress without support—without a strong daily dose of catalysts and nourishers. And that support depends on you. Far too many managers are unaware of the importance of progress and therefore neither worry about it nor act to support it. As crucial as progress is to inner work life, and as obvious as it might seem, we are convinced that most managers simply don't think about it, systematically, every day.

In fact, of all seven companies in our diary study, only one—O'Reilly Coated Materials—had top managers who consistently supported people and their progress. Mark Hamilton, VP of R&D and the head of the O'Reilly division we studied, was neither charismatic nor "warm and fuzzy." Like most of the people on his top management team, Hamilton was a somewhat reserved scientist who had started his career as an individual contributor in an R&D lab. But he was an unusually perceptive and insightful manager. When we interviewed him, we were struck by the lessons he had drawn from his own experience as a lab member, team leader, lab chief, and, most recently, technical director.

Hamilton understood that O'Reilly could succeed only if its individuals and teams succeeded, and that that could happen only if managers focused on consistently supporting the work of their people. Noting that this didn't mean every project would go forward to completion, he insisted that this *did* mean people would always have a sense that they were moving forward on important work—that their managers respected their ideas and supported their efforts to do something meaningful.

This is what *he* did as a manager, whether by encouraging his technical directors to streamline review processes for projects, greeting team leaders' ideas for new experiments with an open mind, or celebrating team successes at all-company gatherings. Through consistent actions,

Hamilton showed an intuitive awareness of the power of progress, catalysts, and nourishers to feed inner work life and fuel high performance.

Awareness is the first step toward action. Knowing how important inner work life is for each person's performance, each day, can sensitize you to its role in your work and the work of everyone around you. Knowing that daily progress, even small wins, can make someone's day—and that even small setbacks can ruin the day—should boost your vigilance for both. In this chapter, we'll show you how to maintain that vigilance and turn that knowledge into action.

A Leader Who Got It Right

When it came to supporting inner work life, Mark Hamilton and his top management team at O'Reilly definitely got it right. But their actions don't offer a close-up perspective on managing effectively, because they did not interact daily with the project teams we studied. For a closer look at what managers can do to facilitate daily progress, we turn to the story of an excellent team leader in a different company—a company whose top managers were ineffective. In the story of this leader's team, we saw abundant examples of just how a manager can make a positive difference day by day.

Graham, a stocky forty-nine-year-old chemical engineer, led the four men on the NewPoly team at Kruger-Bern Chemicals. Whether he was in the company's northern Pennsylvania lab or on one of his frequent visits to customers, this energetic team leader stayed in close touch with his team's progress and what was helping or hindering that progress every day. More importantly, he acted on that information to make things better.

Before we tell this story, a caveat: Graham's *specific* actions to support the team's progress depended on the particular circumstances of the project, the team, and the company. There's no way for us to prescribe in detail what a particular team needs to succeed on a particular project. That requires expertise in the project's field and knowledge about the project's requirements—both of which should reside in the team and its leader. But Graham's actions serve as a powerful example of how managers at any level can approach each day determined to foster progress.

Graham and his team faced an uphill battle. The top brass at Kruger-Bern, a multinational firm headquartered in Europe, was considering a strategic shift that could cause a major reorganization in the U.S. division we studied. The goal of the NewPoly project—developing a safe, biodegradable polymer to replace petrochemicals in cosmetics and eventually in a wide range of consumer products—seemed to fit the new strategic direction, but signals from the European executives weren't clear.

Moreover, Graham had received contradictory signals from two vice presidents in the United States about how his team would be evaluated. The VP of R&D told him to patent as much technology as possible and to avoid partnering with potential customers (large cosmetics manufacturers) until all aspects of the team's new technology had been submitted to the U.S Patent and Trademark Office. The technology development was going to be very complex, with far-reaching applicability if it succeeded, and the R&D head wanted Kruger-Bern to lock up the intellectual property.

But Kruger-Bern's VP of New Business Development pushed Graham to partner with customers immediately, generating revenue as soon as possible. Meanwhile, key individuals in both the corporate patent office and the customer organizations were dragging their feet. And neither VP was willing to give the NewPoly team the additional personnel promised at the start of the project. Although the team understood that this project was important and was making advances in both technology and customer relationships, the uncertainty over goals and the resource constraints threatened to halt its progress.

Despite these challenges, the team did make good progress during the project phase we studied. And, although they had very negative perceptions of the Kruger-Bern organization and its reluctance to provide adequate resources, team members' inner work lives were quite good in most respects. They perceived their work as positively challenging and gave high ratings to their support from the team leader (Graham), mutual support within the team, and autonomy.[1] Their day-by-day positive emotions were strong, on average, and so was their intrinsic motivation. Graham deserves a great deal of the credit.

Setting the Climate, One Event at a Time

On June 5, barely one month into the NewPoly project, a crisis erupted. Late on Friday afternoon, the VP of marketing from the team's most important prospective customer, Mink Industries, called, infuriated about a red lip gloss sample the team had sent earlier in the week. The head buyer from Mink's number-one customer, a major cosmetics retailer, had panned the sample's color and texture. Although the Mink VP had explained that the sample was just the latest experimental result, the buyer declared that Mink should stop working with Kruger-Bern if this was the best they could do.

Shocked by this threat, most members of the team wondered if it spelled the end of their work. Graham promised the customer quick action and immediately mobilized the team. He called an impromptu meeting and, after detailing the nature of the complaint, asked each team member for his analysis of both the technical and the customer management problems. He kept everyone focused on the issues and didn't allow personal accusations. Several team members, starting with Graham himself, noted mistakes that they themselves had made in creating the sample or communicating with the customer. The team huddled long into Friday evening—sustained by Chinese takeout and black coffee—completing their analysis and developing an action plan to deal with the situation.

On Monday morning, Graham and Brady, a somber, sandy-haired research associate, discussed the plan with the Mink vice president— and defused the situation:

Graham and I had a conference call with our customer to exchange information on the complaint situation and to communicate our plans to respond. We also discussed how to deal with [. . .] our customer's customer so as to keep things moving forward. It was a harmonious and productive discussion between two partners committed to a challenging new business opportunity. [Brady, 6/8]

By addressing the problem so swiftly and openly, Graham showed Brady and the rest of the team that he did not shy away from negative information. In effect, he let the team know that he valued and welcomed accurate communication about any situation. By involving the entire team in analyzing the issues and developing a plan, Graham modeled how to respond to crises in the work—not by panicking or pointing fingers to assess personal blame, but by analyzing the problems, identifying causes, and developing a coordinated action plan.

The following Friday, Graham once again called the team to the conference room. Standing before the whiteboard, marker in hand, he focused everyone on debriefing the crisis, assessing the solution they had implemented, and reviewing the knowledge they had gained. Together, they drew several lessons: in the future, they would be more selective in responding to Mink's requests for frequent samples. They would focus on color consistency as well as texture. And they would ask Mink not to show experimental samples to customers until the NewPoly team agreed they were "ready for prime time." What Graham did, essentially, was to show the team how to learn from failure. In helping the team see that they could together solve problems and apply lessons to plan future work, he ratcheted up the climate for smooth coordination.

Brady, with fifteen years' experience at Kruger-Bern and a master's in organic chemistry, was legendary among his fellow research associates for his dedication. Stories circulated about the sleeping bag he kept stashed in his car for those evenings he decided to continue an experiment through the night. He cared deeply about being a valued member of an effective team. Imagine how differently Brady might have described the aftermath of the event if Graham had blamed various team members for the sample's disappointing quality or its premature submission to the customer. That's probably what would have happened in any of the teams we studied at Karpenter Corporation. Brady and his teammates may well have decided to hide problems from Graham in the future. Communication would have been stifled and coordination would have suffered. But, instead, Graham displayed his respect for the team's professional competence and his trust in their effort. And he showed that he respected their ideas by keeping them involved in every aspect of the crisis. His words and actions not only addressed the immediate problems, but also built a positive climate that endured throughout the project.

Staying Attuned Every Day

Without accurate information, no manager can provide the catalysts and nourishers that people need to make progress. Graham was ahead of the game when he established a psychologically safe climate for communication during the customer crisis. Team members knew that his door was always open if he was in the office, and that he welcomed their phone calls if he was away. Moreover, he rolled up his sleeves and worked with them. Day by day, he stayed attuned to the team's progress and needs as he collaborated with them.

For example, Graham often went on customer visits with Brady and Curtis, the NewPoly team's jocular marketing expert. Curtis, a Stanford MBA with twelve years of experience, had been trying to garner interest from Shelton Consumer Products in Minneapolis. Realizing that this business could be even more significant than Mink's, Graham offered to help by joining a trip to Shelton. Curtis didn't hesitate to accept the offer—and the trip went better than expected:

> Met with major customer prospect [. . .] with Brady & Graham.
> [The customer] seemed more enthusiastic about working with us
> [today] than in recent phone conversations [. . .]. We realized
> that [. . .] there may be a very good opportunity here [. . .].
> We all felt good about the meeting. [Curtis, 5/21]

Graham didn't have to wonder about the team's progress on May 21. He saw it for himself.

Graham's nonjudgmental openness to discussing problems in the work led team members to update him frequently—without being asked—on their setbacks, their progress, and their plans. For example, when Brady couldn't get the parameters right on the equipment, he had to abort an experimental trial of a new material. Because the NewPoly team had access to this crucial equipment only one day a week, this caused a significant delay. Brady did not hesitate to share the bad news with Graham:

> I [told] Graham that the trial had to be rescheduled due to operational problems. He didn't like the lost week, but seemed to understand. [Brady, 7/8]

For his part, Graham, though disappointed, did not blame Brady. He accepted the event as unfortunate but unavoidable. More importantly, he focused on diagnosing and correcting the problem:

> Our trial to make a new substrate for a key customer had to be aborted. Although the problem was diagnosed and can be corrected, it means delaying everything a week. [Graham, 7/8]

Notice that Graham took shared ownership of the problem when he referred to "our trial" (rather than "Brady's trial").

Targeting Support

Graham *targeted* his support each day, given what he had seen and heard about recent events in the team and the project. In mid-July, because he was so well attuned to the team, he was able to offer encouragement—a crucial nourisher—when people became jittery about the possible corporate reorganization. A confusing missive had come out from the European headquarters, prompting Graham to immediately seek clarification from his U.S. managers. As soon as he got uplifting information, he relayed it to the team—even though he was on vacation. This made a real difference for team members' inner work lives:

> Graham called to pass along news of a pending organization change that has more positive implications than most of the

rumors. I appreciated his call from vacation to let me know of this glimmer of bright light in the sea of uncertainty. [Brady, 7/17]

Just as crucial as the targeted nourishers that Graham provided were the catalysts he was able to provide. Because of closeness to the team, he could see for himself what specific project support they needed and take appropriate action. He didn't neglect any of the catalysts: clarifying goals; giving autonomy; working to secure sufficient resources and reasonable time-frames; helping with the work directly; fostering an open exchange of ideas; and approaching both problems and successes as learning opportunities.

Graham's targeted provision of catalysts for both major project issues (like the customer complaint) and more mundane challenges was frequent and deliberate. For instance, when Graham traveled to see customers or upper management, he phoned the team every couple of days to see how things were going. In addition, he always asked what he could do to help. Often, he was able to assist even long-distance:

Graham called to inquire about my week. In the course of our chat, Graham observed, from my descriptions, that the poor texture in our problem substrate may be related to some issues with that material reported [in the scientific literature] and observed to a lesser degree in [. . .] yesterday's experiment. I will be following up to see if that idea explains current results. [Brady, 6/19]

Brady and his teammates welcomed Graham's help, largely because he lent his expertise without a trace of condescension.

Although Graham usually knew what the team needed by collaborating with them, he occasionally just *asked*:

Graham asked what we needed to move the project ahead faster. A chorus of voices resounded with our need for more people. While I felt the current reorganization turmoil could make the addition of headcount almost folly, Graham says he will make a strong plea for an engineer and two technicians. That ought to

test management's resolve on this project. I have to admire
Graham's courage to raise that question [. . .] at this time.
[Brady, 8/3]

Three days later Graham was at headquarters making the case. In
this and dozens of other instances, Graham kept himself well-informed
about his team's setbacks, inhibitors, and toxins—and took steps to alleviate them. Not only did his behavior actually propel the project forward, but it also signaled to the team that they and their work had real
value.

Taken separately, none of Graham's actions seems extraordinary. He
simply dealt with problems as they occurred and provided his team
with the resources and help they needed to move ahead in their work.
But what made Graham a great leader was his ability to do this day in
and day out. He consistently provided the team with catalysts and nourishers, and, more importantly, he never allowed inhibitors or toxins to
bring down the project or take over the inner work lives of his team.
Unfortunately, only a minority of the leaders that we studied were able
to do the same.

Checking In, Not Checking Up

There's a fine line between keeping in close touch with how your subordinates are doing and micromanaging them. Some team leaders in our
study stepped way over the wrong side of that line. Operating under a
misguided notion of what management involves, they held themselves
aloof from their teams.[2] Rather than working collaboratively with the
team and *checking in* with team members regularly, as Graham did,
these team leaders spent much of their time *checking up* on people. Subordinates can tell the difference, and the consequences for inner work
life are not good.

Managers who get it wrong make four kinds of mistakes. First, they
fail to allow autonomy in carrying out the work. Unlike Graham, who
gave the NewPoly team a clear strategic goal but respected members'
ideas on how they could meet that goal, micromanagers dictate every

move. Second, they frequently ask subordinates about their work without providing any real help when problems arise. Micromanaging leaders come across as judges and dictators, rather than as coaches and colleagues.

Third, micromanaging leaders are quick to affix personal blame when problems arise, rather than guiding subordinates in an open exploration of causes and possible solutions. Those subordinates end up striving to look good rather than honestly discussing obstacles and how to surmount them. They live in fear, and their perceptions of the manager settle into a permanent trough.

Fourth, the team leaders in our study who got it wrong rarely shared information with team members about their *own* work. Graham and other effective team leaders realized that, by virtue of their special roles, they were privy to vital information about many issues relevant to the team's work. These issues included upper management's views of the project, customers' views and needs, and possible sources of assistance or resistance within and outside the organization. Some team leaders jealously guarded such knowledge as a marker of their status, doling it out as a favor according to their whims. When subordinates realize that a manager withholds potentially useful information like an overcontrolling parent, they feel infantilized, their motivation stalls, and their work is handicapped.

Micromanagement not only poisons inner work life; it stifles creativity and productivity in the long run. When people lack the autonomy, information, and expert help they need to make progress, their thoughts, feelings, and drives take a downward turn—resulting in pedestrian ideas and lackluster output. Managers panic when they see performance lagging, which leads them to hover over subordinates' shoulders even more intrusively and criticize even more harshly— which engenders even worse inner work life. People hide problems from these managers, until those problems erupt into crises. Even when micromanaging leaders try to provide catalysts and nourishers, they don't have enough information about what their subordinates really need. Vicious cycles take hold.

Graham didn't make these mistakes. He effectively managed the conditions affecting progress without micromanaging the people doing the work. Occasionally, without prying, he even got a direct window into their inner work lives—and did what he could to support it. The payoff was an energized, productive team. Learning from Graham and other exemplary leaders in our study, we realized that the payoff depends not on a particular leader personality or background, but on a series of actions. We have codified these actions into a simple daily checklist for managers.[3]

The Daily Progress Checklist

Sometimes the smallest things can make the biggest difference. In his 2009 book, *The Checklist Manifesto*, Harvard surgeon and author Atul Gawande showed that even experienced surgeons can improve the performance of their teams dramatically by using a simple checklist to guide every single operation.[4] The items on the safe surgery checklist seem terribly mundane. They include procedures like self-introductions by everyone on the surgical team, confirming that everyone knows which side of the body is being operated on, and counting the surgical sponges to see that all are removed from the patient before closing the incision.

The results are astonishing. In a three-month experiment in eight different hospitals around the world, the rate of serious complications for surgical patients fell by 36 percent after introduction of the checklist, and deaths fell by 47 percent. Even Gawande himself, a highly trained surgeon with years of operating room experience, found that his own performance improved notably after he started using the checklist. His point is that surgery, like any complex task, requires a regular check of all the fundamentals—to liberate the team to focus on the work and any unexpected circumstances that may arise.

Management may not be brain surgery, but it is a complex task. If you are a top manager, you need to focus on big-picture issues:

economics, science, and society, as well as your business model in the current competitive environment and emerging trends in your industry. You also need to develop your vision for the organization over the long run, your strategy for achieving that vision, and your plan for the next phase of your organization's life. You need to think creatively about resource acquisition and a host of other broad issues that can determine your company's fate. And you must attend to crises as they erupt. Even if you are a lower-level manager—perhaps leading only a single project team—your mind is filled with dozens of concerns, ranging from planning the project's strategy to keeping up on new technologies that could enhance your team's work, not to mention your own work on the project.

But, whatever your level, your strategy is unlikely to succeed unless you also think about the people working to implement it. This is true regardless of whether those people are the top company executives or the members of a project team developing a new product. If you want them to perform at peak levels, you need to support their inner work lives. And you need to do it every day; that's why a daily checklist can be a valuable tool. All it takes is five minutes at the end of the day.

The items on the daily progress checklist (table 8-1) aren't as simple as counting the number of sponges on an operating room tray, but they aren't very complicated, either. They require only that you stay vigilant each day for indications of your team's progress and events influencing it. Stay vigilant, too, for signals about inner work life. Don't expect them to be frequent, and don't constantly probe for them—just be alert for obvious indications. Ruth and Harry, the Infosuite team leaders, didn't need extraordinary emotional intelligence to understand team members' inner work lives on the day of the major terminations. People crying at their desks was a pretty good clue. But often the signs are harder to see, like someone making more errors than usual, or teammates being particularly short-tempered with each other. These can be obvious clues, but only if you are alert to them.

TABLE 8-1

The daily progress checklist

Progress

Which 1 or 2 events today indicated either a small win or a possible breakthrough? (Describe briefly.)

Setbacks

Which 1 or 2 events today indicated either a small setback or a possible crisis? (Describe briefly.)

Catalysts

Did the team have clear short- and long-term *goals* for meaningful work?

Did team members have sufficient *autonomy* to solve problems and take ownership of the project?

Did they have all the *resources* they needed to move forward efficiently?

Did they have sufficient *time* to focus on meaningful work?

Did I give or get them *help* when they needed or requested it?
Did I encourage team members to help one another?

Did I discuss *lessons* from today's successes and problems with my team?

Did I help *ideas flow* freely within the group?

Inhibitors

Was there any confusion regarding long- or short-term *goals* for meaningful work?

Were team members overly *constrained* in their ability to solve problems and feel ownership of the project?

Did they lack any of the *resources* they needed to move forward effectively?

Did they lack sufficient *time* to focus on meaningful work?

Did I or others fail to provide needed or requested *help?*

Did I "punish" failure, or neglect to find *lessons* and/or opportunities in problems and successes?

Did I or others out off the presentation or debate of *ideas* prematurely?

Nourishers

Did I show *respect* to team members by recognizing their contributions to progress, attending to their ideas, and treating them as trusted professionals?

Did I *encourage* team members who faced difficult challenges?

Did I *support* team members who had a personal or professional problem?

Is there a sense of personal and professional *affiliation* and camaraderie within the team?

Toxins

Did I *disrespect* any team members by failing to recognize their contributions to progress, not attending to their ideas, or not treating them as trusted professionals?

Did I *discourage* a member of the team in any way?

Did I *neglect* a team member who had a personal or professional problem?

Is there tension or *antagonism* among members of the team or between team members and me?

Inner work life

Did I see any indications of the quality of my subordinates' inner work lives today?

Perceptions of the work, team, management, firm

Emotions

Motivation

What specific events might have affected inner work life today?

Action plan

What can I do tomorrow to strengthen the catalysts and nourishers identified and provide ones that are lacking?

What can I do tomorrow to start eliminating the inhibitors and toxins identified?

Using the Checklist

Near the end of each workday, use the daily progress checklist as a guide for reviewing the day and planning your managerial actions of the next day. Record your thoughts on a written or electronic copy of the checklist. After using the checklist for a few days, you will be able to efficiently focus on the day's issues by scanning the italicized words in the checklist. First focus on the day's progress and setbacks, then think about specific events—including the catalysts and nourishers—that affected progress. Next consider any clear inner work life clues from the day. Finally, prepare for action. The action plan for the next day is the most important part of your daily review: what is the one thing you can do to best facilitate progress?

Like Graham, use information that you gathered in the normal course of the day. Ideally, you will work closely enough with your subordinates, and remain open enough to what they say, that you will have natural access to this information—as well as to direct signs about the state of their inner work lives. Graham's collaborative mode of interaction invited team members to discuss the status of their work—which supplied him with an ongoing stream of information; he had no need to quiz them constantly. Take a look at the following two journal entries to see this dynamic in play:

> Graham stopped in to review the key project's status and delegate an additional task. [Brady, 7/28]
>
> ———
>
> I learned that Brady has made considerable progress getting materials and equipment for a new phase of the project. [Graham, 7/28]

Through simple interactions like this, Graham reaped new information daily about the team's progress.

If you are like most of the surgeons whom Gawande tried to convince to use his checklist—or even like Gawande himself—you will think the checklist is beneath you. Surely you are far too expert to need such a simplistic crutch. But it's precisely because you are an expert and therefore have so many things to think about, that taking five minutes for the checklist can be so important. We know from our own experience, and from that of the many leaders we have spoken to, just how easy it is to become overwhelmed by the pressures of work and to lose track of those little successes that will eventually lead to that next breakthrough. It's even easier to ignore those little setbacks that can derail it.

Most of us have tendencies to focus either on the positive or the negative. If you tend to focus on the positive, it is all too easy to ignore problems unless the checklist reminds you to do so. Conversely, if you tend to focus on the negative, the checklist will attune you to the things that are going well.

After using the checklist for a few days, you will probably decide that you can run through it mentally. You'll reason that it's so simple, you already have it memorized. Resist that impulse. Without looking at the physical checklist as part of your daily routine and recording your thoughts, you'll be likely to stop doing it altogether. Next thing you know, daily progress, catalysts, and nourishers will have slipped off your mental agenda.

As you review the day to answer the checklist questions, be inclusive. Don't forget the power of small events and negative events. Consider even things that might seem trivial, and look for both positive and negative events. Anything that went well, or better than expected for your team, or for any particular person's work, is a progress event. Any failure or disappointment in the work is a setback.

Consider the full range of work catalysts and inhibitors. Did anything happen that assisted or threatened the team's clarity about goals, autonomy in doing their work, access to necessary resources, time to think creatively, access to needed help, ability to learn from problems and successes, or ability to get their ideas heard? Once in a while, simply ask your people what *you* can do to help *them* move forward. Then, when you next turn to the checklist, your action plan will be clear. Moreover, your inquiry will send the crucial signal that they and the work they do are important.

When you get to the checklist question on nourishers, consider whether your people were respected, recognized, encouraged, and supported as people during the day. Curtis, the marketing specialist on the NewPoly team, was a "man's man," someone who rarely showed a hint of emotion in his diaries or in our meetings with his team. When problems appeared, he described them with taciturn calm and approached them with matter-of-fact efficiency. But, about halfway through our nine-month study of his team, Curtis suffered a brutal personal crisis—his young son was diagnosed with leukemia. Although Curtis missed little work, continued to perform well, and rarely mentioned his troubles, Graham recognized that Curtis was suffering. He reached out to Curtis on more than one occasion:

> Met with two different sets of colleagues from Massachusetts working on related projects; talked to Earl who was [visiting a] customer; counseled Curtis on his personal problems.
> [Graham, 11/23]

Although Curtis mentioned Graham's support in only a few diary entries, it was clear that he appreciated his team leader's empathic awareness of his personal agony.

In scanning the day for relevant incidents, remember that important work events can come from any source—your *own* behavior during the day; technical outcomes that "just happen"; interactions within the team; actions of other managers, employees, or groups; "the system" of procedures and policies in the organization; and even things going on outside the organization. In Graham's own diaries, he noted events across this entire range.

With each item on the checklist, consider whether you need to act immediately or watch for additional signs. You may or may not have sufficient information on the basis of a single day's occurrences. But make a note of anything you want to watch. Keep it on your managerial agenda.

The aim of the checklist is *managing for meaningful progress*, because that is your real job inside the organization. This may require a significant mind-shift. Business schools, business books, and managers themselves usually conceptualize management as *managing organizations* or *managing people*. But if you focus on daily progress in meaningful work, managing people and the entire organization will become much more feasible. You won't have to figure out a way to X-ray subordinates' inner work lives because, if you facilitate their steady progress in meaningful work, make that progress salient to them, and treat them well as people, they *will* experience the perceptions, emotions, and motivation necessary for great performance. Their superior work will contribute much to organizational success. In the bargain, they will be excited about their jobs.

You may be surprised by the checklist's benefits. Completing it at the end of every day will direct you to the fundamentals of inner work life support: the progress principle, the catalyst factor, and the nourishment factor. It will help you avoid focusing only on the most salient event of the day, the most recent event, or your overall feeling about the day.[5] It will also free your mind from having to worry about inner work life all day, so you can throw yourself into your work. Most importantly, it will ensure that your subordinates' daily triumphs and struggles don't fall off your radar screen.

Ironically, such a microscopic focus on what's happening every day is the best way to build a widespread, enduring climate of free-flowing communication, smooth coordination, and true consideration for people and their ideas. It's the accumulation of similar events, day by day, that creates that climate. If you are a manager, the events that you cause are particularly potent. They set the tone and serve as a model for everyone on the receiving end. One event at a time, you shape the climate from which your people take their cues.

Sustaining Virtuous Cycles and Halting Vicious Ones

Focusing on inner work life one day at a time keeps you vigilant, but people make sense of each day's events against the backstory of the days that preceded it. Myopic focus on a narrow timeframe can blind you to the big picture of what's really going on with both inner work life and progress. Because inner work life and progress exert mutual influence, the ideal is to keep positive progress loops—virtuous cycles—going as long as possible and abort negative ones—vicious cycles—as soon as possible. These patterns are often hard to spot unless you keep looking at the right things over time. In fact, we might never have recognized the progress principle had we not been carefully analyzing daily event descriptions, many of which seemed unimportant in isolation. It was focusing on the day-to-day and then stepping back to look for patterns that revealed what was really happening in the teams we studied.

Sustaining virtuous cycles requires recognizing them to begin with. When your private end-of-the-day review indicates a series of days with more progress events than setbacks, and no major signs of negative inner work life, the chances are good that your team is in a virtuous cycle. If your team is fortunate enough to have one going, it's important to stay alert for negative events—especially small hassles—that can sour good inner work life or halt progress. The most fundamental step is watching for and dealing with actual setback events. Graham did this when he acted decisively to address the customer complaint crisis, without fault-finding or melodrama. Other excellent team leaders in our study addressed problems with similar equanimity.

The Vision team of O'Reilly Coated Materials was one of the best teams in our study. Team members experienced many virtuous cycles of progress and inner work life. But not every day we studied the Vision team was rosy—far from it. Because they were doing extremely complex technical work, Dave and his three team members encountered a number of setbacks. Although these men were all professional scientists and technicians who understood the vicissitudes of experimentation, each setback was a disappointment—a negative shock to each team member's inner work life system.

Dave was a master at helping his team deal with these shocks. With no fanfare or panic, he consistently treated these events as business as usual and made it clear that each was an opportunity for learning.

Recall that Tim, the Vision team's senior research engineer, made a mistake running one in a series of experimental trials. When Tim told him, Dave reacted calmly and reasonably, saying, "That is all right, as long as you know what you did."

Remember that statement. This is how a manager creates a climate of psychological safety—by focusing on the work and what can be learned from it, rather than berating subordinates for errors. More generally, this is how a manager can sustain virtuous cycles of progress and positive inner work life in the face of the inevitable setbacks that occur in any complex project. Contrast this to the climate of blame and fear that prevailed throughout Karpenter Corporation. As a member of Karpenter's Domain team said, "Around here, not finding a solution is perceived as not being competent!"

This highlights an important fact. By its very nature, meaningful work is hard; people often get the greatest satisfaction from overcoming the most difficult challenges. Failure is inevitable along the path to innovation. Though you should try to minimize obstacles and setbacks under your control, you can never create a problem-free bubble for your people. You can't nourish inner work life if you drive yourself and your team crazy trying to avoid all problems. Rather, focus on providing people with the catalysts and nourishers they need to overcome the obstacles they will inevitably face. As legendary industrialist Henry Ford once said, "Failure is simply the opportunity to begin again more intelligently."

Turning a bad situation around is always more difficult than keeping a good thing going. But it's possible. Even the heedless top executives at DreamSuite Hotels did manage once to halt the Infosuite team's vicious cycle of negative inner work life and setbacks—if only temporarily and unintentionally. The members of that team fell into negative loops repeatedly as they dealt with a parent company that was by turns neglectful and dismissive, or hostile and demanding. During the reacquisition of the Infosuite team's business unit and the terminations that followed, the management of DreamSuite treated the team as a disposable commodity.

But then there was the golden week of the Big Deal project, during which top management, desperate to avoid losing $145 million, lavished attention on the team. For those eight days, as Infosuite team members worked almost around the clock on the Big Deal, managers freed the team from other obligations, expressed their appreciation for the team's work, and offered constant encouragement in the form of friendly words, bottled water, and food.

The Infosuite team's inner work life hit a peak during those days, and their performance exceeded expectations. The vicious cycle had been broken. Imagine the virtuous cycles that might have ensued if upper management had not gone back to ignoring the team and its needs.

Local Leaders Creating an Oasis

Even in a hostile work environment like DreamSuite's, a deft lower-level manager can sometimes interrupt a vicious cycle of negative inner work life and setbacks. Ruth, the coleader of the Infosuite team, was one such manager. In effect, she created an oasis of support in a harsh, arid organizational climate. Not only did top managers at DreamSuite disrespect and devalue the team, but its department heads—who were the InfoSuite team's internal customers—seldom bothered to clarify their requests or recognize good work. Ruth bucked this foul tide tirelessly, and she usually succeeded in rescuing team members' inner work lives.

The key to her success was the supportive climate she had built with the team in dealing with mundane setbacks, *before* the negative organizational events began to pile up. On many occasions, she injected catalysts. For example, early in our study, Infosuite software engineer Helen was struggling with an indecipherable data file from DreamSuite's marketing department. Although the department administrators needed analyses quickly, they failed to return Helen's calls for clarification. Unable to even read the data, Helen was completely stymied in her attempts to move forward on the assignment. The next day, as soon as Ruth learned of Helen's difficulties, she immediately found someone in the IT group who could help:

I was able to locate a resource in the IT office who was able to read the file provided by Marketing [. . .] This was rewarding, because Helen had been struggling with trying to make the bad file they sent 2 weeks ago work. [Ruth, 2/12]

Ruth's action not only enabled Helen to quickly finish the assignment, it also uplifted Ruth's *own* inner work life.[6] It is not uncommon for such positive effects to reflect back to the manager.[7]

As you saw in chapter 7, Ruth also provided plenty of nourishers to Infosuite team members from the very beginning. Most notably, she encouraged their efforts and provided appreciative recognition when they succeeded. On one occasion, she actually hugged Infosuite software engineer Marsha, who had made outstanding progress:

Today I loaded into production two requests from our Dream-Suite users. I got both requests done in much less time than was estimated, so I saved them some money. My project manager [Ruth] was so happy she hugged me. I'm happy when she's happy! [. . .] I feel very good about all the work I've completed today. [Marsha, 2/18]

You can guess how extraordinarily positive Marsha's inner work life was on this day. Although Ruth's physical expression was unusual, her public display of enthusiasm for good performance was not.

Through Ruth's small acts of good management, the people of Infosuite developed confidence that they could trust in her continued support, even after the DreamSuite terminations began a few weeks into our study. On the day that nearly forty project managers lost their jobs, Marsha's emotions went into a tailspin. On the day after this inner work life assault, Ruth was able to restore Marsha's composure and engagement in the work through a small gesture of emotional understanding:[8]

This morning, my project manager came over and sat next to me and asked me if I was okay after all the firing that went on yesterday. I thought that was really nice. We all had a very rough day yesterday, but I feel better today. In 45 days, we will all know our fate and then we can get on with our lives one way or the other. The outcome of all this is really out of our control. I'm trying to concentrate on what *is* in my control, by doing my job. [Marsha, 5/21]

Thanks in large part to Ruth's management approach from the time she assumed leadership of the Infosuite team, Marsha and her colleagues were indeed able to concentrate on their jobs. Within less than a week, they would throw themselves into the Big Deal project. Ruth's spadework establishing a solid foundation with her team had paid off handsomely. In her constant awareness of subordinates' struggles and accomplishments, and her consistent, daily provision of both catalysts and nourishers for them, Ruth serves as a paragon for any manager who wants to swiftly interrupt vicious cycles of setbacks and inferior inner work life.

Top Managers Taking Responsibility

If you are a top manager, don't let the Infosuite team's story fool you. Ruth was able to rescue her team's inner work life repeatedly, but that doesn't mean that Dreamsuite executives paid no price for their behavior toward the team. The steady stream of negative shocks to the inner work life systems of people on the Infosuite team—shocks originating in the wider organization and its management—constantly interrupted the team's progress in the short term. And the longer-term effects were even more corrosive. Within a year of our research, Ruth, exhausted by her constant battle to neutralize the flow of negative events impinging on her team, accepted another job offer. Many key members of the team left with her. DreamSuite had lost invaluable expertise.

Yes, local leaders can create a temporary oasis for a team, a department, maybe even an entire business unit. But that doesn't excuse top organizational managers from their responsibility to create a positive organizational climate for people and their ideas. It's a waste of local leaders' talent and energy to bear the sole responsibility for sustaining their people's inner work lives. And they can't do it indefinitely. Because negative events pack a stronger punch than positive ones, a hostile organizational climate will have its way in the end.

———————

Progress lives in the everyday, not just in quarterly reports or milestone checkpoints. And building a great organizational climate happens through everyday words and actions, not through a series of major one-time initiatives. Managers can't help but influence subordinates' inner work lives; the only question is how. That's why, if you are a manager, a review of your people's progress should become a daily discipline. This is how you sweat the small stuff that can have magnified effects on inner work life.

Whatever your level in your organization, even if you lead only by your work as a good colleague, you bear some responsibility for the inner work lives of the people around you. You can create catalysts and nourishers; you can reduce inhibiters and toxins. You can become a better contributor to the climate and the success of your organization if you check on these things at the end of the day. But, whether you are a team member or the CEO, there is one more thing you need to keep tabs on: your own inner work life. In our final chapter, we show how.

9

Tending Your Own Inner Work Life

T HROUGHOUT THIS BOOK, we have focused on how events in the workday affect inner work life. By now, you know what role inner work life plays in performance and the impact that specific events can have on inner work life. You also know that these principles apply to each person inside an organization, because everyone has an inner work life. That includes you. If you are a manager, you must tend the inner work lives of your subordinates by supporting them and their progress every day. But don't neglect yourself. Managers perform best when their own inner work lives are positive and strong.

Anne Mulcahy, who headed Xerox corporation from 2000 to 2009, understood the importance of tending inner work life—not only that of her fifty thousand employees, but also her own. Mulcahy was one of the most successful turnaround CEOs in history. Having started her Xerox career as a sales representative in 1976 and moved through the ranks to run her own division, Mulcahy—and the rest of the business world—were taken aback when she was asked to take over the top job. At the time, Xerox was in shambles. The company had long been losing prof-itability and market share in nearly all of its businesses, and had just lost $253 million in a single quarter; it was $18 billion in debt, with no re-maining credit; its bonds had just been downgraded; it was under in-vestigation by the SEC; and its stock price had fallen from $68.00 in 1999 to $6.88 by October 2000. In a meeting on October 23, 2000, ex-ternal advisers recommended filing for bankruptcy.

Mulcahy refused. Her primary reason? The devastating effect that a bankruptcy filing would have on Xerox employees:

> I said, "You just don't get it. You don't understand what it's like to
> be an employee in this company. To fight and come out and win.
> Bankruptcy's never a win. You know what? I'm not going there
> until there's no other decision to be made. There are a lot more
> cards to play." I was angry that anybody could comprehend the
> passion and drive that's required to succeed and not understand
> the impact of filing for bankruptcy on a company's employees.
> I said, "What we have going for us is that our people believe we
> are in a war that we can win."[1]

Mulcahy was right. Her conviction that Xerox employees' motivation would shrivel under bankruptcy, and that only their sustained passion could bring the company back to strong performance, carried Xerox through four years of arduous struggle to undeniable success.

Even as Mulcahy stayed mindful of the inner work lives of Xerox em-ployees, she stayed mindful of her own. At the end of each day, she re-viewed the day's events and the work she had done. No matter how difficult and disappointing the events of the day had been, no matter how small her accomplishments, she was content if she could focus on what she *had* been able to accomplish. Knowing that she had done her best to move Xerox forward, she could face the next day with vigor:

> Even during the worst of times, I can sleep and get up the next
> day and go at it. [. . .] I have this thing that I go to sleep with
> every night. If you review the day and can't think of a thing you

would have done differently, then you just need to be at peace and get up the next day.[2]

Whether you are a CEO or a manager of a small group, you would do well to follow Anne Mulcahy's example. Management responsibilities can take a particular toll on day-by-day perceptions, emotions, and motivations. We saw this repeatedly when we analyzed the diaries of team leaders.[3] Most managers are both superiors and subordinates, sandwiched between people who report to them and people to whom they report. (Even a CEO usually answers to a board of directors.) The team leaders in our study were in that position. Responsible for managing a team and its project, they often had little more formal power than people on the team. Yet they were expected to meet the demands of higher-level management; meet the team's needs for information, help, and resources; and champion the team's work to the rest of the organization and customers.

The dilemma of being squeezed from all directions is almost palpable in the story of Michael, the supply chain manager for Karpenter Corporation's Domain team. The team's contract manufacturer had fumbled an order, threatening a delay in a key customer's urgent order of Spray Jet Mops. On August 2, Michael wrote, "[. . .] we will have to call our number 2 customer and tell them that we will miss the shipping window for their upcoming ad on these mops." Only four days later, the situation repeated itself. Karpenter's upper management came down hard on Michael—and he came down hard on his team:

> The saga [. . .] continues [. . .] with the contract manufacturer
> running out of cartons. As of Friday we have spent $28,000 in air
> freight to send 1,500 $30 mops to our #2 customer. Another 2,800
> remain on this order and there is a good probability that they too
> will gain wings. [I have] turned from the kindly Supply Chain
> Manager into the black-masked executioner. All similarity to
> civility is gone, our backs are against the wall, flight is not possible,
> therefore fight is probable. The VPs are circling this corpse look-
> ing for a likely place to strike. They want a sacrifice. [Michael 8/6]

In virtually all respects, the inner work life dynamics of our team leaders mirrored those of the individuals who worked for them. As with team members, the single type of event that most frequently triggered a positive inner work life experience was progress. But there was an interesting distinction: the progress was more often that of the leader's *subordinates*—the team—rather than the leader alone.

The lesson? To boost your own inner work life as a manager, be sure to provide your people with the catalysts and the nourishers they need to make progress every day, and buffer them from inhibitors and toxins as much as possible. That way, you'll make progress in your own managerial work, setting up your own positive progress loop.

We often hear lower- and midlevel managers say that their administrative roles are a waste of time, detracting from their "real" work— engineering, marketing, product development, and so on. You may feel this way yourself. We hope to change your perspective. You can *find meaning in your managerial work and enhance your own inner work life* if you embrace this critically important role. Most contemporary work is impossible without strong and savvy management support. If you can make providing such support your personal mission, you will contribute much to your organization and the customers it serves. And because great management support makes a measureable difference in your subordinates' perceptions, emotions, and motivation, you will also improve their inner work lives.

At the same time, you can take additional steps to support your own inner work life. Consider Anne Mulcahy's daily practice—similar to the checklist we recommended in the previous chapter—and consider how it might help you stay excited about your work (see "Journaling for Well-Being"). Whether or not you are a manager, a regular review of your day's events can help you sustain good inner work life (or improve bad inner work life) for yourself and your colleagues. It need not take more than five minutes at the end of your day. The benefits can be considerable.

Our research participants taught us the value of reviewing events of the workday. At the end of our study, we asked how, if at all, participating in the study had affected them. A large proportion said that they had

FOOD FOR THOUGHT

Journaling for Well-Being

If you have ever kept a daily journal or even a diary listing of each day's main happenings, you may have experienced some of the powerful effects afforded by this practice. Over the past fifteen years, psychologists have discovered that people in many different situations can benefit from writing regularly about events in their lives.[a] In one experiment, people who wrote briefly about their envisioned "best possible self" for four days in a row reported significantly higher levels of well-being by the end, compared with people who did no such writing.[b] Other experiments have revealed that writing about traumatic or stressful events in one's life results in stronger immune function and physical health, better adjustment to college, a greater sense of well-being, and an ability to find employment more quickly after being laid off.[c]

Aware that physical health can reduce stress and improve performance, many corporate managers offer fitness centers and yoga classes. This research suggests an intriguing addition: maybe employees' inner work lives and performance could also benefit from seminars on journaling.

a. James Pennebaker, a psychologist at the University of Texas, is a pioneer in research on the benefits of expressive writing (e.g., J. W. Pennebaker and S. Beall, "Confronting a Traumatic Event: Toward an Understanding of Inhibition and Disease," *Journal of Abnormal Psychology* 95 [1986]: 274–281).

b. L. A. King, "The Health Benefits of Writing About Life Goals," *Personality and Social Psychology Bulletin* 27 (2001): 798–807.

c. This research is reviewed in J. M. Smyth, "Written Emotional Expression: Effect Sizes, Outcome Types, and Moderating Variables," *Journal of Consulting and Clinical Psychology* 66 (1998): 174–184.

learned something from the study. Most reported that they had found themselves gaining insight from writing about their "event of the day"; in fact, this was often the motivator that kept them sending in their electronic diaries, day after day. Many people also said that they had had "Aha!" experiences while reading through the collected set of their own event narratives, arranged chronologically, that we sent each participant privately a few days after the study ended. Overall, although people reported learning about the team or the organization, self-knowledge was the single most frequent form of insight.[4]

What specific self-knowledge did they gain? Some people told us that thinking about events throughout the day and writing the daily event narrative allowed them to continuously track their own accomplishments, failures, and contributions to the project. Others reported increased mindfulness of their own goals and insight into how they might better achieve those goals at work. And some said they had become more aware of what was really going on at work and why. When ambiguous and unexpected events occur during the workday, people's minds attempt to make sense of those events in a way that is often unconscious and implicit. Journaling can render that sensemaking explicit, enabling fruitful reflection.

Participants also gained insight into how they affected their teammates and the team's overall performance; ideas about interpersonal difficulties and how to improve their interpersonal interactions at work; insight into how their work was affected by various events; and information about their own styles and strengths. Occasionally, a participant would spontaneously report a behavioral change based on these insights. As one wrote on a follow-up survey, "I saw that my comments seemed to reflect a pessimistic tone, which, in retrospect, may have been unwarranted. I now try to approach projects with a more optimistic frame of mind."

Guidelines for Your Own Daily Review

We can offer some guidelines for your daily event review based on feedback from our study participants and the discoveries we have reported in this book (for easy reference, "Guidelines for Daily Journaling" summarizes these tips). If the day was a good one overall, think about why, and bask in the glow of it. Enjoy the sense of accomplishment from progress you or your team made. If the day was a bad one, don't just relegate it to a mental dustbin. No matter how awful you intuitively feel the day was, spend a couple of minutes to recall *any* progress that you or your work group made. Most days, you will be able to find something, and you may be surprised by what was actually accomplished. In addition, if the day was marked by setbacks, consider what caused them. If they occurred simply because of the technical complexity of the work, try to channel your frustration into a plan of action for dealing with the problem. Appreciate the positive aspects of having truly challenging work—in contrast to drudging through a boring job. Consider what you can learn from a setback and try to view those lessons as valuable progress.

TIPS FOR ALL

Guidelines for Daily Journaling

As a starting point for your own journaling, we suggest trying to answer the following questions at the end of each day:

- What event stands out in my mind from the workday, and how did it affect my inner work life?
- What progress did I make today and how did it affect my inner work life?
- What nourishers and catalysts supported me and my work today? How can I sustain them tomorrow?
- What one thing can I do to make progress on important work tomorrow?
- What setbacks did I have today, and how did they affect my inner work life? What can I learn from them?
- What toxins and inhibitors impacted me and my work today? How can I weaken or avoid them tomorrow?
- Did I affect my colleagues' inner work lives positively today? How might I do so tomorrow?

Our guidelines include considering whether you are contributing positively to your colleagues' progress and inner work lives, and how you might do so more effectively. The point of this isn't just to "be nice." Everyone contributes to an organization's climate of communication, coordination, and consideration. As an individual, you will benefit from a climate that facilitates everyone's work and everyone's dignity.

Over time, shape the questions and the format in whatever way is most useful for you. For example, you may wish to make a numerical rating each day on some aspects of inner work life, and graph the patterns weekly or monthly. Several journaling software packages are available, and some have numerical scales that you can customize. A few even include automatic daily reminders. Whatever form you choose for your journal, the important thing is to make entries regularly. Only then will you realize the benefits.

At the end of each month, ask yourself: do I notice trends over time in this journal? What are the implications? As you review trends over time in your journal, you may not like what you see. If, increasingly, there are more bad days than good days, try to understand the root causes. If they are within your control, develop an action plan—and then do it. Maybe you need to talk to your colleagues, boss, or human resource director. Maybe you need to change the way you approach the work or interact with teammates. Maybe, if other efforts fail, you need a new assignment, a new team, a different placement in the organization, or a new employer.

Reviewing each day's main events, even if it only takes five minutes, requires discipline. To ensure that you will adhere to this discipline, an actual journal—paper or electronic—can help. Just be sure to focus on concrete events of the day, and not only inner work life. A daily journal will help you see things you might otherwise miss, facilitate your action planning, and give you greater mastery over the next day's events. Done well, it will help you become a better manager, a stronger contributor to your organization, a more accomplished professional.

How do we know? The wonderful men and women who participated in our diary study told us so. When the time came for us to end our study of their teams, many of them expressed gratitude. At first, we were taken aback. Gratitude? To us? For asking (and occasionally nagging) them to fill out our daily journal form, every workday, for many weeks or even many months? Yes. A number of them told us that, even though it could be a nuisance to complete the journal every day, they were glad they had done it.

Here are some snippets of what they had to say:

> I did find value in doing the questionnaires, especially when I was disciplined enough to do them at the end of the day, when everything was still fresh in my mind. It helped me to reflect on the day, my accomplishments, the team's work, and how I was feeling in general. When you are working at a hectic pace, reflection time is rare, but is really beneficial. Thanks again to all of you.

> It has been a chore doing these [daily journals], but in many ways they have given me a chance to reflect on the day and its activities. Hopefully, then I was able to make adjustments to my actions and directions that made the team a better place to work. I will miss this part [. . .] Thanks to you all for keeping this on the positive side.

One team leader warmed our hearts with his final journal entry. After filling out our form every workday for seven months, he said:

> I am sorry this is coming to an end. It forced me to sit back and reflect on the day's happenings. This daily ritual was very helpful in making me more aware of how I should be motivating and interacting with the team. Thanks again for your help in making me a better person.

It's *we* who are thankful, for the discoveries those journals made possible. When we spoke with Graham at the end of our NewPoly team workshop, he told us that he found meaning in his work by helping his teammates move forward and sharing their joy as the project succeeded. He said that, to him, that's what management really meant.

Having gained the insights about inner work life that we have shared in this book, we couldn't agree more.

We believe that, if management is to have enduring meaning in this world, it should improve people's lives. The obvious route to this goal is to ensure that organizations offer high-quality products and services to customers. But of equal importance, management should enrich the lives of the people working inside the organization—by enabling them to succeed at work that has real value to their customers, the community, and themselves.

Appendix

About the Research

In this appendix, we describe the research program underlying this book. Avoiding excessive technical detail, we describe the companies, teams, and individuals who participated in our diary research; how we disguised their identities to protect confidentiality; what data we collected and how we collected it; what major analytical approaches we took to the data; and the primary studies that serve as the foundation for the book's major conclusions.[1]

Purpose, Participants, and Confidentiality Disguises

Our initial purpose in this research program was to understand the role of inner work life in organizations: what influences it, and how it influences performance. To do this realistically and rigorously, we decided to study people as they did their work in real time inside organizations—rather than retrospectively, as so many previous researchers had done. By studying a large number of people on different project teams, we were able to determine how everyday events affect inner work life and how inner work life affects performance.[2]

We wanted our results to be as general as possible, so, aided by a small group of friends and colleagues in business and academia, we succeeded in recruiting participants from a number of teams in different companies in different industries, from a range of small to large and young to old companies.[3] About half of the companies we approached agreed to allow us to try recruiting teams that met our criteria: teams in which all or almost all members had most of their time dedicated to the team's work, whose members worked interdependently, and where a significant part of the team's work required creativity—new and useful ideas, products, or processes. Table A-1 presents data on the seven participating companies.[4]

TABLE A-1

Participating companies

Data at the time the company's participation began

Pseudonym	Industry	Company age at start of study[a]	Annual revenue[b]	Number of employees[c]	Number of participating teams
HotelData JV, Inc.[d]	High-tech	Young	Small	Medium	1
VH Networks	High-tech	Young	Small	Medium	4
Edgell Imaging Inc.	High-tech	Medium	Small	Small	4
Karpenter Corporation	Consumer products	Old	Medium	Large	4
Lapelle	Consumer products	Medium	Large	Medium	4
O'Reilly Coated Materials	Chemicals	Old	Medium	Large	4
Kruger-Bern Chemicals	Chemicals	Old	Large	Large	5

Notes:

a. Company age at start of study: Young = 18 months–5 years; medium = 10–45 years; old = 65–85 years.

b. Annual revenue: Small = Less than $500 million; medium = $2–$4 billion; large = $15–$25 billion.

c. Number of employees: Small = Less than 1,000; medium = 2,000–6,000; large = 13,000–45,000.

d. A subsidiary of DreamSuite Hotels.

In aiming to explore inner work life in all its complexity, as well as the events that might be influencing it, we knew that each participant would have to feel comfortable being completely honest on the daily diary form (the *daily questionnaire*). This meant that they would all have to participate voluntarily and that we would have to promise confidentiality. In our recruiting meeting with prospective participating teams, we told them that the study was "designed to radically increase our knowledge about how managers and teams can bring about more consistently desirable project outcomes." We explained what participation would involve and said that we could have a team participate only if all or nearly all members wanted to participate, but stressed that the decision had to be theirs. (We had cautioned upper managers against influencing any team's decision to participate.)

We also made it clear to team members that all of their questionnaire responses would come directly to us at Harvard, and that we would fully disguise information about all individuals, teams, projects, and companies in any research reports, including any books using the data. We then let them take a few days to consider participation as a group. About half of the teams we recruited did decide to participate. We made sure that individuals understood that they could confidentially withdraw from the study at any time, without their teammates finding out from us. (A small number of people did, in fact, withdraw.) All teams had a team leader, and five teams had two coleaders. The team leaders always participated. Unless otherwise noted, we treated team leaders as "participants," along with team members, in our analyses. Table A-2 presents data on the participating teams.

Our final sample of 238 employees consisted of 182 men (77 percent) and 56 women. The mean age was 38.2 years (standard deviation = 10.2 years), with a range of 22 to 68 years. On average, at the start of their involvement in the study, our participants had been with their companies for 7.7 years (standard deviation = 8.9 years), ranging from 2 weeks to 36 years. They were highly educated; 82 percent had graduated from college, and most had earned advanced degrees. Most teams participated during most or all of a single significant project or phase of

Participating teams

Data at the time the team's participation began

Company pseudonym	Team pseudonym	Study length (weeks)	Team size*	Gender distribution	Age range (average)
HotelData JV, Inc.	Infosuite	17	9	4M/5F	31–63 (41)
VH Networks	DayRide	9	6	6M	27–32 (29)
	Pixel	9	13	11M/2F	23–30 (26)
	Hampton	14	8	8M	25–40 (30)
	Micro	13	17	12M/4F/1NA	22–40 (29)
Edgell Imaging Inc.	Archive	13	5	3M/2F	39–58 (46)
	Focus	17	8	7M/1F	32–68 (45)
	Value	20	6	5M/1F	31–44 (35)
	Booktext	24	5	4M/1F	42–67 (48)
Karpenter Corporation	Equip	17	13	9M/4F	27–54 (39)
	Domain	17	14	10M/4F	22–55 (36)
	Power	17	17	13M/4F	25–61 (36)
	Color	17	22	19M/3F	23–49 (35)
Lapelle	Mission	13	11	7M/4F	25–45 (35)
	Prospect	8	15	10M/5F	28–48 (36)
	SPF	16	17	10M/6F/1NA	24–50 (40)
	Moisture	16	12	7M/5F	27–53 (36)
O'Reilly Coated Materials	Shield	20	4	3M/1F	23–63 (46)
	Vision	30	4	4M	26–38 (35)
	Flex	28	5	4M/1F	25–64 (43)
	Tent	16	10	9M/1F	26–52 (41)

TABLE A-2

Participating teams

Data at the time the team's participation began

Company pseudonym	Team pseudonym	Study length (weeks)	Team size*	Gender distribution	Age range (average)
Kruger-Bern Chemicals	NewPoly	37	5	5M	37–61 (51)
	Sealant	20	14	11M/3F	26–58 (45)
	Alliance	11	3	2M/1F	44–48 (46)
	Coolant	10	7	6M/1F	30–57 (42)
	Surface	28	11	11M	41–57 (47)

* This is the number of members. In some teams, not every member participated in the study. On average, 92% of a team participated, ranging from 68% to 100%. In teams of five members or fewer, everyone participated.

a project. Teams participated for between 9 and 38 weeks, with an average of 19 weeks.

In disguising participant information in this book, we aimed to protect the privacy of the individuals, their teams, and their companies while retaining the accuracy of the information they provided. Our goals for the disguises were that a company not be identifiable to anyone outside the company; that a team not be identifiable to any other team in the company; and that teammates not discover any personal information about each other that they would otherwise not know. Everything essential about our data, our method, and our findings remains unchanged. For companies, we maintained the general industry classification, but completely changed the company's products, services, clients, and location. Within a range close to the actual value, we modified any identifiable statistics (e.g., company age, revenue, profitability, number of awards won, and workforce data).

For participants, we never disguised gender, job responsibilities, or demographic information (such as education, personality, cognitive style, or number of patents). However, we did change all of their names, obscured their ethnicities by choosing neutral names, made their job titles generic, and presented their age and job tenure as slightly

disguised (i.e., falling within a few years of the actual figure). Any reve-
latory personal information (e.g., having a family member die or being
pregnant) was disguised. We created first-and-last-name pseudonyms
for managers above the team level and used first-name-only pseudonyms for everyone else; we did this to allow readers to easily identify
managers. Spans of time were generally not disguised, and the relative
placement of dates was retained, but all specific dates were disguised.
We do not reveal the exact years in which the data were collected. We
can reveal, however, that the twenty-six teams did not all participate at
the same time, and that all data were collected within fourteen years of
this writing.

The Data

Our findings derived from a variety of surveys, observations, and conversations throughout the study. The most important of these was a
diary-style questionnaire e-mailed daily to all participants.

The Daily Questionnaire

Soon after a team decided to participate in the study, the first author of
this book, Teresa Amabile, met with the team to train its members in
how to respond to the *daily questionnaire*, the daily diary form that they
would receive. (In the case of one company, a trained research associate
ran these meetings, with Amabile joining by conference call.) The most
important part of this training focused on the level of detail in the
diary's event narrative: providing concrete details of what happened
and who was involved. Participants were told to describe one event
from the day that stood out in their minds, regardless of what type of
event it was, as long as it was relevant to the work or the project.
Amabile answered their questions, gave them practice, and provided
feedback. So that we would have independent views of the day's events,
she asked them not to discuss their daily questionnaire responses with
anyone else in the company until after the study was completed.

The idea behind the daily questionnaire was to track both inner work life and the stream of events occurring in the daily work lives of our participants in a way that was both detailed and relatively unobtrusive. In addition, the questionnaire would give us a way to examine specific reactions to the reported events—sensemaking about them, emotional reactions, and motivational responses. We also aimed to track day-by-day work behavior.[5]

Participants were asked to complete the daily questionnaire (which was e-mailed to them by noon, Monday through Friday) at the end of each day or first thing the next morning. Although they were given the option of mailing paper daily questionnaires all of the time or some of the time (e.g., if they were traveling on business), only a small percentage of diaries were submitted this way. Most were submitted at the end of the workday.

In total, participants submitted 11,637 completed daily questionnaires. The overall response rate was 75 percent, with a range across individuals of 16 percent to 100 percent.[6] In most of our quantitative analyses, we eliminated data from participants with response rates below 20 percent. The daily questionnaire took most participants about ten minutes to complete. On average, each participant submitted about fifty questionnaires. The word length of event descriptions varied considerably, from 1 to 855 words; the average was 54 words.

Table A-3 summarizes the daily questionnaire.

Other Questionnaires

In addition to the daily questionnaire, participants completed a number of other questionnaires at various points during the study. Our aim was to gather background data on the individuals (demographics and personality), the team, and the project. These additional questionnaires are described in table A-4.

Additional Data

While a team was participating, Teresa Amabile called each member once per month to see if she or he had any questions or concerns about

TABLE A-3

Questions on the "daily questionnaire"—daily diary form

Sections and their content[a]	Number and type of questions	Sample questions
Basics about the workday	6 fill-in-the-blank	• Today's date • Number of hours spent working on the project today • Work done on the project today (brief description) • Number of team members worked with today
Own work and motivation	12 scale ratings[b]	Today, in my work on the project, I felt . . . • Progress was made on my part • I did creative work • My work was high quality • Challenged by my work • Motivated by recognition I might earn • Motivated by interest in my work
The team and its work	6 scale ratings[c]	Based on the team's work on the project today, I felt . . . • The team worked well together • The team did quality work • The team made progress
Perceptions of the work environment	14 scale ratings	To what extent does each item describe the work environment of the project as you perceived it today? • Freedom or autonomy in the work • Time pressure in the work • Clarity of goals for the project • Encouragement and support from the project supervisor • High-level management encouragement of our team's creativity

Sections and their content[a]	Number and type of questions	Sample questions
Emotions	6 scale ratings	Today, overall, I felt . . . • Frustrated • Happy
Today's event	1 narrative	Briefly describe *one* event from today that stands out in your mind as relevant to the project, your feelings about this project, your work on this project, your team's feelings about this project, or your team's work on this project. Remember to specify who was involved and what happened. The event can be positive, negative, or neutral.

Questions about the event	5 scale ratings[d]	• How many individuals on your team are aware of this event?
		
		• Rate the effect of this event on each of the following:
		
		  • Your feelings about the project
		
		  • Your work on the project today
		
		  • Other team members' work on the project today
		
		  • The project overall, in the long term

Anything else (optional)	1 narrative	Please add anything else that you would like to report today.

Notes:

a. Sections are listed in order of appearance on the questionnaire.

b. Unless otherwise specified, the scale for all scale-rated items was the following: 1 = not at all; 2 = slightly; 3 = somewhat; 4 = moderately; 5 = quite a bit; 6 = very much; 7 = extremely.

c. This section and the following section gave participants the option of responding "N" to any given item, if they had no basis for answering the question that day (e.g., if they had had no contact with the team that day).

d. The scale for the first of these questions was: 1 = only myself; 2 = only myself and one other team member; 3 = less than half the team; 4 = more than half the team; 5 = the entire team. The scale for the second of these questions was: 1 = very negative effect; 2 = moderately negative effect; 3 = slightly negative effect; 4 = neutral or no effect; 5 = slightly positive effect; 6 = moderately positive effect; 7 = very positive effect.

TABLE A-4

Questionnaires completed by participants[a]

Questionnaire[b]	Frequency	Description
Daily questionnaire	Daily	Combined quantitative scale-rated items and qualitative narrative items.
Final project assessment	Once (at end of study)	Collected quantitative scale-rated data from each participant concerning the team's overall performance on a number of dimensions.
Individual assessment form	Monthly	Asked participants to rate every team member, including him- or herself, on four dimensions based on the previous month's work: creative contribution to the project, contribution to quality of the project, commitment to the project, and contribution to team cohesiveness.
Kirton Adaptation-Innovation Inventory[c]	Once, at start of study	Assessed cognitive style, specifically creative thinking style.
KEYS: Assessing the Climate for Creativity[d]	Three times (at start, middle, and end of study)	Assessed the work environment, oriented toward the work environment for creativity.
NEO Five-Factor Inventory (Form S)[e]	Once (at start of study)	Measured the "Big Five" personality dimensions: neuroticism, extraversion, openness to experience, agreeableness, and conscientiousness.
Work Preference Inventory[f]	Once (at start of study)	Assessed an individual's stable extrinsic and intrinsic motivational orientations toward work.

Notes:

a. Other questionnaires were completed, but we only list those whose data were analyzed for this book.

b. Unless otherwise noted, all questionnaires were created for this research program.

c. M. J. Kirton, "Adaptors and Innovators: A Description and Measure," *Journal of Applied Psychology* 61 (1976): 622–629. The KAI was obtained from, and used with the permission of, the Occupational Research Centre (www.kaicentre.com).

d. T. M. Amabile, R. Conti, H. Coon, J. Lazenby, and M. Herron, "Assessing the Work Environment for Creativity," *Academy of Management Journal* 39 (1996): 1154–1184. The KEYS questionnaire was obtained from, and used with the permission of, the Center for Creative Leadership (www.ccl.org).

e. P. T. Costa and R. R. McCrae, *NEO-PI-R: Professional Manual* (Odessa, FL: Psychological Assessment Resources, 1992). The NEO Five-Factor Inventory (Form S) was obtained from and used with the permission of Psychological Assessment Resources (www3.parinc.com).

f. T. M. Amabile, K. G. Hill, B. A. Hennessey, and E. M. Tighe, "The Work Preference Inventory: Assessing Intrinsic and Extrinsic Motivational Orientations," *Journal of Personality and Social Psychology* 66 (1994): 950–967.

the daily questionnaire or the study. (In the case of one company, a senior research associate made these calls.) Each team leader was called twice per month. Occasionally, these conversations revealed useful data about the individuals, projects, teams, or companies. We never divulged any information gathered about the project, team, company, or individuals during these conversations.

About halfway through the projected time period for a team's participation, we held a brief "mid-study meeting" with the team. The purpose was to informally gather additional data about the team, project, or organization, as well as maintain the team's enthusiasm for participation and answer any questions they might have had. We divulged no information we had received to that point, aside from giving each individual his or her confidential scores on the NEO and Work Preference Inventory.

Within one month of the end of data collection on a team, Amabile (accompanied by a research associate) held a half-day final meeting with the team. The purpose was to present preliminary aggregated results for that team, using both quantitative and qualitative data, and to get feedback as to the accuracy of our tentative conclusions about the team's story.[7] Amabile invited team members to meet with her individually after the meeting, and several did. Although we intended these final meetings to serve as "payback" for the participants in the form of useful information for their future work, we invariably found that we gathered a great deal of new and useful data.

In the final meetings, we asked team members what motivated them to keep sending in the completed forms day after day. Most commonly, they replied that they were very curious about the knowledge they would gain about themselves and their team. They also said they wanted the organization to be able to learn from the study of all of the teams. In the final (optional) section of the last daily questionnaire, a number of participants spontaneously mentioned that they found filling out the questionnaire useful. Some examples appear in chapter 9.

Within one month of the final meeting, Amabile and the research associate collaborated to write a research case on the team. The case was intended to serve as a primary source of qualitative data, capturing fresh observational information about the team, team members, project, organization, management, and events that occurred during the study period. These cases drew on repeated readings of both the individual team members' diary narratives and the notes from the four meetings with the team, meetings with individual team members, telephone conversations with or e-mails received from individual team members (including the team leader), and conversations or meetings with higher-level managers. The research cases were developed through an iterative process in which one author would draft a section that would be reviewed and edited by the other, then passed back to the original author, until both were satisfied as to its accuracy. In most instances, they would meet multiple times to discuss the case at various stages of its development. The final research cases are extensive documents.

After all data collection within a company had been completed, Amabile and a research associate met with top managers of the company (or, in some larger companies, top managers of the relevant unit). These executives were presented with aggregated quantitative and qualitative data from the participating teams in their company, with no identifying information on any teams or individuals. Amabile pointed out particular strengths and weaknesses in the organizational work environment revealed by the study, and invited the managers to engage in discussion of the results. To what extent did the results match their own views of the organization? What thoughts did the managers have on patterns of positive and negative events within the organization? As with the individual team meetings, we gained a great deal of useful data from these meetings with top management and from conversations we had with top managers at various points during the study.[8] New information was added to the team research cases, as appropriate.

Analyses

Because we collected both qualitative and quantitative data, we used a variety of analysis techniques.

Qualitative Analyses (Used in All Chapters)

Over several years, we conducted detailed qualitative analyses of participants' open-ended diary narratives, as well as the other written materials (research cases and notes). Two features of these data are worth highlighting. First, because we gathered daily data from each participant over several weeks, we were able to see patterns in events and inner work life over time. Second, because multiple people on the same team often mentioned the same events, we have greater confidence in what our participants described.

Qualitative analyses proceeded in seven waves, each yielding information useful for different purposes.

First, Teresa Amabile and Steven Kramer repeatedly read the narrative sections of all 11,637 diaries (all 26 teams, 238 participants), as well as the 26 research cases. Through an iterative process, we kept extensive notes and discussed our emerging ideas with each other. This process led to our description of the inner work life system (chapter 2), the ways in which inner work life influences performance (chapter 3), the progress loop (chapter 5), and the essential climate elements (chapter 6).[9]

Second, we did an extremely detailed "index" coding of everything mentioned in all 11,637 diary narratives. The coding scheme developed for this purpose was called DENA (Detailed Event Narrative Analysis).[10] Five research associates were trained in its use.[11] Agreement between independent coders on the several dimensions of this scheme was generally quite good.[12] The purpose of this detailed coding was to catalogue various aspects of each specific event reported in each narrative—for example, what the event was; who the source of the event was; who the target of the event was; whether it was a concrete event that actually happened on the day in question (versus a recollection from a previous time, an expectation of the future, an opinion about something, or a reaction to something); and what sort of emotionality was attached to the participant's report of the event (positive, negative, or neutral).[13] Although the daily questionnaire requested one "event of the day," the average event description reported about five interrelated specific events.

Third, we developed a somewhat broader coding scheme, with fewer dimensions, to capture the major types of events, for the best days–worst days studies. Acceptable agreement between coders was established between Teresa Amabile and the research associate who carried out most of the coding for these studies.[14] The best days–worst days studies, as described in chapter 4, led to identification of the *key three* influences on inner work life: the progress principle, the catalyst factor, and the nourishment factor.

Fourth, both book authors and various research associates created detailed stories describing the inner work lives, major events, and performance outcomes of fourteen of the twenty-six teams, including at least one team from each of the seven companies.[15] Each story was a collaborative effort including at least one author and at least one research associate. Each story was created through an iterative process of both individuals reading all diary narratives and other materials on the team, one person drafting the story, then the other person giving feedback, discussing, and revising—until both were satisfied that the story accurately captured the events, the experiences, and the performance of the individuals and the team overall.

These stories were then used in a weeklong workshop with both authors and one research associate.[16] During that workshop, the fourteen teams that had detailed stories were examined on daily quantitative measures and qualitative accounts of progress and inner work life. This examination led to identification of the progress loop (chapter 5). In addition, at the workshop we created a large matrix of the fourteen teams against all measures of progress and inner work life. We then identified, for each of the teams, the major positive and negative events that stood out in their stories. This process led to identification of the seven specific catalyst-inhibitor pairs of event types and the four specific nourisher-toxin pairs of event types (chapters 6 and 7). We checked these lists against results of the best days–worst days studies, as well as quantitative analyses of all twenty-six teams. Finally, discussions in this workshop led us to identify the teams we would use as illustrations of the key three influences on inner work life in this book (chapters 4, 5, 6, and 7).

Fifth, Steven Kramer carried out a detailed coding of the diaries from teams chosen as illustrations of the progress principle (chapters 4 and 5), the catalyst factor (chapter 6), the nourishment factor (chapter 7), and daily progress support (chapter 8), as well as the diaries of several team leaders from additional teams (for chapter 9).[17] This coding was based on the coding scheme for the best days–worst days studies, but was focused on the particular elements of catalysts, inhibitors, nourishers, and toxins that had been identified in the workshop. It also included a few additional codes (such as "possible diary quote for the book"). Teresa Amabile checked portions of this coding against her own reading of portions of the diary narratives from the chosen teams, and discussed disagreements with Kramer until consensus was reached.

Sixth, for studies of team-leader behavior, we created a coding scheme from a taxonomy of leader behaviors developed by previous researchers.[18] Using this scheme, and after we had established an acceptable level of agreement between independent coders, one research associate coded every mention of a team leader behavior in any of the 11,637 diary narratives. Results derived from this coding appear in chapters 5, 6, and 7.

Seventh, for the purposes of studies in which we wanted to examine very specific emotions that were spontaneously expressed in the diary narratives, we trained a completely separate set of individuals to carry out this coding.[19] Several specific emotions were coded, including: joy; love (i.e., affection, warmth, or pride); anger; fear; and sadness.

Quantitative Analyses

We conducted statistical analyses on the numerical data collected from the study participants, such as the numerical items on the daily questionnaire and the monthly teammate assessments. We also conducted statistical analyses on numerical data that came from the qualitative analyses, such as the frequency of a certain coded event.

In the main body of this book, we have presented only descriptive data. However, the reliability of our findings and our conclusions is based on a variety of statistical methods.[20] We relied most heavily on a particular type of regression called a *multilevel model* because our data had three distinct levels. Coming from 26 different *teams*, 238 different *participants* each provided data on many different *days*. The regressions took all of this into account, and also took into account several individual characteristics on which participants can differ (e.g., gender, age, company tenure, educational level, and—often—personality, cognitive style, and/or motivational orientation).[21] Moreover, some of these regressions looked for effects across multiple days using *lagged analyses*. For example, we used lagged multilevel regression to find that a person's mood on a particular day predicted the person's creative thinking that day *and* the next day.[22]

Note that regressions cannot establish cause-and-effect relationships. Even the prediction of a given day's measure (like creative thinking) from a prior day's measure (like mood) using lagged analyses can only suggest causality from temporal precedence. That is why, throughout the book, we rely on two other sources to reinforce our causal conclusions: controlled experiments done by ourselves or other researchers, and statements made in participants' diary narratives indicating that something led to something else.

Major Studies

We have already described how we used qualitative analyses to arrive at our descriptions of the inner work life system, the progress loop, and organizational climate. We also relied primarily on qualitative analyses to describe the mechanisms by which inner work life influence performance, and mechanisms by which the key three types of events influence inner work life. We used many simple descriptive statistics throughout this book. For example, when quoting diary excerpts in many chapters, we made frequent reference to the numerical self-ratings of perceptions, emotions, and/or motivations on those individual participants' daily diaries.[23]

In this section, we briefly describe each of the major quantitative studies underlying the main conclusions in the book.

Small Events (Chapter 1)

Throughout the book, we have remarked on the surprising power of many seemingly small, mundane, even trivial events to strongly influence daily inner work life. We first presented the results of our small-events study in chapter 1, along with a brief description of our method. Here, we provide a bit more detail. On the daily questionnaire, immediately following the event report section, there was a question asking participants to rate the impact of the event on their *feelings about the project* that day. This was our measure of how "big" the person's reaction was to the event (on a 7-point scale ranging from very negative, through neutral, to very positive).[24] In addition, about two weeks after our study of their team had ended, we sent all individuals a chronological log of all of their own diary event narratives. Next to each day's event description, we asked them to rate *how big an impact the event had had on the project overall*, now that the project had ended (on the same 7-point scale). This was our measure of how "big" the event was.[25] Using these ratings, we found that over 28 percent of the small events evoked big reactions.

Creativity and Emotions (Chapter 3)

One of the major studies underlying our conclusion that inner work life influences performance (chapter 3) examined the influence of emotions on creativity.[26] Multilevel regressions used three different measures of emotion to predict two different measures of creativity. The measures of emotion were (1) general positive mood, a composite of six ratings by the participant on the daily diary form; (2) general positive mood, as assessed by coders of the participant's event description on the diary form; and (3) specific emotions of joy, love, anger, fear, and sadness, as rated by different coders of the participant's event description. The measures of creativity were (1) creative thinking, as coded from the event description (that is, evidence that the participant personally had made a discovery, had an idea, solved a problem in a non-rote way, or was actively involved in trying to do so); and (2) creativity of the participant as rated monthly by the team leader and teammates on the individual assessment form.

Both measures of general positive mood and the emotion of joy were positive predictors of creativity on the same day; the negative emotions of anger, fear, and sadness were all negative predictors. Then we looked for effects on the *subsequent* days. If emotions predicted creativity a day or two later, it would support the conclusion that inner work life influences creativity and that people were not simply happy or frustrated because they solved or failed to solve a problem. This is exactly what we found. Controlling for the subsequent days' mood, we found that both measures of general positive mood predicted creative thinking the next day. And self-rated general positive mood seemed to predict creative thinking two days later.[27]

In this same study of emotion and creativity, qualitative analyses of each diary that contained a creative thinking event also revealed a reverse-causality effect: creativity leads to joy. Note that creative thinking is a type of progress (or performance). Taken together, these results provide evidence for both influences in the progress loop (chapters 3, 4, and 5): an aspect of inner work life (emotion) influences performance (creativity), and an aspect of performance (creativity) influences an aspect of inner work life (emotion).

Creativity, Perceptions, and Motivation (Chapter 3)

Two studies using data from this research program support the conclusion that people's perceptions of their work environment relate to their creativity on the job. In one study, we focused on perceived team leader support (as indicated by three scale-rated questions on the daily diary form). Regression analysis showed that perceived team leader support significantly predicted participants' creativity as assessed by their peers on the monthly ratings.[28]

The second study used perceptions of many aspects of the work environment to predict creativity with regression analyses.[29] Perceptions of the work environment came from participants' daily ratings on the diary form, as well as ratings they made on the longer, more detailed KEYS survey of the work environment three times during our study of their team (beginning, middle, and end of the study). Perceptions of the work environment ranged from the local (such as the work itself, the team, and the team leader) to the broad organizational environment (such as top management encouragement of creativity). Measures of creativity included the monthly peer ratings, monthly self-ratings, and coding of creative thinking from the diary narratives. This series of regressions identified several positive perceptions of the work environment as positive predictors of creativity, and several negative perceptions as negative predictors.

We also did regressions to examine intrinsic motivation and creativity. We created a measure of a participant's intrinsic motivation on a given day from responses to several items on the daily diary form, and used that measure to predict creative thinking as coded from behavior reported in the diary's event description. The regression showed a strong, significant, positive effect; people were more likely to do creative thinking on days when they were more highly intrinsically motivated to do their work.

Productivity and Inner Work Life (Chapter 3)

Individuals in our study were more likely to be productive on days when their inner work lives were better. These effects appeared at the team level, too. Overall, teams were more productive, yielding higher-quality work and more successful projects, when their members' inner work lives had been more positive throughout the project.

We conducted a study predicting productivity from *emotion*, using regressions identical to those in the study of creativity and emotion, described earlier. The productivity measure was an aggregate of several coded events from the day's diary narrative (e.g., making progress, resolving a problem, using time or resources efficiently). The emotion measures were the same as those in the creativity study. The results were essentially identical to those of the creativity study, except that the effects were mostly limited to the same day. There were few carryover effects to subsequent days. For the same day, the results were strong: the more positive emotions were, the higher the productivity; the more negative emotions were, the lower the productivity.

A second aspect of inner work life, *perceptions of the work environment*, was analyzed as a predictor of productivity in a series of regressions. Work environment perceptions came from the brief daily ratings on the diary form as well as the more detailed ratings made on the longer KEYS work environment questionnaire administered three times. Productivity was measured as monthly peer-rated work quality, monthly self-rated work quality, and daily self-rated work quality on the diary form. We found that many dimensions of the perceived work environment predicted productivity. These dimensions included support from the team leader; support from the team; perceived challenge in the work; and perceived autonomy in carrying out the work. The broad organizational environment was predictive, too, with productivity being helped by collaborative, open organizational climates and hindered by climates rife with political problems and conservatism.

The third aspect of inner work life, motivation, was analyzed in the same way. As with creativity, we used several daily self-rated items on the diary form to create the measure of intrinsic motivation. In regressions, this measure positively predicted monthly self-rated work quality and daily self-rated work quality. The result is consistent for the monthly peer-rated work quality measure, but that result is not statistically significant.

Commitment to the Work and Inner Work Life (Chapter 3)

We used a series of regressions to determine if the three aspects of inner work life predicted participants' commitment to their work as rated monthly by their peers. As described for the previous regressions, we obtained measures of inner work life from the daily questionnaires—either the numerical scale ratings or coded emotions from the daily event description. We obtained additional measures of work environment perceptions from the more detailed KEYS work environment questionnaire administered three times.

Our analyses revealed that positive mood and positive specific emotions predict people's demonstrated commitment to the work. In addition, commitment was higher when people perceived their work environments more positively—specifically, when they perceived more freedom and positive challenge in the work; encouragement from their team leaders; support from their teammates as well as managers and coworkers outside the team; and fewer impediments in the form of political infighting, harsh evaluation norms in the organization, or biases toward the status quo. Finally, daily intrinsic motivation predicted commitment.

Collegiality and Inner Work Life (Chapter 3)

The analyses for this study were identical to those that we just described for commitment to the work. Here, however, the predicted measure was the monthly peer-rated measure of contribution to team cohesiveness. These regressions revealed that each aspect of inner work life predicts collegiality. Results were similar to those for commitment. Collegiality was higher when people experienced more positive emotions, higher intrinsic motivation, and more positive perceptions of the work, the team, and the organization.

Best Days–Worst Days (Chapters 4, 5, 6, and 7)

The best days–worst days studies enabled our discovery of the key three influences on inner work life (chapter 4): the progress principle, the catalyst factor, and the nourishment factor. These studies highlighted the power of progress and setbacks to influence inner work life; the number-one factor is the progress principle. The catalyst factor and the nourishment factor are second and third, respectively, in influence (see figures 4-1 and 4-2). Follow-up qualitative analyses allowed us to discover the specific elements of the catalyst factor (chapter 6) and the nourishment factor (chapter 7).

The logic behind the best days–worst days studies is simple. Since we wanted to know what types of events made for good and bad inner work life, we investigated what types of events most strongly differentiated the best inner work life days from the worst inner work life days.[30]

We conducted eight best days–worst days studies for each of seven aspects of daily inner work life: intrinsic motivation, joy, love, anger, fear, sadness, and overall mood. The first seven studies were all done the same way, and the eighth (a second study on the overall mood aspect of inner work life) was done differently, as a check. To illustrate the method for the first seven studies, we will use overall mood. After eliminating participants who had submitted fewer than twenty diary entries, we were left with 221 of the original 238. For all 221 people, we then computed each person's average (mean) and standard deviation on overall daily mood across all of the diaries that person submitted. This gave us the person's baseline.[31] Next, we computed a standard score for each of the person's diary days on the particular aspect of inner work life—in this case, overall mood.[32] In other words, for each person, each day, we created a number telling us how good the person's overall mood was that day, relative to his or her own baseline mood.

From these thousands of standard scores for overall mood from all 221 people, we created a pool of the 1,000 most positive scores (days of best mood), 1,000 most negative (days of worst mood), and 1,000 average (for comparison purposes). From the 1,000 in each sample, we randomly selected 100 days to be coded for events. But we placed some constraints on the random sampling to ensure that we had a good representation across the individuals and the teams in the study. Our goal was to have at least 25 of the 26 teams and at least 75 different participants represented in each sample of 100.[33] All 300 diary narratives were then coded for all events using the best days–worst days coding scheme that we described earlier.

After the coding was done, we analyzed the frequency and percent of event types in each sample (best days, worst days, and average days). As we reported in chapter 4, on the best-mood days, progress stood out as the major event type. And, on the worst-mood days, setbacks stood out. Moreover, a comparison of progress and setbacks produced the biggest differential on both best days and worst days, bigger than any other opposite-type pairs of events.

This was true not only for the study of overall mood. For every single aspect of inner work life on which we did a best days–worst days study, progress and setbacks were the top differentiators. Average days were always intermediate between the best and worst days.

These best days–worst days analyses left us with two concerns. First, we were concerned that certain participants might have been overrepresented and therefore might have biased our findings. Second, we were worried that the participants represented in the best-days samples might have differed in some way from those in the worst-days and average-days samples. So we did a final study, again using overall mood, as a check against these two possibilities.[34] For this study, we randomly selected two participants from each of the twenty-six teams and coded the events in their best overall mood day, worst overall mood day, and an average overall mood day. As with the first seven studies, *best*, *worst*, and *average* were defined relative to the person's own baseline. The same coding scheme was used, and one of the original coders did all of this coding. The results were virtually identical to the results of the overall mood study conducted with the original sampling method, validating that method.

Comparison of Progress Days and Setback Days (Chapter 4)

The other major study behind our conclusion about the power of progress used data from all 11,637 submitted diaries. Using the fine-grained "index" coding of all the diary narratives, we flagged each diary as having one or more reports of progress that day, one or more reports of a setback that day, or neither. We then used these events—progress and setbacks—to predict various ratings of inner work life that the participants had made on the diary form that day. The summary of the regression results, presented in table A-5, shows that progress and setbacks predicted several aspects of each element of inner work life.

TABLE A-5

Comparisons relative to days without progress or setback events

Elements of inner work life	How days with progress events compare	How days with setback events compare
Emotions	• More positive overall mood	• More negative overall mood
	• More happiness	• Less happiness
	• More warmth/love/pride	• Less warmth/love/pride
	• Less frustration	• More frustration
	• Less fear	• More fear
	• Less sadness	• More sadness
Motivations	• More intrinsically motivated (by the interest, enjoyment, challenge of, and involvement in the work itself)	• Less intrinsically motivated (by the interest, enjoyment, challenge of, and involvement in the work itself)
		• Less motivated by recognition
Perceptions	• More positive challenge in the work	• Less positive challenge in the work
	• Team more mutually supportive	• Team less mutually supportive
	• More positive interactions between the team and the supervisor	• Supervisor less supportive
		• Less freedom in the work
	• More time pressure	• Insufficient resources available for the work

Managerial Survey (Chapter 5)

After discovering the progress principle, we created a survey to determine whether managers are aware of the power of progress.[35] Aiming for a wide range of respondents, we solicited 669 volunteers from attendees of various executive education programs and the alumni lists of a top business school. These volunteers represented dozens of different companies across a variety of industries and companies around the world, and all levels of management from team leaders to CEOs.

The survey asked our respondents to rank the importance of five factors that could influence employees' motivations and emotions at work.

Four of the factors came from conventional management wisdom: "recognition for good work (either public or private)," "monetary incentives (compensation, benefits, bonuses, and other rewards)," "interpersonal support (respect, camaraderie, emotional understanding, etc.)," and "clear goals in the work (vision, priorities, etc.)." The fifth item, representing the progress principle, was "support for making progress in the work (help, resources, time, etc.)." (This item actually appeared fourth on the survey list, after interpersonal support and before clear goals.[36])

The results revealed that most managers are unaware of how strongly progress can affect inner work life. On average, these 669 managers ranked "support for making progress" fifth out of the five factors as a motivator, and third as an influence on emotion. Instead, they ranked "recognition for good work (either public or private)" as the most important factor in motivating workers and making them happy. Only 35 (5 percent) of the 669 managers ranked "support for making progress" as the most important way in which managers can motivate employees.

Negative Events Stronger Than Positive (Chapter 5)

Chapter 5 describes our discovery that, in general, negative events appeared to have a stronger impact on inner work life than positive events. The first of our studies that revealed this finding involved a series of multi-level regressions using all of the data, in which we investigated the effect of the two key events—progress and setbacks—on two key emotions—happiness and frustration. Although regressions cannot establish causality, the results show a strong asymmetry. Setback events had a stronger effect on both happiness and frustration than progress events did. In fact, the negative effect of a setback event on happiness was over twice as strong as the positive effect of a progress event on happiness, and the power of a setback event to increase frustration was over three times as strong as that of a progress event to decrease frustration.

The second study examined this negativity bias in *small events*. Here, we analyzed only the days where small events had a strong impact on feelings about the project. (See our discussion of small events earlier in this appendix.) Even though the dataset was dramatically reduced (only 1,666 diaries in the analysis, rather than 11,637), and the results were therefore not all statistically significant, the same asymmetry showed up. The effect of a setback event on happiness was over three times as strong as the effect of a progress event on happiness,[37] and the effect of a setback event on frustration was almost twice as strong as that of a progress event on frustration.[38]

The third study was designed to see if the impact of team leader behavior on inner work life was subject to the negativity bias. We did a series of multilevel regressions in which we predicted each aspect of inner work life—perceptions, emotions, and motivations—from positive, neutral, and negative team leader behaviors as reported in the diary narratives. (We described the coding of these team leader behaviors earlier in this appendix, as our sixth form of qualitative analysis.[39]) Negative team leader behaviors significantly predicted more inner work life elements than did positive or neutral team leader behaviors, and only negative team leader behaviors significantly predicted motivation.[40] The effects were all in the direction you would expect: Positive team leader behaviors related positively to the positive perceptions and emotions, but negatively to the negative perceptions and emotions. Negative team leader behaviors related negatively to motivation, and negatively to the positive perceptions and emotions, but positively to the negative perceptions and emotions.

Finally, we found that, the more negative participants' self-rated feelings about the event they reported on the daily questionnaire, the longer the event narrative tended to be.[41]

Effects of Time Pressure (Chapter 6)

Initially, we looked at the overall effect of time pressure on creativity without regard to the type of time pressure. Using a regression analysis, we found that, overall, the more time pressure people reported on a particular day, the less likely they were to do creative thinking that day.[42] This effect was not owing to a simple decrease in the overall available work time that people had on time-pressured days. In fact, they actually spent more time working as time pressure increased. The negative effect of time pressure on creativity carried over to the next day and the day after that.[43]

However, as reported in chapter 6, the type of time pressure does matter. We delved more deeply into this issue by looking at the type of work that people were doing on high-time-pressure and low-time-pressure days, the context in which they were doing it, and whether or not their diary narrative contained a creative thinking event. For this, we developed a coding scheme for categorizing participants' reports in the brief "Work done today" section at the beginning of the daily questionnaire. Our aim in developing this coding scheme was to capture the number of different activities participants were doing on a given day, the number of people they were doing them with, the degree of focus they had in their day, the number and type of meetings they attended, and so on. We then created four random samples of 100 days each from the database of 11,637 days. These four samples represented four very different kinds of days: (1) days of very high time pressure when creative thinking did happen (of which there were only about 100 in the entire database); (2) days of very high time pressure when creative thinking didn't happen (of which there were a great many days to choose from); (3) days of very low time pressure when creative thinking did happen; and (4) days of very low time pressure when creative thinking did not happen.[44] Very low time pressure was rather rare, but we had over 100 days to choose from for each of the latter two samples.

We then coded the 400 daily reports in the four samples (using multiple coders to ensure reasonable agreement), and examined the final codes for consistent patterns within samples as well as differences between samples. It was from this work that we generated the typology of time pressure, in terms of impact on creative productivity. As reported in chapter 6, the very common *on a treadmill* high time pressure undermines creativity, but the rare *on a mission* high time pressure can facilitate it. However, creativity was more likely to flourish under low *on an expedition* time pressure. The unusual low time pressure of *being on autopilot* is negative for productivity of any kind, creative or otherwise.[45]

Team Leader Behaviors (Chapters 6 and 7)

We did this study to focus on the ways in which managers' specific actions might influence one aspect of inner work life: perceptions of managerial support. Because team leaders were the managers mentioned most frequently in the daily diaries, we focused on them. Using reports of all team leader behaviors from the diaries of all participants who were not team leaders, we analyzed the relationship between those behaviors and perceptions of team leader support.[46] Team leader behaviors included both catalysts and nourishers. We found that certain catalysts (or inhibitors) and certain nourishers (or toxins) significantly predicted perceived team leader support.

The Power of Local Context (Chapters 6, 7, and 8)

For most of our twenty-six teams, there was a fairly close match between the local work environment (created by the team leader, the team, and the work itself) and the broader organizational work environment (created by the rest of the organization and its management). However, for six teams, there was a mismatch. For three of these teams, the organizational context was much better than the local context. (None of those teams is featured in this book.) For the other three teams, the local context was much better than the organizational context. Two of these, the Infosuite team of HotelData and the NewPoly team of Kruger-Bern Chemicals, are featured in this book.

Through regression analyses using all twenty-six teams, we investigated whether the local or the organizational environment might consistently have a more powerful influence on inner work life when the two are discordant. The results were quite striking. In a regression where a composite measure of the local environment and a composite measure of the organizational environment were both used to predict daily mood, only the local environment had a significant effect. In another regression, where these composite measures were both used to predict daily intrinsic motivation, once again only the local environment had a significant effect.[47] We interpret this to suggest that, although the organizational environment influences a person's inner work life in important ways, much of the influence may be indirect—filtered through the more immediate experience the person has of the everyday work, the team, and the team leader.

Conclusion

We had one overarching goal in conducting this research. We wanted to understand inner work life, the events influencing it, and its impact on people as well as performance. Our goal in writing this book was to convey our findings, their meaning, and their practical implications to you. We hope that we have succeeded.

Notes

Introduction

1. Excerpt from "Founders' IPO Letter" (2004), written by Larry Page and Sergey Brin, http://investor.google.com/corporate/2004/ipo-founders-letter.html.

2. T. M. Amabile, C. N. Hadley, and S. J. Kramer, "Creativity Under the Gun," *Harvard Business Review*, August 2002, 52–61; T. M. Amabile and S. J. Kramer, "Inner Work Life: The Hidden Subtext of Business Performance," *Harvard Business Review*, May 2007, 72–83; T. M. Amabile and S. J. Kramer, "Breakthrough Ideas for 2010: 1: What Really Motivates Workers," *Harvard Business Review*, January 2010, 44–45.

3. We give more details about this survey in chapter 5, the appendix, and in Amabile and Kramer, "What Really Motivates Workers."

4. In using the first person plural to describe the research, we refer to ourselves (Teresa Amabile and Steven Kramer), as well as a team of researchers whose names appear in the acknowledgments.

5. We first described inner work life and presented some of these results in Amabile and Kramer, "Inner Work Life."

6. This phrase comes from, but is not suggested as the only important management task in, Jim Collins's book, *Good to Great: Why Some Companies Make the Leap . . . And Others Don't* (New York: HarperCollins, 2001).

Chapter 1

1. Although factual information is accurate, all specific identifying information on the companies, teams, and individuals we studied has been disguised throughout the book. Certain details about the weather, physical surroundings, and individuals' appearances are fictional. See the appendix for details about the disguise procedure.

2. This and other team member quotes are taken from the daily diaries we collected in our research, as described more fully in the appendix. The diary quotes presented throughout the book are verbatim excerpts from the diary narratives, except that (a) we corrected grammatical, spelling, and typographical errors in order to improve readability; (b) we inserted [in brackets] relevant background information or missing words in order to facilitate comprehension; and (c) we changed all names, dates, and other identifying information to protect confidentiality. We never inserted "emotional" punctuation, like exclamation points, that did not appear in the original. Dots in brackets [. . .] indicate that we removed irrelevant material.

3. Management scholar Jeffrey Pfeffer has provided evidence and written extensively about the importance of "people-centered management" in high performance organizations. At a broad level, his findings are entirely consistent with ours. For example, see J. Pfeffer, *The Human Equation: Building Profits by Putting People First* (Boston: Harvard Business School Press, 1998); J. Pfeffer, "Building Sustainable Organizations: The Human Factor," *Academy of Management Perspectives* 24 (2010): 34–45. More recently, David Sirota and his colleagues have made similar arguments based on their own data; see D. Sirota, L. A. Mischkind, and M. I. Meltzer, *The Enthusiastic Employee: How Companies Profit by Giving Workers What They Want* (Upper Saddle River, NJ: Wharton School Publishing, 2005).

4. Management scholar Robert Sutton, an expert on organizational behavior, has shown through much of his work that everyday managerial actions can exert profound effects on employees' well-being and motivation. His conclusions about management and performance reinforce many of the points we make throughout this book. For example, see R. Sutton, *Good Boss, Bad Boss: How to Be the Best. . . and Learn from the Worst* (New York: Business Plus, 2010).

5. P. T. Kilborn, "Strikers at American Airlines Say the Objective Is Respect," *New York Times*, November 21, 1993. The preceding flight attendant quotes are taken from this article.

6. Quoted in Sirota, Mischkind, and Meltzer, *The Enthusiastic Employee*, 115.

7. Survey by the Aon Hewitt Company, cited in G. A. Kohlrieser, "Engaging Employees Crucial for Their Morale," *The Nation (Thailand)*, November 29, 2010.

8. Scholars who study organizational behavior have found that, at work, people generally control their displays of strong feelings or personal perceptions about what is going on around them (e.g., J. E. Bono, H. J. Foldes, G. Vinson, and J. P. Muros, "Workplace Emotions: The Role of Supervision and Leadership," *Journal of Applied Psychology* 92 [2007]: 1357–1367). Fear has been identified as a central reason for "silence" concerning even important issues (J. J. Kish-Gephart, J. R. Detert, L. K. Trevino, and A. E. Edmondson, "Silenced by Fear: The Nature, Sources, and Consequences of Fear at Work," *Research in Organizational Behavior* 29 [2009]: 163–193).

9. Throughout this book, we use the terms *motivation* and *drive* interchangeably. Formal psychological definitions distinguish between biological drives (like hunger) and motivation (like the impetus to do one's work). In this book, we draw on the more colloquial use of *drive* as equivalent to motivation. For example, Daniel H. Pink used the term this way in *Drive: The Surprising Truth About What Motivates Us* (New York: Riverhead Books, 2009). Also, we use the colloquial term *feelings* interchangeably with *emotions*, and the terms *thoughts* and *cognitions* interchangeably with *perceptions* (although psychologists make fine distinctions between cognitions and perceptions).

Chapter 2

1. D. Watson and L. A. Clark, "Negative Affectivity: The Disposition to Experience Negative Emotional States," *Psychological Bulletin* 96 (1984): 465–490; T. M. Amabile, K. G. Hill, B. A. Hennessey, and E. M. Tighe, "The Work Preference Inventory: Assessing Intrinsic and Extrinsic Motivational Orientation," *Journal of Personality and Social Psychology* 66 (1994): 950–967.

2. As described in the appendix, most of the analyses we did controlled for personality. Generally, most aspects of personality were not significant predictors and, when they were, they did not account for a great deal of the variance in inner work life.

3. T. M. Amabile and S. J. Kramer, "Inner Work Life: The Hidden Subtext of Business Performance," *Harvard Business Review*, May 2007, 72–83.

4. The more precise term, scientifically, is *affect*, with *emotion* reserved for sharply defined reactions to specific events and *moods* referring to more general feeling states. We use the term *emotion* to refer to both because we believe it is a more generally understood term. See A. P. Brief and H. M. Weiss, "Organizational Behavior: Affect in the Workplace," *Annual Review of Psychology* 53 (2002): 279–307.

5. See S. G. Barsade and D. E. Gibson, "Why Does Affect Matter in Organizations?" *Academy of Management Perspectives* 21 (2007): 36–59.

6. D. Goleman, *Emotional Intelligence: Why It Can Matter More Than IQ* (New York: Bantam Books, 1997); D. Goleman, R. Boyatzis, and A. McKee, *Primal Leadership: Learning to Lead with Emotional Intelligence* (Boston: Harvard Business School Press, 2002); P. Salovey and J. D. Mayer, "Emotional Intelligence," *Imagination, Cognition, and Personality* 9 (1990): 185–211.

7. A. M. Isen, "Positive Affect and Decision-Making," in M. Lewis and J. Haviland-Jones, eds., *Handbook of Emotions*, 2nd ed. (New York: Guilford, 2000), 417–435.

8. According to the literature, sensemaking gears up most strongly in ambiguous, uncertain, or unexpected situations. At work, because people generally expect their managers and coworkers to be competent and supportive, sensemaking engages most deeply when these expectations are violated. Some basic readings on sensemaking include: E. Goffman, *Frame Analysis* (Cambridge, MA: Harvard University Press, 1974); K. E. Weick, *Sensemaking in Organizations* (Thousand Oaks, CA: Sage Publications, 1995); G. Klein, B. Moon, and R. F. Hoffman, "Making Sense of Sensemaking I: Alternative Perspectives," *IEEE Intelligent Systems* 21 (2006): 70–73; G. Klein, B. Moon, and R. F. Hoffman, "Making Sense of Sensemaking II: A Macrocognitive Model," *IEEE Intelligent Systems* 21 (2006): 88–92; A. Wrzesniewski, J. E. Dutton, and G. Debebe, "Interpersonal Sensemaking and the Meaning of Work," *Research in Organizational Behavior* 25 (2003): 93–135.

9. D. J. Campbell and R. Pritchard, "Motivation Theory in Industrial and Organizational Psychology," in *Handbook of Industrial and Organizational Psychology*, ed. M. D. Dunnette (Chicago: Rand McNally, 1976), 63–130; J. P. Campbell, "Modeling the Performance Prediction Problem in Industrial and Organizational Psychology," in *Handbook of Industrial and Organizational Psychology*, 2nd ed., vol. 1, eds. M. D. Dunnette and L. M. Hough (Palo Alto, CA: Consulting Psychologists Press, 1990), 687–732.

10. Many scholars have elaborated on the forms of human motivation (e.g., S. E. Cross, P. L. Bacon, and M. L. Morris, "The Relational-Interdependent Self-Construal and Relationships," *Journal of Personality and Social Psychology* 78 [2000]: 191–208; E. L. Deci and R. M. Ryan, "The 'What' and 'Why' of Goal Pursuits: Human Needs and the Self-Determination of Behavior," *Psychological Inquiry* 11 [2000]: 227–268; M. J. Gelfand, V. S. Major, J. L. Raver, L. H. Nishii, and K. O'Brien, "Negotiating Relationally: The Dynamics of the Relational Self in Negotiations," *Academy of Management Review* 31 [2006]: 427–451; A. M. Grant and J. Shin, "Work Motivation: Directing, Energizing, and Maintaining Research," *Oxford Handbook of Motivation*, ed. R. M. Ryan [Oxford: Oxford University Press, forthcoming, 2011]; F. Herzberg, *The Motivation to Work* [New York: Wiley, 1959]; and R. M. Ryan and E. L. Deci, "Self-Determination Theory and the Facilitation of Intrinsic Motivation, Social Development, and Well-Being," *American Psychologist* 55 [2000]: 68–78). Recent research shows that different forms of motivation can interact in complex ways (A. M. Grant, "Does Intrinsic Motivation Fuel the Prosocial Fire? Motivational Synergy in Predicting Persistence, Performance, and Productivity," *Journal of Applied Psychology* 93 [2008]: 48–58).

11. K. R. Lakhani and E. von Hippel, "How Open Source Software Works: 'Free' User-to-User Assistance," *Research Policy* 32 (2003): 923–943.

12. Psychological researchers often distinguish between relational motivation and altruistic, or *prosocial*, motivation. The former is defined as the desire to connect with other people, and the latter as the desire to protect and promote the well-being of other people. Since both are focused on relationships with other people, we combine them here.

13. See: T. M. Amabile, *Creativity in Context* (Boulder, CO: Westview Press, 1996). We discuss these dynamics in more detail later in the book.

14. In a classic article, Frederick Herzberg presented evidence showing that, although employees are dissatisfied by inadequate pay and benefits, they are not motivated to do excellent work by such factors. Rather, they are motivated by having interesting, challenging work that allows them to achieve. See F. Herzberg, "One More Time: How Do You Motivate Employees?," *Harvard Business Review*, January–February 1968, 53–62.

15. What is an *event*? Recent psychological research has resulted in a fascinating theory about how people get a sense that something is a discrete event ("what is happening now"). The theory suggests that the human brain's "working memory" constructs representations of events because they improve perception and the ability to predict what will happen next. See: J. M. Zacks, N. K. Speer, K. M. Swallow, T. S. Braver, and J. R. Reynolds, "Event Perception: A Mind/Brain Perspective," *Psychological Bulletin* 133 (2007): 273–293. This research expands on earlier findings about people's cognitive segmentation of behavior into events (e.g., D. Newtson, "Attribution and the Unit of Perception of Ongoing Behavior," *Journal of Personality and Social Psychology* 28 (1973): 28–38.

16. Evidence is mounting from psychology and neuroscience that emotions and thoughts are inextricably intertwined (e.g., E. A. Phelps, "Emotion and Cognition: Insights from Studies of the Human Amygdala," *Annual Review of Psychology* 57 [2006]: 27–53).

17. P. J. Lang, M. M. Bradley, J. R. Fitzsimmons, B. N. Cuthbert, J. D. Scott, B. Moulder, and V. Nangia, "Emotional Arousal and Activation of the Visual Cortex," *Psychophysiology* 35 (1998): 199–210.

18. For more on the fascinating interactions between emotions and cognition, see the work of Antonio Damasio and Joseph LeDoux (e.g., A. Damasio, *Descartes' Error: Emotion, Reason and the Human Brain* [New York: Putman, 1994]; A. Damasio, *The Feeling of What Happens: Body and Emotion in the Making of Consciousness* [New York: Harcourt, Inc., 1999]; J. LeDoux, *The Emotional Brain: The Mysterious Underpinnings of Emotional Life* [New York: Simon & Schuster, 1996]).

19. This hypothetical example is drawn from Damasio, *Descartes' Error*.

Chapter 3

1. The latter quote is generally attributed to the American businessman and political figure Joseph P. Kennedy, Sr. (1888–1969), father of President John F. Kennedy and Senators Robert F. Kennedy and Edward M. Kennedy.

2. For example, N. Anderson, C. K. De Dreu, and B. A. Nijstad, "The Routinization of Innovation Research: A Constructively Critical Review of the State-of-the-Science," *Journal of Organizational Behavior* 25 (2004):147–173; F. M. Andrews and G. F. Farris, "Time Pressure and Performance of Scientists and Engineers: A Five-Year

Panel Study," *Organizational Behavior and Human Performance* 8 (1972): 185–200; R. Eisenberger and J. Cameron, "Detrimental Effects of Reward: Reality or Myth?," *American Psychologist* 51 (1996): 1153–1166; S. Fineman, "On Being Positive: Concerns and Counterpoints," *Academy of Management Review* 31 (2006): 270–291; J. M. George, "Review of Kim S. Cameron, Jane E. Dutton, and Robert E. Quinn, eds.: *Positive Organizational Scholarship: Foundations of a New Discipline*," *Administrative Science Quarterly* 49 (2004): 325–329; and G. Kaufmann, "Expanding the Mood-Creativity Equation," *Creativity Research Journal* 15 (2003): 131–135.

3. J. M. George, J. Zhou, "Dual Tuning in Supportive Context: Joint Contributions of Positive Mood, Negative Mood, and Supervisory Behaviors to Employee Creativity," *Academy of Management Journal* 50 (2007): 605–622.

4. http://news.bbc.co.uk/2/hi/programmes/working_lunch/2985501.stm.

5. For example, T. M. Amabile, *Creativity in Context* (Boulder, CO: Westview Press, 1996); T. M. Amabile, S. G. Barsade, J. S. Mueller, and B. M. Staw, "Affect and Creativity at Work," *Administrative Science Quarterly* 50 (2005): 367–403; T. M. Amabile, R. Conti, H. Coon, J. Lazenby, and M. Herron, "Assessing the Work Environment for Creativity," *Academy of Management Journal* 39 (1996): 1154–1184; J. Andrews and D. C. Smith, "In Search of the Marketing Imagination: Factors Affecting the Creativity of Marketing Programs for Mature Products," *Journal of Marketing Research* 33 (1996): 174–187; K. Byron and S. Khazanchi, "A Meta-Analytic Investigation of the Relationship of State and Trait Anxiety to Performance on Figural and Verbal Creativity Tasks," *Personality and Social Psychology Bulletin* (forthcoming, 2011); K. S. Cameron, J. E. Dutton, and R. E. Quinn, eds., *Positive Organizational Scholarship: Foundations of a New Discipline* (San Francisco: Berrett-Koehler, 2003); A. M. Grant, "Does Intrinsic Motivation Fuel the Prosocial Fire? Motivational Synergy in Predicting Persistence, Performance, and Productivity," *Journal of Applied Psychology* 93 (2008): 108–124; J. R. Kelly and J. E. McGrath, "Effects of Time Limits and Task Types on Task Performance and Interaction of Four-Person Groups," *Journal of Personality and Social Psychology* 49 (1985): 395–407; A. K. Kirk and D. F. Brown, "Latent Constructs of Proximal and Distal Motivation Predicting Performance Under Maximum Test Conditions," *Journal of Applied Psychology* 88 (2003): 40–49; B. M. Staw and S. G. Barsade, "Affect and Managerial Performance: A Test of the Sadder-But-Wiser vs. Happier-And-Smarter Hypotheses," *Administrative Science Quarterly* 38 (1993): 304–331; and B. M. Staw, R. I. Sutton, and L. H. Pelled, "Employee Positive Emotion and Favorable Outcomes at the Workplace," *Organization Science* 5 (1994): 51–71.

6. Job satisfaction is essentially a combination of perceptions and emotions about one's job. This analysis suggests that job satisfaction leads to better performance, and not vice versa: M. Riketta, "The Causal Relation Between Job Attitudes and Performance: A Meta-Analysis of Panel Studies," *Journal of Applied Psychology* 93 (2008): 472–481.

7. Staw, Sutton, and Pelled, "Employee Positive Emotion and Favorable Outcomes at the Workplace." The performance measures in the second time period controlled for evaluations in the first time period. This means that emotion in the first period predicted performance in the second, regardless of performance in the first period.

8. In fact, the research landscape is more nuanced than a stark two-sided divide. We have simplified the debate for expository purposes. A 2008 paper that analyzed dozens of studies found that, overall, positive moods produce more creativity than neutral moods, but not always more than negative moods (M. Baas, C. K. W. De Dreu, and B. A. Nijstad, "A Meta-Analysis of 25 Years of Mood-Creativity Research: Hedonic

Tone, Activation, or Regulatory Focus?," *Psychological Bulletin* 134 [2008]: 779–806). Our own work has found that certain forms of pressure and extrinsic motivation can support creativity under the right conditions (see T. M. Amabile, "Motivational Synergy: Toward New Conceptualizations of Intrinsic and Extrinsic Motivation in the Workplace," *Human Resource Management Review* 3 [1993]: 185–201; and T. M. Amabile, C. N. Hadley, and S. J. Kramer, "Creativity Under the Gun," *Harvard Business Review,* August 2002, 52–61).

9. As soon as they agreed to participate, we asked participants to complete standard questionnaires assessing personality, thinking style, motivational orientation, educational level, organizational tenure, and other demographic characteristics. As explained in the appendix, we took these individual differences into account in our statistical analyses.

10. Amabile, Barsade, Mueller, and Staw, "Affect and Creativity at Work."

11. Theorists have made convincing cases for incubation effects in creativity (e.g., D. K. Simonton, *Origins of Genius: Darwinian Perspectives on Creativity* [New York: Oxford University Press, 1999]). Although our study is the first demonstration of an incubation effect in organizational creativity, several researchers have recently found incubation effects in learning: R. Stickgold, L. James, and A. J. Hobson, "Visual Discrimination Learning Requires Sleep After Training," *Nature Neuroscience* 3 (2000): 1237–1238; R. Stickgold, L. Scott, C. Rittenhouse, and J. Hobson, "Sleep-Induced Changes in Associative Memory," *Journal of Cognitive Neuroscience* 11 (1999): 182–193; R. Stickgold and M. Walker, "To Sleep, Perchance to Gain Creative Insight?," *Trends in Cognitive Sciences* 8 (2004): 191–192; U. Wagner, S. Gais, H. Haider, R. Verleger, and J. Born, "Sleep Inspires Insight," *Nature* 427 (2004): 352–355; and M. P. Walker, T. Brakefield, J. Seidman, A. Morgan, J. Hobson, and R. Stickgold, "Sleep and the Time Course of Motor Skill Learning," *Learning and Memory* 10 (2003): 275–284.

12. B. L. Fredrickson, "What Good Are Positive Emotions?", *Review of General Psychology* 2 (1998): 300–319.

13. Fully 80 percent of those creative thinking days followed days on which Marsha's general mood was more positive than average for her, and 65 percent followed particularly joyful days (i.e., days when her joy was higher than average for her). Her negative emotions on the days preceding creative thought days were the mirror image. Her anger was below average on 75 percent of the preceding days, her fear was below average on 65 percent, and her sadness was below average on 60 percent of them.

14. On the self-rated mood scale, constructed from several items on the daily diary questionnaire, Marsha's mood was nearly one standard deviation above her average that day.

15. These findings build on prior organizational creativity research. The following paper not only reports an empirical study investigating the effects of the work environment on creativity in organizations, but it also reviews much previous research: Amabile et al., "Assessing the Work Environment for Creativity." The following source also reviews empirical research on the topic: M. A. West, and A. W. Richter, "Climates and Cultures for Innovation and Creativity at Work," in *Handbook of Organizational Creativity*, eds. J. Zhou and C. Shalley (New York: Lawrence Erlbaum Associates, 2008), 211–236.

16. Our own previous research has shown a strong connection between perceived positive challenge in a task and creativity on the task (e.g., Amabile et al., "Assessing the Work Environment for Creativity"). A 2006 paper reported a connection between

empowerment and creativity (B. J. Alge, G. A. Gallinger, S. Tangirala, and J. L. Oakley, "Information Privacy in Organizations: Empowering Creative and Extrarole Performance," *Journal of Applied Psychology* 91 [2006]: 221–232). In two studies, organizations that respected the privacy of employees' personal information enhanced employee perceptions of empowerment which, in turn, enhanced employee creativity. An earlier paper reported a laboratory experiment in which high task autonomy was one of three environmental variables that, taken together, interacted to produce superior levels of participant creativity on a workplace simulation task. (The other two variables were positive feedback delivered in an informational style: J. Zhou, "Feedback Valence, Feedback Style, Task Autonomy, and Achievement Orientation: Interactive Effects of Creative Performance," *Journal of Applied Psychology* 83 [1998]: 261–276.)

17. This research includes controlled experiments, showing that events undermining intrinsic motivation also undermine creativity, as well as non-experimental studies showing a positive relationship between intrinsic motivation and creativity in different fields. The experiments include: T. M. Amabile, "Effects of External Evaluation on Artistic Creativity," *Journal of Personality and Social Psychology* 37 (1979): 221–233; T. M. Amabile, "Children's Artistic Creativity: Detrimental Effects of Competition in a Field Setting," *Personality and Social Psychology Bulletin* 8 (1982): 573–578; T. M. Amabile and J. Gitomer, "Children's Artistic Creativity: Effects of Choice in Task Materials," *Personality and Social Psychology Bulletin* 10 (1984): 209–215; T. M. Amabile, "Motivation and Creativity: Effects of Motivational Orientation on Creative Writers," *Journal of Personality and Social Psychology* 48 (1985): 393–399; T. M. Amabile, "The Motivation to Be Creative," in S. Isaksen, ed., *Frontiers of Creativity Research: Beyond the Basics* (Buffalo, NY: Bearly Limited, 1987); T. M. Amabile, B. A. Hennessey, and B. S. Grossman, "Social Influences on Creativity: The Effects of Contracted-for Reward," *Journal of Personality and Social Psychology* 50 (1985): 14–23; T. M. Amabile, P. Goldfarb, and S. C. Brackfield, "Social Influences on Creativity: Evaluation, Coactions, and Surveillance," *Creativity Research Journal* 3 (1990): 6–21; B. A. Hennessey, "The Effect of Extrinsic Constraints on Children's Creativity While Using a Computer," *Creativity Research Journal* 2 (1989): 151–168; and B. A. Hennessey, T. M. Amabile, and M. Martinage, "Immunizing Children Against the Negative Effects of Reward," *Contemporary Educational Psychology* 14 (1989): 212–227. The non-experiments include: T. M. Amabile, K. G. Hill, B. A. Hennessey, and E. M. Tighe, "The Work Preference Inventory: Assessing Intrinsic and Extrinsic Motivational Orientations," *Journal of Personality and Social Psychology* 66 (1994): 950–967; J. Ruscio, D. M. Whitney, and T. M. Amabile, "Looking Inside the Fishbowl of Creativity: Verbal and Behavioral Predictors of Creative Performance," *Creativity Research Journal* 11 (1998): 243–263. In recent years, Robert Eisenberger and his colleagues have challenged the intrinsic motivation principle of creativity in a series of studies. (You can find a summary in R. Eisenberger and L. Shanock, "Rewards, Intrinsic Motivation, and Creativity," *Creativity Research Journal* 15 [2003]: 121–130.) Specifically, they argue that rewards can enhance intrinsic motivation and creativity; our experiments found that rewards can be perceived as controlling and, therefore, often undermine intrinsic motivation and creativity. However, we have found that, under certain specific conditions, reward can have positive effects (see T. M. Amabile, "Motivational Synergy: Toward New Conceptualizations of Intrinsic and Extrinsic Motivation in the Workplace," *Human Resource Management Review* 3 [1993]: 185–201). We believe, though, that these conditions must be managed carefully and that, more generally, focusing on reward as the reason for doing something does undermine creativity.

18. T. M. Amabile, "Motivation and Creativity." This experiment was conducted at Brandeis University, as were most of our motivation and creativity experiments. Amabile conducted the earliest of these experiments at Stanford University.

19. F. X. Frei, R. J. Ely, and L. Winig, "Zappos.com 2009: Clothing, Customer Service, and Company Culture," Case 9-610-015 (Boston: Harvard Business School, 2009), 4.

20. J. K. Harter, F. L. Schmidt, J. W. Asplund, E. A. Killham, and S. Agrawal, "Causal Impact of Employee Work Perceptions on the Bottom Line of Organizations," *Perspectives on Psychological Science* 5 (2010): 378–389. In this study, although business unit performance at earlier points in time did predict employee perceptions at later points in time (showing some reverse causality), employee perceptions at earlier points in time were much stronger predictions of later business unit performance (supporting the forward causality we report here).

21. A. Damasio, *The Feeling of What Happens: Body and Emotion in the Making of Consciousness* (San Diego: Harcourt, 1999), 60–71. Recent research using neuro-imaging of people's brains as they experience different emotions shows distinct patterns for "approach" (positive) emotions and "withdrawal" (negative) emotions (e.g., A. Bartels and S. Zeki, "The Neural Correlates of Maternal and Romantic Love," *NeuroImage* 21 [2004]: 1155–1166; and F. C. Murphy, I. Nimmo-Smith, and A. D. Lawrence, "Functional Neuroanatomy of Emotions: A Meta-Analysis," *Cognitive, Affective & Behavioral Neuroscience* 3 [2003]: 207–233). Negative emotions like fear and sadness can lead to brain activity and thought patterns that are detrimental to creative, productive work: (a) avoidance of risk (J. S. Lerner and D. Keltner, "Beyond Valence: Toward a Model of Emotion Specific Influences on Judgment and Choice," *Cognition and Emotion* 14 [2000]: 473–493); (b) difficulty remembering and planning (N. I. Eisenberger, "Identifying the Neural Correlates Underlying Social Pain: Implications for Developmental Processes," *Human Development* 49 [2006]: 273–293); and (c) rational decision making (E. B. Andrade and D. Ariely, "The Enduring Impact of Transient Emotions on Decision Making," *Organizational Behavior and Human Decision Processes* 109 [2009]: 1–8). The negative effect on decision making persists even after the negative emotion itself has dissipated.

22. Fredrickson presented this "broaden-and-build" theory in two papers (Fredrickson, "What Good Are Positive Emotions?"; B. L. Fredrickson, "The Role of Positive Emotions in Positive Psychology: The Broaden and Build Theory of Positive Emotions," *American Psychologist* 56 [2001]: 218–226). Other psychologists have proposed similar mechanisms. Alice Isen's research has found that positive emotion leads people to see more connections between things, but negative emotion leads them to think more narrowly (A. M. Isen and K. A. Daubman, "The Influence of Affect on Categorization," *Journal of Personality and Social Psychology* 47 [1984]: 1206–1217; A. M. Isen, P. Niedenthal, and N. Cantor, "The Influence of Positive Affect on Social Categorization," *Motivation and Emotion* 16 [1992]: 65–78; B. E. Kahn and A. M. Isen, "Variety Seeking among Safe, Enjoyable Products," *Journal of Consumer Research* 20 [1993]: 257–270). Isen and her colleagues have theorized that these differences are due to differential levels of brain dopamine released under positive and negative emotion (F. G. Ashby, A. M. Isen, and A. U. Turken, "A Neuropsychological Theory of Positive Affect and Its Influence on Cognition," *Psychological Review* 106 [1999]: 529–550). In 1959, Easterbrook proposed that negative emotions like anxiety and fear narrow attention (J. A. Easterbrook, "The Effect of Emotion on Cue Utilization and the Organization of Behavior" *Psychological Review* 66 [1959]: 183–201). In 1994, Derryberry and Tucker hypothesized that positive emotions broaden the scope of attention (D. Derryberry

and D. M. Tucker, "Motivating the Focus of Attention," in P. M. Neidenthal and S. Kitayama, eds., *The Heart's Eye: Emotional Influences in Perception and Attention* [San Diego, CA: Academic Press, 1994], 167–196).

23. B. L. Fredrickson and C. Branigan, "Positive Emotions Broaden the Scope of Attention and Thought-Action Repertoires," *Cognition and Emotion* 19 (2005): 313–332.

24. T. M. Amabile and R. Conti, "Changes in the Work Environment for Creativity During Downsizing," *Academy of Management Journal* 42 (1999): 630–640.

25. J. Welch and S. Welch, *Winning: The Answers Confronting 74 of the Toughest Questions in Business Today* (New York: Harper Collins, 2006).

Chapter 4

1. In chapter 3, we also showed that inner work life influences two other dimensions of performance, commitment, and collegiality. Because those are not aspects of daily work progress, they are not directly relevant to this chapter.

2. Interestingly, on progress days, people also reported more time pressure. As we discuss in chapter 6, time pressure relates to inner work life in fascinating and complex ways. From the analyses reported here, it is impossible to say what causes what. It may be that, when people feel more time pressure, they are likely to get more work done (that is, make more progress).

3. This is our formal definition of a progress event: *The person or the team made progress, finished a task, moved forward, was productive, or achieved an accomplishment in the work; this could include a creative accomplishment.*

4. This is our formal definition of a setback event: *The person or the team had setbacks or lack of progress or accomplishment in the work; the person or the team encountered work difficulties or obstacles.*

5. The emotion we label *love* is a combination of warmth and pride (including pride in oneself).

Chapter 5

1. M. Dewhurst, M. Guthridge, and E. Mohr, "Motivating People: Getting Beyond the Money," *McKinsey Quarterly*, November 2009, 1–5.

2. T. M. Amabile and S. J. Kramer, "What Really Motivates Workers," *Harvard Business Review,* January 2010, 44–45. The managers surveyed represented all levels, from team leaders to CEOs. Drawn from attendees of executive education programs and the alumni records of a top business school, they represented dozens of different companies across a variety of industries.

3. Since the publication of the classic *Built to Last* in 1994, managers' awareness of the importance of progress in *firms* has been heightened. A central thesis of that book is that, to achieve long-lasting success for a firm, top executives must stimulate progress (continuous change through new strategies, new methods, and so on), while preserving the core ideology on which the firm was established. J. C. Collins and J. I. Porras, *Built to Last: Successful Habits of Visionary Companies* (New York: HarperCollins, 1994).

4. S. D. Dobrev and W. P. Barnett, "Organizational Roles and Transition to Entrepreneurship," *Academy of Management Journal* 48 (2005): 433–449; N. Wasserman, "Founder-CEO Succession and the Paradox of Entrepreneurial Success," *Organization Science* 14 (2003): 149–172; N. Wasserman, *Founding Dilemmas* (Princeton, New Jersey, Princeton University Press, forthcoming).

5. http://techcrunch.com/2011/03/03/jack-dorsey-twitter-punched-stomach/.

6. Several psychological theorists have described the role of self-efficacy and related concepts. All suggest that it is a central facet of human motivation (e.g., A. Bandura, *Self-Efficacy: The Exercise of Control* [New York: Freeman, 1997]; E. L. Deci and R. M. Ryan, *Intrinsic Motivation and Self-Determination in Human Behavior* [New York: Plenum Press, 1985]; M. E. Gist, "Self-Efficacy: Implications for Organizational Behavior and Human Resource Management," *Academy of Management Review* 12 [1987]: 472–485).

7. G. Fitch, "Effects of Self-Esteem, Perceived Performance, and Choice on Causal Attributions," *Journal of Personality and Social Psychology* 16 (1970): 311–315; S. Streufert and S. C. Streufert, "Effects of Conceptual Structure, Failure, and Success on Attribution of Causality and Interpersonal Attitudes," *Journal of Personality and Social Psychology* 11 (1969): 138–147.

8. L. F. Lavallee and J. D. Campbell, "Impact of Personal Goals on Self-Regulation Processes Elicited by Daily Negative Events," *Journal of Personality and Social Psychology* 69 (1995): 341–352.

9. Research on people suffering from depression shows that they often engage in chronic self-focus (e.g., R. E. Ingram and T. S. Smith, "Depression and Internal Versus External Locus of Attention," *Cognitive Therapy and Research* 8 [1984]: 139–152; T. W. Smith and J. Greenberg, "Depression and Self-Focused Attention," *Motivation and Emotion* 5 [1981]: 323–331; T. W. Smith, R. E. Ingram, and D. L. Roth, "Self-Focused Attention and Depression: Self-Evaluation, Affect, and Life Stress," *Motivation and Emotion* 9 [1985]: 381–389). Other research shows a link between depression and discrepancies between people's views of their "ideal" and "real" selves (e.g., E. T. Higgins, R. Klein, and T. Strauman, "Self-Concept Discrepancy Theory: A Psychological Model for Distinguishing among Different Aspects of Depression and Anxiety," *Social Cognition* 3 [1985]: 51–76; R. Laxer, "Self-Concept Changes of Depressed Patients in General Hospital Treatment," *Journal of Consulting Psychology* 28 [1964]: 214–219; M. Nadich, M. Gargan, and L. Michael, "Denial, Anxiety, Locus of Control, and the Discrepancy Between Aspirations and Achievements as Components of Depression," *Journal of Abnormal Psychology* 84 [1975]: 1–9). In social psychology, self-regulatory theory proposes that nonchronic depressive episodes result when an event confronts a person with the difficulty (or seeming impossibility) of achieving a goal that is important to that person's identity or sense of self-worth (T. Pyszczynski and J. Greenberg, "Self-Regulatory Perseveration and the Depressive Self-Focusing Style: A Self-Awareness Theory of Reactive Depression," *Psychological Bulletin* 102 [1987]: 122–128).

10. Pyszczynski and Greenberg, "Self-Regulatory Perseveration and the Depressive Self-Focusing Style."

11. C. S. Carver and M. F. Scheier, "Origins and Functions of Positive and Negative Affect: A Control Process View," *Psychological Review* 97 (1990): 19–35; E. Diener, "Subjective Well-Being," *Psychological Bulletin* 95 (1984): 542–575.

12. In our study, there was a statistically significant correlation between the number of words in the "event of the day" narrative and participants' rating of how the event affected their feelings about the project (–.22); the more negative the feelings, the more participants wrote about the event.

13. A. Bandura and D. Cervone, "Self-Evaluative and Self-Efficacy Mechanisms Governing the Motivational Effects of Goal Systems," *Journal of Personality and Social Psychology* 45 (1983): 1017–1028; M. E. Gist, "Self-Efficacy"; C. Harris, K. Daniels, and

R. B. Briner, "A Daily Diary Study of Goals and Affective Well-Being at Work," *Journal of Occupational and Organizational Psychology* 76 (2003): 401–410.

14. B. L. Chaikin, "The Effects of Four Outcome Schedules on Persistence, Liking for the Task, and Attributions for Causality," *Journal of Personality* 3 (1971): 512–526.

15. J. A. Conger and R. N. Kanungo, "The Empowerment Process: Integrating Theory and Practice," *Academy of Management Review* 13 (1988): 471–482.

16. Researchers Richard Hackman and Gregory Oldham identified three essential elements of work meaningfulness: skill variety ("the degree to which the job requires a variety of different activities in carrying out the work"), task identity ("the degree to which a job requires completion of a 'whole' and identifiable piece of work, that is, doing a job from beginning to end with a visible outcome"), and task significance ("the degree to which the job has a substantial impact on the lives of other people, whether those people are in the immediate organization or in the world at large"); see J. R. Hackman and G. R. Oldham, *Work Redesign* (Reading, MA: Addison-Wesley, 1980), 78–79.

17. http://en.wikipedia.org/wiki/John_Sculley.

18. W. F. Cascio, "Changes in Workers, Work, and Organizations," in *Handbook of Psychology* 12, *Industrial and Organizational Psychology*, eds. W. Borman, R. Klimoski, and D. Ilgen (New York: Wiley, 2003), 401–422.

19. Ideally, the company's and the individual employees' views of "contributing" will have a strong ethical component. Many managers at disgraced companies such as Enron probably thought they were managing for progress, and it's quite likely that their employees felt great as they saw the money rolling in month after month. Although these individuals may have been creating (temporary) monetary value for themselves and shareholders, their actions ultimately destroyed value.

20. In itself, the meaningfulness of work can have powerful psychological effects. Essentially, people are more likely to experience personal well-being when their work is more meaningful to them. Several sources provide evidence, including: K. A. Arnold, N. Turner, J. Barling, E. K. Kelloway, and M. C. McKee, "Transformational Leadership and Psychological Well-Being: the Mediating Role of Meaningful Work," *Journal of Occupational Health Psychology* 12 (2007): 193–203; R. F. Baumeister and K. D. Vohs, "The Pursuit of Meaningfulness in Life," in C. R. Snyder and S. J. Lopez, eds., *The Handbook of Positive Psychology* (New York: Oxford University Press, 2002), 608–618; S. Cartwright and N. Holmes, "The Meaning of Work: The Challenge of Regaining Employee Engagement and Reducing Cynicism," *Human Resource Management Review* 16 (2006): 199–208; A. M. Grant, "The Significance of Task Significance: Job Performance Effects, Relational Mechanisms, and Boundary Conditions," *Journal of Applied Psychology* 93 (2008): 108–124; and J. R. Hackman, *Leading Teams: Setting the Stage for Great Performances* (Boston: Harvard Business School Press, 2002).

21. N. Wiener, *Cybernetics or Control and Communication in the Animal and the Machine* (Cambridge, MA/Paris: MIT Press/Hermann et Cie, 1948); B. Arthur, "Positive Feedbacks in the Economy," *Scientific American*, February 1990, 80.

22. Across the 26 teams and thousands of diary narratives we analyzed, we saw both the virtuous cycle and the vicious cycle playing out repeatedly. Subsequent chapters describe some of these cycles, through the stories of the companies, teams, and individuals we studied. It is through those stories, rather than single diary narratives, that the entire cycle of the progress loop truly reveals itself.

Chapter 6

1. Notice the implication: one of the key three influences on inner work life, catalysts (the catalyst factor), influences another, progress (the progress principle).

2. A number of researchers have pointed to the importance of clear goals for effective performance. Generally, this research emphasizes that goals should be clear, meaningful, and challenging, but achievable. (See E. A. Locke, and G. P. Latham, *A Theory of Goal-setting and Task Performance* [Englewood Cliffs, NJ: Prentice-Hall, 1990].) For an overview of the importance of "compelling direction" for team performance, see: J. R. Hackman, *Leading Teams: Setting the Stage for Great Performances* (Boston: Harvard Business School Press, 2002). An earlier paper suggested that unclear goals present the major obstacle to team performance (H. J. Thamhain and D. L. Wilemon, "Building High Performance Engineering Project Teams," *IEEE Transactions on Engineering Management* 34 [1987]: 130–137). Another study found that managers' private experiences of fear at work were most commonly associated with uncertainty (K. Mignonac and O. Herrbach, "Linking Work Events, Affective States, and Attitudes: An Empirical Study of Managers' Emotions," *Journal of Business and Psychology* 19 [2004]: 221–240). Finally, goal clarity can be important for creating psychological safety within a work team (A. C. Edmondson and J. P. Mogelof, "Explaining Psychological Safety in Innovation Teams: Organizational Culture, Team Dynamics, or Personality?" in *Creativity and Innovation in Organizational Teams,* eds. L. L. Thompson and H. S. Choi [New York: Lawrence Erlbaum Associates, 2006]). Most simply, without clear goals, it is impossible to set priorities or to work effectively either as individuals, teams, or organizations (H. H. Stevenson and J. L. Cruikshank, *Do Lunch or Be Lunch: The Power of Predictability in Creating Your Future* [Boston: Harvard Business School Press, 1998]).

3. Several studies have shown that restricting autonomy lowers intrinsic motivation. For reviews of this research, see: E. L. Deci and R. M. Ryan, *Intrinsic Motivation and Self-Determination in Human Behavior* (New York: Plenum Press, 1985); A. M. Grant and J. Shin, "Work Motivation: Directing, Energizing, and Maintaining Research," in *Oxford Handbook of Motivation*, ed. R. M. Ryan (Oxford: Oxford University Press, 2011, forthcoming); R. M. Ryan and E. L. Deci, "Self-Determination Theory and the Facilitation of Intrinsic Motivation, Social Development, and Well-Being," *American Psychologist* 55 (2000): 68–78. Research has also shown that autonomy increases creativity (T. M. Amabile and J. Gitomer, "Children's Artistic Creativity: Effects of Choice in Task Materials," *Personality and Social Psychology Bulletin* 10 [1984]: 209–215).

4. Considerable research has demonstrated the importance of resource availability for high performance (e.g., M. Tushman and R. Nelson, "Technology, Organizations and Innovation: An Introduction," *Administrative Science Quarterly* 35 [1990]: 1–8; B. Wernerfelt, "A Resource-Based View of the Firm," *Strategic Management Journal* 5 [1984]: 171–180). However, although effective performance requires a sufficiency of resources, it is possible to have too many resources of certain types. For example, having too many people on a team can lead to motivation problems, in which individuals exert less effort than they might with fewer people (B. Latane, K. Williams, and S. Harkins, "Many Hands Make Light the Work: The Causes and Consequences of Social Loafing," *Journal of Personality and Social Psychology* 37 [1979]: 822–832). Moreover, although it is important to have enough people for good project completion, having too many people can lead to coordination problems (Hackman, *Leading Teams*, 116–122). Some scholars have suggested that a surplus of all types of resources can

result in risk aversion, passivity, and decreased innovation (e.g., D. Levinthal and J. March, "The Myopia of Learning," *Strategic Management Journal* 14 [1993]: 95–112).

5. Jeffrey Pfeffer, a professor of organizational behavior at Stanford University's Graduate School of Business, described the negative effects of downsizing on people and on companies in a 2010 article, "Lay Off the Layoffs" (*Newsweek*, February 15, 2010, 32–37).

6. More research than not suggests that time pressure undermines complex forms of work (e.g., T. M. Amabile, R. Conti, H. Coon, J. Lazenby, and M. Herron, "Assessing the Work Environment for Creativity," *Academy of Management Journal* 39 [1996]: 1154–1184; J. Andrews and D. C. Smith, "In Search of the Marketing Imagination: Factors Affecting the Creativity of Marketing Programs for Mature Products," *Journal of Marketing Research* 33 [1996]: 174–187). However, some research has uncovered a positive relationship (e.g., F. M. Andrews and G. F. Farris, "Time Pressure and the Performance of Scientists and Engineers: A Five-Year Panel Study," *Organizational Behavior and Human Performance* 8 [1972]: 185–200). One recent study even found a curvilinear relationship, with the highest level of creativity at a moderate level of time pressure—but only for certain types of people under certain circumstances (M. Baer and G. Oldham, "The Curvilinear Relation between Experienced Creative Time Pressure and Creativity: Moderating Effects of Openness to Experience and Support for Creativity," *Journal of Applied Psychology* 91 [2006]: 963–970).

7. Research suggests that jobs have become increasingly interdependent and that organizations are increasingly using teams as the basic work units (D. R. Ilgen and E. D. Pulakos, *The Changing Nature of Performance: Implications for Staffing, Motivation, and Development* (San Francisco: Jossey-Bass, 1999). Moreover, there is research evidence that helping within teams is beneficial not only for the team but for the organization more broadly. For example, see S. E. Anderson and L. J. Williams, "Interpersonal, Job, and Individual Factors Related to Helping Processes at Work," *Journal of Applied Psychology* 81 (1996): 282–296; W. C. Borman and S. J. Motowidlo, "Expanding the Criterion Domain to Include Elements of Contextual Performance," in *Personnel Selection in Organizations*, eds. N. Schmitt and W. C. Borman (San Francisco: Jossey-Bass, 1993), 71–98; D. W. Organ, *Organizational Citizenship Behavior: The "Good Soldier" Syndrome* (Lexington, MA: Lexington Books, 1988); L. Van Dyne, L. L. Cummings, and J. McLean Parks, "Extra Role Behaviors: In Pursuit of Construct and Definitional Clarity (a Bridge over Muddied Waters)," in *Research in Organizational Behavior*, vol. 17, eds. L. L. Cummings and B. M. Staw (Greenwich, CT: JAI Press, 1995), 215–285. In general, help-giving is vitally important in organizations (S. J. Motowidlo, "Some Basic Issues Related to Contextual Performance and Organizational Citizenship Behavior in Human Resource Management," *Human Resource Management Review* 10 [2000]: 115–126). A recent study of professional service firms showed that *seeking help* can also be important, particularly in setting the stage for moments of group creativity (A. B. Hargadon and B. A. Bechky, "When Collections of Creatives Become Creative Collectives: A Field Study of Problem Solving at Work," *Organization Science* 17 [(2006]: 484–500). That study also revealed the importance of an organizational culture that encourages and rewards both help-seeking and help-giving.

8. Psychologist Carol Dweck and her colleagues have carried out over three decades of research showing that performance benefits when people view ability as something that can develop over time, rather than something inherently fixed. In this research, mistakes and setbacks are essential vehicles for learning (C. S. Dweck, *Mindset: The New Psychology of Success* [New York: Random House, 2006]).

9. There is considerable research and theory suggesting that groups and organizations will perform more effectively and more creatively when the culture is one of psychological safety. (For example: A. Edmondson, "Psychological Safety and Learning Behaviors in Work Teams," *Administrative Science Quarterly* 44 [1999]: 350–383; W. A. Kahn, "Psychological Conditions of Personal Engagement and Disengagement at Work," *Academy of Management Journal* 33 [1990]: 692–724.)

10. A summary of research on the importance of idea flow for creativity and innovation in organizations appears in T. M. Amabile, *Creativity in Context* (Boulder, CO: Westview Press, 1996). R. Keith Sawyer summarizes a great deal of the research linking collaborative idea flow in groups to creative group performance (R. K. Sawyer, *Group Genius: the Creative Power of Collaboration* [New York: Basic Books, 2007]). A number of scholars have been fascinated by the phenomenon of creative collaboration (e.g., V. John-Steiner, *Creative Collaboration* [New York: Oxford University Press, 2000]). A more general review of the effectiveness of work team collaboration appears in R. A. Guzzo and M. W. Dickson, "Teams in Organizations: Recent Research on Performance and Effectiveness," *Annual Review of Psychology* 47 (1996): 307–338.

11. Although organizational scholars draw distinctions between climate and culture, various definitions of the two constructs overlap a great deal. Almost all include perceived values, norms, and procedures. (See: J. R. Rentsch, "Climate and Culture: Interaction and Qualitative Differences in Organizational Meanings," *Journal of Applied Psychology* 75 [1990]: 668–681; M. L. Tushman and C. O'Reilly, "Managerial Problem Solving: A Congruence Approach," in *Managing Strategic Innovation and Change: A Collection of Readings*, eds. M. L. Tushman and P. Anderson [New York: Oxford University Press, 2004], 194–205.)

12. E. H. Shein, "The Role of the Founder in Creating Organizational Culture," *Organizational Dynamics* 12 (Summer 1983): 13–28.

13. We discerned these three central forces of climate from all the journals, interviews, and observations we made across all seven companies and 26 teams in our diary study. These same three climate forces spawn the interpersonal events of the nourishment factor—nourishers and toxins—that we discuss in chapter 7.

14. In the Arthur Conan Doyle story "The Silver Blaze," Sherlock Holmes finds it telling that a dog did *not* bark on the night of a crime. (He deduced that someone familiar to the animal must have committed the murder, since the dog would have barked at a stranger.) The relative absence of inhibitors in the Vision daily journals led us to suspect that inhibitors seldom impinged on the team's work. When we met with the team after our study ended and asked them to describe their working conditions, our suspicions were confirmed.

15. Jim Collins, *Good to Great: Why Some Companies Make the Leap . . . And Others Don't* (New York: HarperCollins, 2001).

16. Dave's self-rated mood this day was one-quarter standard deviation above his average.

17. M. Moskowitz, R. Levering, and C. Tkaczyk, "100 Best Companies to Work For," *Fortune,* January 13, 2010, 75–88. W. L. Gore has also received awards for its subsidiaries around the world. Gore has repeatedly been ranked high on the lists of the Best Workplaces in the United States, the United Kingdom, France, Sweden, Italy, and Germany. According to the W. L. Gore Web site, "Associates (not employees) are hired for general work areas. With the guidance of their sponsors (not bosses) and a growing understanding of opportunities and team objectives, associates commit to projects that match their skills. All of this takes place in an environment that combines freedom with

cooperation and autonomy with synergy" (http://www.gore.com/en_xx/aboutus/culture/index.html). According to the most recently available information, Gore has been profitable every year since its founding in 1958 (A. Harrington, "Who's Afraid of a New Product?", *Fortune,* November 10, 2003, 189–192).

18. Sophie's mood on April 26 was nearly two standard deviations below her average.

19. Ben's intrinsic motivation this day was a full standard deviation below his average.

Chapter 7

1. There are three basic sources of evidence. First, in the best days–worst days study reported in chapter 4, the nourishment factor was a major differentiator between the best and the worst inner work life days. We defined nourishers (or interpersonal support) as the person's report (in the diary narrative) of receiving support oriented toward encouraging, comforting, and/or providing other forms of socio-emotional help that day. *Socio-emotional help* simply means that the person's emotions or views were validated in some way (even if only by being really listened to), or that some sort of comfort and encouragement were given—whether about the work or about a personal matter. Sometimes this could mean just having fun with coworkers or enjoying their presence. The second source of evidence is a finding about collaboration in the best days–worst days study. Although not as strong a differentiator as the key three, collaboration (simply working with someone else) was more frequent on best days than worst days. The third source of evidence comes from analyses we did of people's moods, as reported on the numerical scale questions of the daily diary questionnaire. In an initial analysis, we found that moods were significantly more positive on days when people reported collaboration. However, to reduce the possibility that this result was due to people simply making more progress when they combined their efforts with someone else, we then eliminated from the analysis all days that people reported both collaboration and progress. We still found that moods were significantly more positive on collaboration days, suggesting that there is something about simply being with other people that can be uplifting.

2. Some research suggests that, when people talk about their work with interviewers, they focus more on the meaning derived from their connections with coworkers than on the meaning derived from the work itself. See: L. E. Sandelands and C. J. Boudens, "Feeling at Work," in *Emotion in Organizations,* ed. S. Fineman (London: Sage, 2000), 46–63.

3. People who give their colleagues and subordinates nourishers not only benefit from others' inner work lives, they may also benefit the organization and their own careers. In one study, employees who tended to make their colleagues feel energized (or motivated) got better performance evaluations, advanced more quickly, and sparked more innovation than those who were "de-energizers" (R. Cross and A. Parker, *The Hidden Power of Social Networks: Understanding How Work Really Gets Done in Organizations* [Boston: Harvard Business School Press, 2004]).

4. One recent study found that human-service professionals working in emotionally challenging settings, such as pediatric hospitals, a drug-treatment center, and a hospice facility, not only felt better emotionally but also reported being able to more effectively handle their work demands when the negative emotions they confided to coworkers were validated by those coworkers (C. N. Hadley, "The Social Processing of Positive and Negative Emotions in Work Groups" [PhD diss., Harvard University, 2005]).

5. Researchers have found important relationships between respect and both inner work life and performance. In one study, researchers combined the results of 183 studies and found that being treated with politeness, dignity, and respect results in higher job satisfaction, higher commitment to the organization, better organizational citizenship, and higher performance; see J. A. Colquitt, D. E. Conlon, M. J. Wesson, O. L. H. Porter, and K. Y. Ng, "Justice at the Millennium: A Meta-Analytic Review of Organizational Behavior Research," *Journal of Applied Psychology* 86 (2001): 425–445. Increasing respect also leads to lower levels of emotional exhaustion; see L. Ramarajan, S. G. Barsade, and O. R. Burack, "The Influence of Organizational Respect on Emotional Exhaustion in the Human Services," *Journal of Positive Psychology* 3 (2008): 4–18. Respectful interactions between leaders and subordinates have been linked to higher satisfaction, commitment, role clarity, and perceived competence; see C. R. Gerstner and D. V. Day, "Meta-Analytic Review of Leader-Member Exchange Theory: Correlates and Construct Issues," *Journal of Applied Psychology* 82 (1997): 827–844. Incivility or lack of respect has been linked to lower satisfaction and poorer mental health; see S. Lim, L. M. Cortina, and V. J. Magley, "Personal Workgroup Incivility: Impact on Work and Health Outcomes," *Journal of Applied Psychology* 93 (2008): 95–107.

6. Expressing confidence in subordinates, along with high expectations for performance, leads to a stronger sense of empowerment and higher motivation; see W. Burke, "Leadership as Empowering Others," in *Executive Power*, ed. S. Srivastra (San Francisco: Jossey-Bass, 1986), 51–77; and J. A. Conger, "Leadership: The Art of Empowering Others," *Academy of Management Executive* 32 (1989): 17–24. Setting inspirational and/or meaningful goals also leads to a sense of empowerment and higher motivation in workers; see W. Bennis and B. Nanus, *Leaders: The Strategies for Taking Charge* (New York: Harper & Row, 1985); and J. A. Conger and R. N. Kanungo, *Charismatic Leadership in Organizations* (Thousand Oaks, CA: Sage Publications, 1998).

7. When leaders show concern or express support, followers are both more satisfied and more motivated; see T. A. Judge, R. F. Piccolo, and R. Ilies, "The Forgotten Ones? The Validity of Consideration and Initiating Structure in Leadership Research," *Journal of Applied Psychology* 89 (2004): 36–51. Supervisor support turns out to be an antecedent of organizational support, which in turn is related to higher levels of commitment, job satisfaction, positive mood, and lower levels of strain and turnover; see L. Rhoades and R. Eisenberger, "Perceived Organizational Support: A Review of the Literature," *Journal of Applied Psychology* 87 (2002): 698–714.

8. Team building is among the most effective ways to increase job satisfaction and improve work attitudes; see G. A. Neuman, J. E. Edwards, and N. S. Raju, "Organizational Development Interventions: A Meta-Analysis of Their Effects on Satisfaction and Other Attitudes," *Personnel Psychology* 42 (1989): 461–489. Affiliation also influences inner work life by creating a sense of trust. Perceived trust is associated with higher job satisfaction and commitment; see K. T. Dirks and D. L. Ferrin, "The Role of Trust in Organizational Settings," *Organization Science* 12 (2001): 450–467.

9. Our survey of 669 managers, reported in chapter 5, suggests as much; see T. M. Amabile and S. J. Kramer, "What Really Motivates Workers," *Harvard Business Review*, January 2010, 44–45.

10. K. A. Jehn, "A Multimethod Examination of the Benefits and Detriments of Intragroup Conflict," *Administrative Science Quarterly* 40 (1995): 256–282; K. A. Jehn, "A Qualitative Analysis of Conflict Types and Dimensions in Organizational Groups," *Administrative Science Quarterly* 42 (1997): 530–557.

11. Not surprisingly, researchers have found that conflict within a team can undermine performance, and that the way in which conflict is handled makes a significant difference for team performance over the long run (K. J. Behfar, R. S. Peterson, E. A. Mannix, and W. M. K. Trochim, "The Critical Role of Conflict Resolution in Teams: A Close Look at the Links Between Conflict Type, Conflict Management Strategies, and Team Outcomes," *Journal of Applied Psychology* 93 [2008]: 170–188).

12. On this day, Barbara's overall mood was more than one standard deviation below her average.

13. The problem-solving style measure on which Barbara and Roy differed so widely was the Kirton Adaption-Innovation Inventory (KAI). Relative to the rest of the team, Barbara was an extreme "innovator" on the KAI and Roy was an extreme "adaptor." According to adaption-innovation theory, problem-solving style is independent of creative potential; that is, people with either style can produce quite creative results. Moreover, having different styles on a team can be an advantage, if the differences are managed well. If they are not, damaging interpersonal conflict can result; see M. J. Kirton, "Adaptors and Innovators: A Description and Measure," *Journal of Applied Psychology* 61 (1976): 622–629; M. J. Kirton, "Adaptors and Innovators in Organizations," *Human Relations* 33 (1980): 213–224.

14. According to adaption-innovation theory, problem-solving style differences between two team members can be managed in a number of ways. For example, a facilitator can help the individuals and their teammates understand and appreciate the differences. In addition, one or more people whose style is intermediate can act as a "bridger" between the two, mediating their communication. In the Focus team, Donald could have played this role, because his style was intermediate between Roy's and Barbara's. Unfortunately, because he was so new to the company, he was ill-equipped to serve as a bridger. If noticeable style differences between team members are not managed effectively, destructive interpersonal conflict can derail a team's work; see Kirton, "Adaptors and Innovators," and Kirton, "Adaptors and Innovators in Organizations."

15. For example, on March 17, Dustin's intrinsic motivation was more than one standard deviation below his average, and his overall mood was more than a half standard deviation below his average.

16. "Agreeableness" is one of five personality dimensions assessed by the test we used (P. T. Costa and R. R. McCrae, *NEO-PI-R: Professional Manual* [Odessa, FL: Psychological Assessment Resources, 1992]). *Agreeableness* includes a person's belief in the sincerity and good intentions of others, frankness in expression, active concern for the welfare of others, modulated response to interpersonal conflict, tendency to be humble about achievements, and attitude of sympathy for others.

17. Repairing trust is more difficult than establishing it in the first place. Moreover, it requires not only rebuilding positive expectations, but first wiping out negative expectations; see P. H. Kim, D. L. Ferrin, C. D. Cooper, and K. T. Dirks, "Removing the Shadow of Suspicion: The Effects of Apology vs. Denial for Repairing Ability vs. Integrity-Based Trust Violations," *Journal of Applied Psychology* 89 (2004): 104–118.

18. Of the twenty-six teams in our study, five had two coleaders.

19. This was a common pattern across our twenty-six teams.

20. C.-Y. Chen, J. Sanchez-Burkes, and F. Lee, "Connecting the Dots Within: Creative Performance and Identity Integration," *Psychological Science* 19 (2008): 1178–1184.

21. Helen's mood score on this day was nearly two standard deviations above her average.

22. Information about Shackleton's leadership was drawn from: M. Morrell and S. C. Capparell, *Shackleton's Way: Leadership Lessons from the Great Antarctic Explorer* (New York: Viking, 2001); D. Perkins, M. Holtman, P. Kessler, and C. McCarthy, *Leading at the Edge: Leadership Lessons from the Extraordinary Saga of Shackleton's Antarctic Expedition* (New York: Amacom, 2000); N. Koehn, "Leadership in Crisis: Ernest Shackleton and the Epic Voyage of *Endurance*," Case 9-803-127 (Boston: Harvard Business School, 2002).

23. You can learn more about this fascinating story of survival from a 2002 episode of the PBS Television series *Nova*, "Shackleton's Voyage of Endurance."

24. Shackleton intuitively used the progress principle and the catalyst factor, in addition to the nourishment factor. Above all, Shackleton understood the importance of progress on meaningful tasks. In the long hike toward land, the group set out dragging two lifeboats full of supplies over the rough ice. They walked during the night when the ice was hardest and slept during the day when it was warmest. Their progress was so difficult and slow that one of the crew suggested they simply wait until the ice drifted toward shore. Shackleton's response was to try to move forward: "It will be much better for the men in general to feel that even though progress is slow, they are on their way to land, than it will be simply to sit down and wait for tardy northwesterly drift to take us out of this cruel waste of ice" (Perkins et al., *Leading at the Edge*). Though they were eventually forced to abandon the march, Shackleton continued leading his crew toward their eventual rescue.

25. R. K. Greenleaf, *The Power of Servant Leadership: Essays* (San Francisco: Berrett-Koehler, 1998); M. J. Neubert, D. S. Carlson, J. A. Roberts, K. M. Kacmar, and L. B. Chonko, "Regulatory Focus as a Mediator of the Influence of Initiating Structure and Servant Leadership on Employee Behavior," *Journal of Applied Psychology* 93 (2008): 1220–1233; F. Jaramillo, D. B. Grisaffe, L. B. Chonko, and J. A. Roberts, "Examining the Impact of Servant Leadership on Sales Force Performance," *Journal of Personal Selling & Sales Management* 29 (2009): 257–275.

26. P. F. Drucker, *The Essential Drucker: The Best of Sixty Years of Peter Drucker's Essential Writings on Management* (New York: Harper Collins, 2005), 81.

Chapter 8

1. Of all twenty-six teams in our study, the NewPoly team ranked highest in their perceptions of having positively challenging work.

2. In theory at least, all of the team leaders in our study should have been engaged with the team and the project every day. We selected teams for the study using several criteria (see appendix). One of these was that the team leader had to be assigned full-time to the team's project.

3. The exemplary leaders include several we have introduced in this book: Mark Hamilton, the head of the O'Reilly division we studied; Dave, the leader of O'Reilly's Vision team; Ruth and Harry, the Infosuite team leaders; and Graham, the NewPoly team leader.

4. A. Gawande, *The Checklist Manifesto: How to Get Things Right* (New York: Metropolitan Books, 2009).

5. Without a disciplined approach to drawing conclusions and making decisions, all humans are subject to certain cognitive biases and errors. For a good review of how such biases and errors can affect managers, see M. Bazerman and D. Moore,

Judgment in Managerial Decision Making, 7th ed. (New York: John Wiley and Sons, Inc., 2008).

6. Ruth's intrinsic motivation on this day was 1.62 standard deviations above her average.

7. Some of these benefits extend beyond inner work life. Rob Cross and his colleagues have documented that people who make their colleagues feel "energized" (or motivated) tend to receive more favorable performance reviews, advance more quickly in their careers, and spark more innovation than those who are "de-energizers" (R. Cross and A. Parker, *The Hidden Power of Social Networks: Understanding How Work Really Gets Done in Organizations* [Boston: Harvard Business School Press, 2004]).

8. Although Marsha's mood was 2.13 standard deviations below her average on May 20, it was .43 standard deviations above her average on May 21.

Chapter 9

1. W. George and A. N. McLean, "Anne Mulcahy: Leading Xerox Through the Perfect Storm," Case 9-405-050 (Boston: Harvard Business School, 2005), 11.

2. Ibid., 10.

3. For our study of team leaders, we used qualitative analysis identical to that used to study the influences on inner work life. We focused on at least one team leader from each of the seven companies in the study. In total, thirteen team leaders' complete diaries were analyzed, covering ten different teams.

4. On our open-ended survey question about what, if anything, they got out of the study, 33 percent of participants spontaneously reported that they had gained self-knowledge.

Appendix

1. We are deeply grateful to research associate Yana Litovsky for her invaluable assistance in drafting this appendix. In addition, she collaborated with us to create the data disguises, implemented the disguises, and carried out and/or summarized many of the analyses presented here.

2. We discuss some of the advantages and disadvantages of our research method in T. M. Amabile and S. J. Kramer, "Meeting the Challenges of a Person-Centric Work Psychology," *Industrial and Organizational Psychology* 4 (2011): 116–121.

3. We describe and analyze this unusual and fruitful collaboration in T. M. Amabile, C. Patterson, J. S. Mueller, T. Wojcik, P. Odomirok, M. Marsh, and S. Kramer, "Academic Practitioner Collaboration in Management Research: A Case of Cross-Profession Collaboration," *Academy of Management Journal* 44 (2001): 418–431.

4. Several excellent research associates were involved in participant contact and data collection, including Susan Archambault, Melanie Paquette, Jeremiah Weinstock, and Dean Whitney.

5. We drew our inspiration for this method from prior research that aimed to understand psychological experience in real time. (See M. Csikszentmihalyi and I. S. Csikszentmihalyi, eds. *Optimal Experience: Psychological Studies of Flow in Consciousness* [Cambridge: Cambridge University Press, 1998]; and M. Csikszentmihalyi and R. Larson, "Validity and Reliability of the Experience Sampling Method," *Journal of Nervous and Mental Disorders* 175 [1987]: 526–536.)

6. We took into consideration each person's reported vacation and sick days. Lack of response on those days did not count against the response rate.

7. We contacted individual team members in advance to ask their permission to use any specific quotes from their diaries that we wished to include in this team presentation.

8. At no point during the study did we divulge to the top managers any identifying information about the individuals or teams that matched specific data-points. In the one company that had only one participating team, we did not have a final meeting with upper management, because it would have been impossible to disguise the identity of the participating team.

9. We are grateful to our friend and colleague, Barbara Feinberg, who was invaluable in helping us to flesh out the concept of inner work life and its relationship to work and progress.

10. T. M. Amabile, J. S. Mueller, and S. M. Archambault, "Coding Manual for the DENA Coding Scheme (Detailed Event Narrative Analysis)," working paper 03-071, Harvard Business School, Boston, 2003; and T. M. Amabile, J. S. Mueller, and S. M. Archambault, "DENA Coding Scheme (Detailed Event Narrative Analysis)," working paper 03-080, Harvard Business School, Boston, 2003.

11. Our friend and colleague Jennifer Mueller was particularly helpful in the development of the DENA coding scheme, training the research associates in its use, and checking their reliability throughout the many months of coding (which stretched over more than a calendar year). Coders were trained on sample diary narratives until they achieved an acceptable degree of agreement. They then worked independently, coding separate subsets of the 11,637 diary narratives. Throughout the months of coding, their reliability was periodically rechecked to ensure that high levels were maintained. We are grateful to the primary DENA coders, Susan Archambault, Talia Grosser, Jennifer Mueller, Debbie Siegel, and Rasheea Williams.

12. On most dimensions of the coding scheme, intercoder reliability exceeded the .70 level (Cohen's kappa).

13. Throughout this book, our reports of findings about "events" are limited to concrete events that happened on the day in question. However, findings about perceptions and emotions are not restricted to concrete events.

14. Again, acceptable intercoder reliability is considered to be >.70. We are grateful to Elizabeth Schatzel for carrying out most of this coding. Research associate Yana Litovsky also helped.

15. We chose these 14 teams (at least one from each of the seven companies) to represent the entire range of inner work life experiences, work events, and outcomes that we saw across all 26 teams. After satisfying that criterion, we chose teams whose members wrote rich and clear event descriptions.

16. Research associate Yana Litovsky was enormously helpful in preparing background data for this workshop and collaborating in it.

17. These teams were Infosuite, Vision, Equip, Focus, and NewPoly.

18. This was the Managerial Practices Survey (MPS) of Yukl, Wall, and Lepsinger (G. A. Yukl, S. Wall, and R. Lepsinger, "Preliminary Report on Validation of the Managerial Practices Survey," in *Measures of Leadership*, eds. K. E. Clark and M. B. Clark [Greensboro, NC: Center for Creative Leadership, 1990], 223–237). We expanded the original fourteen MPS categories by creating three forms of each: positive, negative, and neutral. We also created a fifteenth category, "Other," for team leader behaviors that did not fit well into any of the existing MPS categories. We are indebted to our

colleague Elizabeth Schatzel for carrying out the initial work in locating the MPS, determining its appropriateness for our study, and coding leader behaviors. The leader behavior study for which this coding was originally carried out is reported in: T. M. Amabile, E. A. Schatzel, G. B. Moneta, and S. T. Kramer, "Leader Behaviors and the Work Environment for Creativity: Perceived Leader Support, *Leadership Quarterly* 15 (2004): 5–32.

19. We are indebted to our colleague Sigal Barsade for developing this coding scheme and overseeing the training of these coders and execution of the coding. Coders were trained on sample diary narratives until they achieved an acceptable degree of agreement. They then worked independently coding separate subsets of the 11,637 diary narratives.

20. We are grateful to a number of collaborators and research associates for their help in conducting statistical analyses and summarizing those analyses. In particular, we wish to single out Jennifer Mueller, Giovanni Moneta, Elizabeth Schatzel, and Yana Litovsky. The staff of the Research Computing Center at Harvard Business School provided invaluable assistance on many analyses. In particular, we thank DeYett Law, Debbie Strumsky, Bill Simpson, and Toni Wegner.

21. The specific type of regression conducted depended on whether the outcome (predicted) variable was continuous or dichotomous (yes/no). In the multilevel models, the first level was individual daily or monthly response, the second level was participant, and the third level was team. We used mixed models, with random effects for individuals and fixed effects for teams (S. W. Raudenbush and A. S. Bryk, *Hierarchical Linear Models: Applications and Data Analysis Methods* [Thousand Oaks, CA: Sage Publications, 2002]). We used SAS software Version 9.1, PROC MIXED for analyses (Cary, NC: SAS Institute, 2003). The regressions took into account that we had repeated measures across individual respondents, and also controlled for autocorrelation—the tendency of one day's data to correlate with the previous day's data.

22. A note about the data for these lagged analyses: Because our data was collected only Monday through Friday, with occasional breaks for vacations, holidays, sickness, and other nonresponse days, we used the *previous observation* for a given participant, even if it was not the previous calendar day. Still, since most of these days were in fact consecutive, we did take autocorrelation into account.

23. We often used endnotes to provide numerical values for these measures of inner work life. However, we often omitted these because we believed that comprehensive inclusion would be too tedious for even the most diligent reader.

24. Using the 7-point scale, we considered *big* to be the extremes—the two lowest or two highest ratings. The three middle ratings were considered *small*.

25. We checked this measure in the following way. On the daily diary form, after the narrative describing the day's event, we included the same numerical scale, asking participants to rate the impact they *expected* the event to have on the project overall. This same-day rating correlated very highly (.66) with the rating we used——the retrospective rating of the *actual* impact, made several weeks (sometimes months) later, after the study was ended.

26. T. M. Amabile, S. G. Barsade, J. S. Mueller, and B. M. Staw, "Affect and Creativity at Work," *Administrative Science Quarterly* 50 (2005): 367–403.

27. This latter effect was only marginally significant ($p < .10$).

28. Amabile et al., "Leader Behaviors and the Work Environment for Creativity."

29. In these regressions and most regressions described below, controls were included for sex, age, tenure with the company, education level, cognitive style (KAI),

personality (NEO openness scale), trait intrinsic motivation (WPI intrinsic motivation scale), and team size.

30. This logic is put forth by Boyatzis in his treatise on qualitative analysis (R. E. Boyatzis, *Transforming Qualitative Information: Thematic Analysis and Code Development* [Thousand Oaks, CA: Sage Publications, 1998]). He argues that codes should be developed from events appearing in samples of all of the qualitative data in a given study, with an effort to be theoretically comprehensive. Then, to identify the most important events for a given outcome, the researcher can compare code frequencies in extreme samples on that particular outcome. This is the procedure we followed.

31. We could do these numerical computations because all seven aspects of inner work life had numerical ratings. Intrinsic motivation and overall mood came from ratings the person had made on the daily diary form. The specific emotions came from numerical ratings of emotion expressed in the diary narrative, made by independent raters.

32. The standard score was a z-score.

33. The intrinsic motivation study, which was the first study we did, differed in the size of the samples. We had 300 in each sample, rather than 100. After we saw how long the coding took, we decided to reduce the sample size to 100.

34. We are grateful to colleague Ramana Nanda and other members of the MIT Sloan School of Management OSG seminar for suggesting this study.

35. T. M. Amabile and S. J. Kramer, "What Really Motivates Workers," *Harvard Business Review*, January 2010, 44–45.

36. We asked the question four ways: factors that can influence employee motivation; tools managers can use to influence employees' motivation; factors that can influence employee emotions; and tools managers can use to influence employees' emotions. We counterbalanced the order of asking the question these four ways. It turned out that order was irrelevant to the results. Moreover, the results were the same regardless of whether the question asked about factors that influence employees or tools managers can use to influence employees.

37. The progress effect was not significant at the .05 level, but was significant at the .10 level.

38. The progress effect was not statistically significant. The setback effect was not significant at the .05 level, but was significant at the .10 level.

39. We based this coding scheme on the Managerial Practices Survey (MPS) of Yukl, Wall, and Lepsinger ("Preliminary Report on Validation of the Managerial Practices Survey"). We expanded the original 14 MPS categories by creating three forms of each: positive, negative, and neutral. We also created a fifteenth category, "Other," for team leader behaviors who did not fit well into any of the existing MPS categories.

40. A composite of negative team leader behaviors significantly predicted sixteen aspects of inner work life, including perceptions, emotions, and intrinsic motivation. A composite of positive team leader behaviors significantly predicted only nine aspects of inner work life, including perceptions and emotions but not motivation. Similarly, a composite of neutral team leader behaviors significantly predicted only nine aspects of inner work life, including perceptions and emotions but not motivation.

41. We correlated the word count of the event description with the participant's ratings on the 7-point scale for the question (following the event description) about the effect of the event on their feelings about the project that day. The correlation was −.22, significant at the .01 level.

42. T. M. Amabile, J. S. Mueller, W. B. Simpson, C. M. Hadley, S. J. Kramer, and L. Fleming, "Time Pressure and Creativity in Organizations: A Longitudinal Field Study," working paper 02-073, Harvard Business School, Boston, 2002.

43. The lagged effects appeared to be substantial. For example, a one standard deviation increase in time pressure on a given day decreased the probability of a creative thinking event the following day by 19 percent.

44. We defined "very high" time pressure as 6 or 7 on the 7-point scale; "very low" was 1 or 2 on the 7-point scale.

45. T. M. Amabile, C. N. Hadley, and S. T. Kramer, "Creativity Under the Gun," *Harvard Business Review*, August 2002, 52–61.

46. Amabile et al., "Leader Behaviors and the Work Environment for Creativity."

47. In these analyses, measures of the environment all came from the KEYS instrument that was administered three times, at the beginning, middle, and end of each team's participation in the study. Responses from the three administrations were aggregated. The local environment was a composite of three KEYS scales: Supervisory Encouragement, Work Group Supports, and Challenge (positive challenge in the work). The organizational environment was a composite of two KEYS scales: Organizational Encouragement and Organizational Impediments (reverse-scored). The mood and intrinsic motivation measures were both scales created from multiple items on the daily questionnaire.

Index

Acknowledgments

This book is about making progress and enjoying good inner work life. We are grateful to many people who nourished our inner work lives while helping us make progress in our research and writing. We can thank only the major contributors, and our research participants stand at the top of the list. Without the companies that invited us in, and the hundreds of individual employees who gave so generously of their time doing daily diaries over weeks and months (not to mention the other questionnaires and the meetings with us), the discoveries described in this book would have been impossible. Because we promised confidentiality, we will not name names. But you know who you are; know also that we are profoundly grateful.

The research and the book would not have been possible without the encouragement of Harvard Business School (HBS) deans Kim Clark and Jay Light and the generous support of the School's Division of Research and Faculty Development over the several years of this research program. People in HBS Research Computing Services and Baker Research Services helped tremendously with survey design, database construction, coding program creation, company data collection, and statistical analysis—particularly Katherine Codega, Sarah Eriksen, Robyn Heller, DeYett Law, Bill Simpson, Debbie Strumsky, Jessica Tobiason, Toni Wegner, and Sarah Woolverton. Teresa's HBS faculty assistants, especially Nicole Dutton and Joyce Majewski, were especially helpful in organizing the literature reviewed. Normand Peladeau of Provalis Research, who created the QDA Miner software that we used for much of our qualitative analysis, was generously responsive to our suggestions for enhancements.

We are indebted to the colleagues and research associates who worked with us on the research. Jennifer Mueller started as a doctoral RA for one summer, then became a highly valued colleague and coauthor through several years of this research program. Connie Hadley, too, started as a doctoral student and grew into the roles of coauthor and long-time collaborator. At the very start of this research program, we enjoyed the wise counsel, recruiting and data collection assistance, and tireless encouragement of several practitioners who started as acquaintances and became close friends—some even coauthors—through our years of "IRG Team" meetings: Candis Cook, Mel Marsh, Lynn Miller, Paul Odomirok, Chelley Patterson, John Reiners, and Tom Wojcik. We were also fortunate to benefit from the brilliant colleagueship of faculty coauthors Sigal Barsade, Giovanni Moneta, and Barry Staw. And we enjoyed a succession of incredible research associates, some of whom became valued collaborators on published research papers, case studies, or both. We appreciate not only their dedicated work but also their creative contributions to this research program. Roughly in chronological order, they were: Dean Whitney, Jeremiah Weinstock, Melanie Paquette, Susan Archambault, Debbie Siegel, Rasheea Williams, Talia Grosser, Danielle Hootnick, Elizabeth Schatzel, Reut Livne-Tarandach, Yana Litovsky, and Julianna Pillemer.

In carrying out the research for and the writing of this book, we enjoyed the great benefit of insights and suggestions from outstanding colleagues and friends. He may not realize it, but Richard Hackman set off this research program with some challenging questions he asked in a seminar that Teresa gave several years ago. His advice in the planning year of this research was extremely helpful, as was the advice of John Pratt, Bob Rosenthal, and Arthur Schleifer. As we struggled to mine the data and break it down into interpretable chunks, we received expert guidance from colleagues Jay Brinegar, Amy Edmondson, Robin Ely, Dorothy Leonard, Leslie Perlow, and Scott Snook. As we extracted results and interpreted their meaning, the challenging give-and-take at several academic meetings helped hone our methods and conclusions: the HBS ARG research group, QUIET Group, and Entrepreneurial Management seminar; the Harvard Social Psychology lunch series; the NBER "New Ideas about New Ideas" conference; and seminars at MIT, Stanford, Yale, the University of Chicago, the University of Minnesota, the London Business School, the University of Michigan, the University of California (Berkeley), Rutgers University, Washington University in St. Louis, and Boston College. We have also learned a great deal from testing our ideas with groups of business executives and employees at HBS and around the world.

As we developed various drafts, we received invaluable feedback and suggestions from Andy Brown, Candis Cook, Connie Hadley, Josea Kramer, Michele Rigolizzo, Carolyn Amabile Ross, Richard Seaman, Walter Swap, Marjorie Williams, and participants in the Book Seminar at HBS. Beyond this specific help, we were buoyed by a much wider circle of family and friends who encouraged us during the darkest days of research and writing.

Barbara Feinberg spent many days talking with us as our ideas for this book took shape, nudging the ideas along, writing us memos that synthesized and challenged those ideas, reading our drafts, and suggesting improvements. We are immensely grateful for her insight, encouragement, and friendship. We also extend warm gratitude to Connie Hale, the author and writing guru whose talents as an editor guided us through the final revision.

Finally, we are grateful for the people of Harvard Business Review Press. Allison Peter, the senior production editor on this book, not only pulled everything together with a sure hand but also engaged the skills of our extraordinary copyeditor, Monica Jainschigg. Most of all, we deeply appreciate our editor, Melinda Merino. She began conversations with us during the years that data collection was still in progress, having received a tip about what she considered a promising study. Melinda, thank you for your consistent interest, your provocative ideas, and your unflagging support.

About the Authors

Teresa Amabile is the Edsel Bryant Ford Professor of Business Administration and a Director of Research at Harvard Business School. Originally educated as a chemist at Canisius College, Amabile received her doctorate in psychology from Stanford University. Her research investigates how everyday life inside organizations can influence people and their performance. Initially focusing on individual creativity, Amabile's research has expanded to encompass subjective experience at work (inner work life), individual productivity, team creativity, and organizational innovation.

Amabile was awarded the E. Paul Torrance Award by the Creativity Division of the National Association for Gifted Children in 1998, and *The Leadership Quarterly* Best Paper Award by the Center for Creative Leadership in 2005. She has spoken to dozens of groups in business, government, and education around the world, and has taught courses on creativity, leadership, and ethics at Harvard Business School. Before moving to Harvard, she was a psychology professor at Brandeis University.

Amabile was the host/instructor of *Against All Odds: Inside Statistics*, a twenty-six-part instructional series originally broadcast on PBS. She has served on the boards of Seaman Corporation and other organizations. Amabile is the author of *Creativity in Context* and *Growing Up Creative*, as well as over one hundred articles, chapters, and case studies.

Steven Kramer is an independent researcher, writer, and consultant in Wayland, Massachusetts. He received his undergraduate degree in psychology from UCLA and his doctorate in developmental psychology from the University of Virginia. He has served as a postdoctoral research associate at Vanderbilt University, a psychology professor at Brandeis University, and a researcher at Epidemiological Resources, Inc. Kramer's current research interests include adult development, the meaning of work in human life, and the subjective experience of everyday events inside organizations (inner work life). Previously, he researched the perceptual and cognitive development of infants and young children.

Kramer has published several articles in *Harvard Business Review* on topics including inner work life, managerial awareness of work motivators, and the influence of time pressure on creativity. He has also published in the *Academy of Management Journal* and *The Leadership Quarterly*. In 2005, he won *The Leadership Quarterly* Best Paper Award from the Center for Creative Leadership.

Kramer is an avid landscape photographer.

Teresa Amabile and Steven Kramer have been married for over twenty years.